HERBAL

The Essential Guide to Herbs for Living

Female Emperor Moth

HERBAL

THE ESSENTIAL GUIDE TO HERBS FOR LIVING

BARNES
&NOBLE
BOOKS
NEW YORK

This edition published for Barnes & Noble, Inc.,
by arrangement with Pavilion Books, Ltd

2001 Barnes & Noble Books

MI0987654321

ISBN 0-7607-2768-6

First published in Great Britain in 2001 by
Pavilion Books, Ltd
London House
Great Eastern Wharf
Parkgate Road
London SW11 4NQ

Design by: David Fordham
Colour origination by: Anglia Graphics, Bedford
Printed by: Giunti Industrie Grafiche

DISCLAIMER

The Chelsea Physic Garden Company does not endorse or recommend any of the medicinal uses of plants referred to in the work, whether historic or current; neither will it endorse or disavow testing of any products on animals. Readers should consult a medical practitioner before making use of any plant for medical purposes. The Chelsea Physic Garden Company accepts no liability for any reliance placed on the advice contained in this work.

Herbal is intended to increase your knowledge, enjoyment, and appreciation of herbs. It is not meant to encourage self-medication. Herbs and herbal supplements can improve health and vitality as part of a balanced diet and lifestyle but are not a substitute for professional medical diagnosis or care. The author and the publisher can accept no responsibility for any illness, harm or other effects arising from the use or misuse of herbs described in this book.

Contents

Plate 337.

Coffee.

Eliz. Blackwell delin. sculp. et Pinx.

1. Flower.
2. Fruit.
3. Back of the Seed.
4. Face of the Seed.

Coffee.

FOREWORD

I AM VERY HAPPY TO BE ABLE TO INTRODUCE this new celebration of the power of plant material to contribute not only to human health but also to beauty, cooking and our environment. Deni Bown has compiled a wide-ranging review of which plants are used in herbal treatments of many kinds. She pays appropriate attention to European herbs, to the important contribution of North American plants and plants borrowed from the Ayurvedic and Chinese medical traditions as well as to a wide variety of tropicals, many of which first entered Europe through the spice trade, and others of which, collected from rainforests because of their long histories of tribal use, are currently enjoying almost cult status in the West.

When the Society of Apothecaries first founded the Chelsea Physic Garden in 1673, they were interested in both native and newly introduced exotics of potential medicinal value. One of their primary concerns was with correct identification for, without this, patients would either be ineffectively treated or, worse, even poisoned. This concern is still with us today, but to it have been added new worries about over-extraction from the wild to serve the huge recent boom in herbal medicine in the West. Species such as blue cohosh, echinacea, goldenseal, Siberian and American ginseng, bogbean and yellow gentian are becoming rare, sometimes because of loss of habitat, but more often from unsustainable use. Deni has highlighted many of these problems. The 'green' consumer should ask for cultivated source herbs or for some evidence of sustainable wild crafting.

I have been interested to learn from Deni about the ways in which long traditions of herb use have affected our colloquial language. To this she has added information about ethnobotanical uses and tips for the gardener on how to grow the plants successfully. Whether she is reviewing aromatics, aphrodisiacs, balsams, gums and resins, or colourants, salads and tonics, the reader is given a good insight into the sheer variety of plant material which can be termed 'herbal'.

The Chelsea Physic Garden has been very pleased to contribute to the illustrations in this book from the resources of its own library, once the library of the Society of the Apothecaries. The earliest illustrations are from Leonard Fuchs's *De Historia Stirpium* of 1542, of which this library holds one of the finest hand-coloured copies. Other images were produced by William Curtis who was Praefectus Horti (Director) and Demonstrator of Plants here from 1772 to 1777, or painted by Elizabeth Blackwell, a resident of neighbouring Swan Walk, in her *Curious Herbal* of 1737–9. This extraordinary work of plants used in physic (and all cut from the Garden) was a successful attempt by Blackwell to raise money to release her husband from the debtors' gaol. The Garden's history is full of such happy schemes and I hope that this herbal will be yet another addition to it.

In today's world, where 80 per cent of the world's population relies on plants for its healthcare, herbal medicine is a matter of no little importance. In 1673 the Apothecaries could not have foreseen today's pharmaceutical industry. Nor could they have known that, of the top 25 best-selling pharmaceutical drugs today, half owe their origin to the natural world rather than to synthetic chemistry. Plants still rule where medicine is concerned, just as they did in 1673.

SUE MINTER, CURATOR, CHELSEA PHYSIC GARDEN

Plate 473.

Elecampane.

1. Flower.
2. Flower separate
3. Seed

Helenium.

Eliz. Blackwell delin. sculp. et P.

INTRODUCTION

THE ORIGINAL PROPOSAL FOR A BOOK ABOUT HERBS, linked with Chelsea Physic Garden and illustrated with both contemporary photographs and historical plates, came from Vivien James, Publishing Director of Pavilion. My contribution to its evolution was to suggest that the book should be called simply *Herbal* and that it should focus on 150 key herbs for the twenty-first century, selected on the basis that they are enduringly popular, widely used, or up-and-coming, and grown – with rare exception – at the Chelsea Physic Garden. I wanted, in addition, to explore in special features herbs that are important for health and vitality – from aphrodisiacs and natural colourings to salad herbs and tonics. Our first exploratory meeting to discuss these ideas was held in the Garden on a sunny August day, sitting outside near the venerable old olive tree that was planted in the late 1880s and fruits regularly in the genial microclimate created by the enclosing walls and surrounding buildings of London's 'secret garden'. Nowhere else in the land is there a garden where the plants generate such a sense of place and history.

The Chelsea Physic Garden dates back to 1673, making it the third oldest botanical garden in Great Britain after Edinburgh (1670) and Oxford (1621), and the only one today using the earlier term of 'physic garden'. Physic gardens were so called because their purpose was to grow medicinal plants for physicians – mainly for teaching students and providing research materials, and also to some extent for producing drugs. The archaic word 'physic' means 'art of healing' – a skill rather more holistic than simply 'medical'. In the seventeenth century (and long before) almost all medicines came from plants, and physicians and apothecaries were familiar with their identification, cultivation and harvesting. They had to be something of a naturalist and a gardener too. Botany was part and parcel of medicine, and plants were studied seriously with the sole purpose of understanding more clearly how they could benefit human health.

By the mid-nineteenth century this situation had changed radically. Not only did the choice of cultivated plants increase considerably through colonial explorations, but the Victorian

TRIFOLIUM PRATENSE

BORAGO OFFICINALIS

LINIUM USITATISSIMUM

CALENDULA OFFICINALIS

passion for collecting, categorizing and experimenting resulted in the birth of science as we know it today. After the Industrial Revolution and the shift of focus from rural to urban living, traditional herbal medicine no longer held centre stage, and the study of *materia medica* – the origins and properties of medicinal herbs – was axed from the medical syllabus in 1895. Instead, the separate sciences of botany, pharmacognosy and pharmacology were developed. As a consequence, the role of the physic garden became largely obsolete, and the old physic gardens evolved into modern botanical gardens. Indeed, the Society of Apothecaries gave up the Chelsea Physic Garden in 1899.

By great good fortune, however, the Garden continued as a botanical teaching and agricultural research institution from 1901 funded, bizarrely, by a charity founded to support London's poor. It remained, horticulturally, something of a botanical Noah's ark, where perhaps more rare, unusual and historically interesting plants could be found than in any comparable area. When the resurgence of interest in herbs began in the late twentieth century, the Chelsea Physic Garden was perfectly poised to display herbal collections and expertise that outrank those of much larger institutions. I remember taking a group along on a Sunday afternoon in the early 1980s and being able to show them herbs that they had only ever read about before, or seen in illustrations. I had arranged the tour for my class, who were attending a course on Herbs for Health I was teaching at a college of further education. All were adults, some were health professionals, yet they were as thrilled as children to discover sassafras and toothache trees, cardamom and liquorice – and all within a few steps of each other.

Over the years I have visited Chelsea Physic Garden many times and found much to delight both the intellect and the senses. Quite a number of the photographs for my *Encyclopedia of Herbs & Their Uses* were taken there and it made the perfect venue for the launch of the Royal Horticultural Society's edition of the book. What I enjoy most about the garden is that in some ways it has remained unchanged; the basic layout is pretty much as it was a century ago, and although certain plants are the object of serious study, they are collectively enjoyed for their beauty and associations. It is, after all, a garden, not just a laboratory, library or a lecture room, and a walled garden at that. Our word for 'paradise' comes from *pairidaeza*, a word in Avestan, an ancient Iranian language, that

TANACETUM PARTHENIUM

OCIMUM BASILICUM

meant an enclosed garden. As you turn your back on the London traffic and step through the gate in the wall, you recognize the sense in which such a place is heaven.

Yet, having said that one of the garden's great strengths is the connection to its past, there is always something new to discover. On one level, a garden is always changing, through the seasons and from day to day through light and weather, and Chelsea Physic Garden is as magical as any other in this respect. On another level, the garden changes in terms of its displays and exhibitions, and increasingly through its contribution to information and issues concerning our use of the world's plant resources for health and healing. Like many of its plants, Chelsea Physic Garden is a rarity: for being one of the few botanical gardens – if not the only one – whose main sphere of interest is herbs.

I have had a passion for herbs since the 1960s, when they were far from fashionable. In those days, there were no fresh herbs in the shops, apart from the parsley decorating a fishmonger's display and few, if any, skin and hair-care products contained herbal extracts. In the northern city

ECHINACEA PURPUREA

EUCALYPTUS SPECIES

ROSA CANINA

ALOE VERA VAR. OFFICINALIS

where I grew up, there was a strange little shop in a back street that sold crudely packaged, old-fashioned herbal remedies to a mostly elderly clientele, but the closest to herbal products in a chemist's pharmacy were Sennatabs, castor oil or Vick's. Today, herbs seem to be added to everything and their names and images appear everywhere. International trade in herbs increased by about 20 per cent a year in the late 1990s. The nineteenth century saw the Gold Rush; the twentieth century struck oil; the wealth of the twenty-first century, I am sure, lies in herbs. Sustainable wealth, whether of gold, oil or herbs, depends on sensible management of resources. The conservation and production of herbs will be a significant factor in protecting and regenerating the countryside, whether rural England, American woodland, African desert or tropical rainforest.

The new millennium will, I believe, bring new meaning to the word herbal. There will be a new generation of phytomedicines, plant-based cosmetics, 'nutriceuticals' (therapeutic foods containing herbal extracts), and fusion cuisine that sources herbs from around the world. We will rediscover what we owe to plants and learn to respect, even worship them again. Plants are, after all, the basis for life on earth and our continuing life-support system. We may also come to redefine what we mean by a herb. The usual definition is that herbs are plants used for flavouring, medicinal or aromatic purposes. More precisely, herbs are plants that have therapeutic properties when used in the right amounts. In the words of Paracelsus, the sixteenth-century physician and alchemist, 'All substances are poisons. The right dose differentiates a remedy from a poison.' A more controversial definition I have used before is that a herb is a plant with a human face. Herbs are defined only by our use of them. A herb in one region may not be recognized as such elsewhere; it is a cultural phenomenon. Will our new definition embrace the brave new world of genetically modified plants? Could a tree carrying a human gene, that can be tapped safely and renewably as a source of disease-free proteins or antibodies, be defined as a herb? Might this be the first human herb? Whatever we make of it, the future's herbal.

HERBAL
A–Z

Achillea millefolium   YARROW

PORTRAIT

An aromatic perennial reaching 30–60cm (12–24in), with tough stems and very finely cut leaves – hence the name '*millefolium*', thousand-leaf. The long-lasting flowers are dull white to pink and are borne in flat clusters over a very long period from summer to early winter. Yarrow is a common plant of grassland in many parts of Europe and is widely naturalized in North America, Australia and New Zealand.

HISTORY

According to the sixteenth-century herbalist John Gerard, the genus *Achillea* was named after Achilles who used yarrow to heal injuries on the battlefield. Another side to yarrow is its role in

Achillea Millefolium.

Published by Dr Woodville Jany 1. 1791.

divination. Yarrow stalks were originally cast when consulting the I Ching, the ancient Chinese book of divination. More mundanely in English folklore, a youngster would twiddle a yarrow leaf inside the nostrils while chanting a rhyme and if it caused a nosebleed, he or she could be sure 'my love loves me'. Similarly, putting yarrow under the pillow would reveal a future husband or wife in a dream.

HEALING

Traditionally, yarrow was a wound herb, giving rise to names such as soldier's woundwort, staunchweed, sanguinary, and *Herba Militaris.* It is actually quite effective in stopping bleeding — worth remembering if you are on a hike and need some first aid. For this purpose, crush the leaves, or chew them before applying, to release the astringent juices. When taken internally, yarrow lowers fever and is often recommended, combined with elderflower and peppermint, for the early stage of colds and flu. Herbalists also find it useful in helping to lower blood pressure after a stroke or heart attack.

ACHILLEA MILLEFOLIUM 'RED BEAUTY'

ACHILLEA MILLEFOLIUM

NOTES FOR GARDENERS

Yarrow grows happily in most soils but romps away in moist, well-drained soil in sun. Wild yarrow is very invasive and certainly needs the fierce competition of its grassland neighbours to keep it in check. Though ideal for perennial wildflower meadows, cultivars such as the deep pink 'Cerise Queen', orange-red 'Paprika' or mauve 'Lilac Beauty', are less invasive and more colourful for borders. As a bonus, the blooms attract beneficial insects, such as ladybirds, and are long-lasting as cut flowers.

Actaea racemosa   BLACK COHOSH

PORTRAIT
A hardy, clump-forming perennial, with a woody rootstock and elegant, broadly triangular leaves, which are divided into leaflets. In summer, branched stems, up to 2.5m (8ft) tall, bear slender spikes of malodorous white flowers. Black cohosh belongs to the buttercup family, Ranunculaceae, and grows in rich, open woodland in eastern North America.

HISTORY
Native Americans traditionally used black cohosh for female complaints, hence the common name, squaw root. It was described scientifically in 1705 and cultivated at the Chelsea Physic Garden in London in 1737. Another common name is bugbane, referring to its past use as an insect repellent, reflected in its earlier scientific name of *Cimicifuga racemosa*, from *cimex*, a bug, and *fugo*, to drive away.

HEALING
The resinous rhizomes contain oestrogenic, sedative substances that are effective in treating menstrual and menopausal problems, and pains during labour and after childbirth. They also stimulate the uterus and have anti-rheumatic and expectorant effects. Black cohosh has a good track record in relieving a range of conditions, from tinnitus and asthma to arthritic and rheumatic complaints. For obvious reasons, it should not be taken during pregnancy. The closely related *A. foetida* and *A. dahurica* are both known in Chinese medicine as *sheng ma*, a traditional remedy for asthma, colds, and feverish infections, such as measles.

NOTES FOR GARDENERS
Black cohosh is a magnificent ornamental for moist, humus-rich soil in the woodland garden, among shrubs, or at the back of a shaded border. Propagate plants by seed sown when ripe or by division in early spring or autumn. As they come up to their full flowering height, plants may need staking but are otherwise trouble-free.

Agastache foeniculum

ANISE HYSSOP
LAVENDER HYSSOP

PORTRAIT
Anise hyssop belongs to the mint family (Lamiaceae) and grows wild in North American priaries and upland woods. It is an upright perennial with pointed, toothed, anise-scented leaves and bold spikes of violet-blue, tubular flowers in summer. Plants reach 60–90cm (24–36in) in cool areas, and nearer 1.5m (5ft) in their homelands.

HISTORY
The native American name for anise hyssop is *wahpe' yata'pi*, meaning 'leaf that is chewed'. The leaves were made into a tea to lift the spirits, strengthen a weak heart or to relieve coughs. Anise hyssop leaves were also used in sweat lodges to induce perspiration, and as a powder to cool the body during a fever. The Cree tribe included the flowers in medicine bundles. Anise hyssop was

AGASTACHE FOENICULUM

widely planted by American beekeepers in the 1870s to produce a fine honey with a slight aniseed flavour.

COOKING
The leaves are worth experimenting with in salads and as a slightly sweet, pleasant flavour in herb teas.

HEALING
The main properties of anise hyssop are diaphoretic (inducing perspiration) and decongestant but it is seldom used medicinally. More important in herbal medicine is its Asian relative, *A. rugosa*, which has been used in Chinese medicine for almost 2,000 years. Commonly known as Korean mint, or in Chinese terminology as *huo xiang*, this mint-flavoured herb improves digestion and appetite, and relieves digestive upsets. It is also good for colds that are characterized by chills rather than fever.

eniculum

Notes for Gardeners

Agastaches are easily grown from seed sown at temperatures above 13°C (55°F) in early spring, or by division in spring or semi-ripe cuttings in late summer. Being a prairie species, *A. foeniculum* tolerates poorer soil and drier conditions than *A. rugosa*, which often grows near mountain streams. Both make excellent plants for the border. Anise hyssop looks particularly good with tall grasses and usually self-sows generously. The white form, 'Alabaster', is attractive too, as are hybrids that may have mint- or anise-scented leaves and lavender, pink or white flowers.

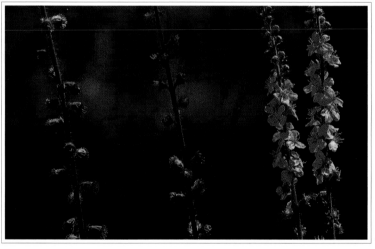

AGRIMONIA EUPATORIA

Agrimonia eupatoria   AGRIMONY

Portrait

Widely distributed along fields, hedges and roads from Europe to North Africa and Iran, this upright perennial reaches 30–60cm (12–24in) and bears downy leaves with three to five pairs of leaflets. Spires of small, faintly scented yellow flowers are produced in summer, followed by bristly fruits that cling to fur, feathers or clothing, dispersing them to pastures new and giving the plant names such as cocklebur and sticklewort.

History

In Anglo-Saxon times agrimony was an important wound herb known as 'garclive'. It was an ingredient of *eau d'arquebusade*, a French herbal lotion originally used to treat wounds caused by an arquebus (a fifteenth-century long-barrelled gun). In the Tyrol, agrimony was one of five plants (the others being broom, rue, maidenhair fern and ground ivy) that were bound together and either carried as an amulet to enable the bearer to see witches, or placed over a door to prevent a witch from entering — a custom that appears to have persisted well into the nineteenth century.

HEALING

Agrimony does indeed have astringent properties and controls bleeding, so it is still used for minor injuries, haemorrhoids and such like. It also makes an effective gargle for sore throats and chronic catarrh. Herbalists today might prescribe agrimony for urinary problems, such as cystitis, and gastro-intestinal disorders. In traditional Chinese medicine, the closely related *A. pilosa* (shaggy speedwell) is known to increase blood clotting, due to its high vitamin K content, by as much as 50 per cent. Combined with bletilla (*Bletilla striata*) and great burnet (*Sanguisorba officinalis*), it controls internal haemorrhage and has proved effective in relieving symptoms of silicosis, a serious lung disease. It has anti-tumour activity too.

NOTES FOR GARDENERS

Agrimony is a well-behaved, good-looking plant and though obviously at home in a wildflower meadow would not be out of place in the border. It likes full sun and well-drained soil, tolerating the dry and alkaline conditions that are enjoyed by herbs such as sage, lavender and thyme. It is easily grown from seed sown in spring.

Alchemilla species   # LADY'S MANTLE

PORTRAIT

Two species are used medicinally: *A. alpina* and *A. xanthoclora*, which was previously known as *A. vulgaris*. The former is a distinctive plant, reaching only 10–20cm (4–8in), with a creeping rootstock and dark green leaves that are round to kidney-shaped in outline and cut almost to the base into between five and seven lobes. The leaf undersides are clad in silky hairs, seen from above as a silver edge to the margins. *Alchemilla xanthoclora* is nearer 50cm (20in) in height and spread, and quite different in appearance, having a woody rootstock and lighter green, finely toothed, kidney-shaped leaves with nine to eleven shallow lobes. Both produce clusters of tiny yellow-green flowers. The two species are variable in the wild, and a number of variations have at times been given species status, giving rise to a plethora of names. To complicate the picture further, *A. alpina* — as the name suggests — is an alpine plant that is difficult to grow at low elevations, and is often replaced in cultivation by the look-alike *A. conjuncta*. Worse still, they all hybridize readily.

HISTORY

The name *Alchemilla* refers to the exquisite drops of dew that form on the leaves of these plants and were once used in the concoctions of alchemists. The common name, lady's mantle, indicates that these herbs were primarily used for female disorders. Lady's mantles of one sort or another are often grown in herb gardens, though seldom correctly labelled — identifying alchemillas is no easy task, even for botanists. Nevertheless, there is no excuse for passing off *A. mollis* as a herb. Though easily grown and arguably the loveliest of the genus, it has no history of use as a medicinal herb and even as a garden plant was virtually unknown until the 1960s. This is not to say that it definitely has no medicinal properties. It may have, but at the moment, no one knows.

HEALING

Historically, *A. xanthoclora* is the more important, though both are basically astringent, anti-inflammatory herbs that control bleeding and promote healing. Though traditionally used for menstrual and menopausal disturbances, womb problems, and during childbirth, the Commission E Monographs — set up in Germany in 1978 by the Federal Health Agency to evaluate herbal medicines — describe it merely as an astringent for mild diarrhoea. In contrast, though herbalists less often use *A. alpina*, the Monographs report that in addition to treating female complaints, there are unsubstantiated claims that it also has diuretic, antispasmodic and cardioactive effects.

ALCHEMILLA XANTHOCLORA

NOTES FOR GARDENERS

Both species are hardy and may be propagated by seed sown without heat in spring, or by division in early spring or autumn. They thrive in sun or partial shade and in any moisture-retentive soil, though *A. xanthoclora* dislikes lime. Most plants self-sow freely but if you grow more than one species, chances are that their offspring will be hybrids.

Allium sativum   GARLIC

PORTRAIT

Garlic is unknown in the wild but probably derived from a central Asian species. It is a hardy, clump-forming perennial with a rounded to pyramidal bulb, composed of up to fifteen bulblets or cloves, clad in a papery white tunic. Flat, keeled leaves, up to 60cm (24in) long, appear early in the

Alchenulla vulgaris.

353.

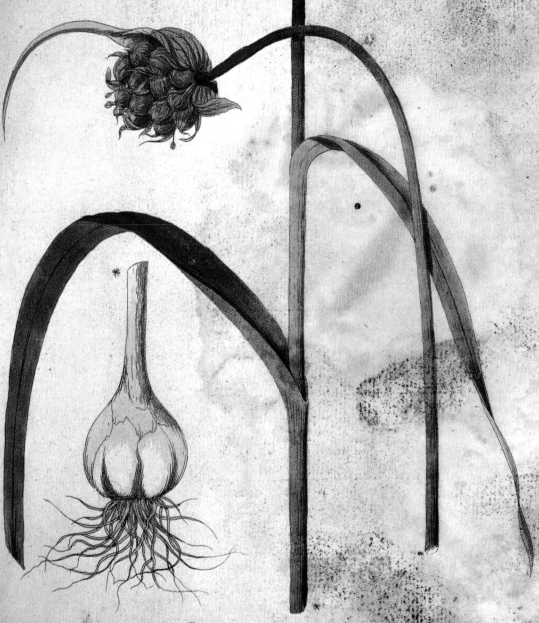

Allium sativum L.

growing season, followed by a flower head bearing many bulbils and a few greenish-white flowers, or bulbils only.

HISTORY
Garlic was cultivated 5,000 years ago in the Middle East and found in the tomb of Tutankhamun (*c.*1370–1352BC). Though popular in ancient Greek and Roman times, those eating it were not allowed in temples. In the first century AD, Pliny listed dozens of complaints for which garlic was effective; around a hundred years later Galen referred to it as the peasants' 'theriac' or cure-all. Records of garlic in Chinese medicine began around AD510. By Chaucer's time, garlic became known as 'poor man's treacle'. Stories about garlic abound. According to Muslim legend, garlic sprang up from Satan's left footstep and onion from his right. On the positive side, it is said to protect against vampires and prevent competitors from getting ahead if chewed during a race.

COOKING
Regional dishes in many parts of the world rely on garlic, making it the ultimate flavour enhancer for meats, fish, seafood, many vegetables, and staple foods such as potatoes and pasta. It is a condiment in its own right when added to oil, butter, vinegar, or even to salt, and a vital ingredient of sauces such as *aïoli*. Crushed or chopped garlic has a greater pungency than whole cloves or bulbs which, when roasted until soft, have an almost sweet, nutty flavour.

HEALING
Fresh garlic bulbs are a cornucopia of vitamins, minerals, amino acids, and sulphur compounds that produce the pungent taste and odour, and also most of the medicinal properties. A clove of garlic, with all the constituents intact, is undoubtedly more effective than an apple a day in keeping the doctor away. Thousands of scientific papers have been published on garlic over the past 20 years. Results support the traditional use of garlic as an anti-infective for both bacterial and viral infections, especially of the respiratory tract and digestive system. It is also a useful expectorant for bronchial and nasal congestion. More controversial is garlic's role in lowering blood pressure and cholesterol levels, and thinning the blood – all of which benefit cardiovascular health. Anti-cancer and anti-oxidant effects have also been reported. Some controversy surrounds the efficacy of the way garlic is taken – fresh or dried, freeze-dried, or as essential oil or deodorized oil – making results difficult to compare.

NOTES FOR GARDENERS
Garlic enjoys full sun and moist, light, humus-rich soil that is neutral to slightly alkaline. Plant individual cloves of garlic 2.5cm (1in) deep in autumn or winter, depending on climate (in very cold areas plant in early spring). You can use any kitchen garlic, but bear in mind that the variety may not be well-suited to your area. For more certain results, buy from a local seed merchant. Autumn planting gives the largest bulbs, as garlic starts to grow on the shortest day and finishes on the longest. Keep an eye on newly planted cloves, re-planting any tweaked out by birds. As large quantities are usually required, and as it is not a particularly attractive plant, garlic is best planted in rows in the vegetable garden. Dotted about among the roses and other flowers, however, it is supposed to deter pests and diseases.

Herbal

ABELMOSCHUS MOSCHATUS

SERENOA REPENS

TURNERA ULMIFOLIA

THE SEARCH FOR APHRODISIACS that really work has obsessed human beings since the dawn of time. It was a quest second in importance only to that for elixirs of life, and cure-alls or panaceas, and just as difficult to define. Just what are aphrodisiacs and do they work? The word 'aphrodisiac' refers to Aphrodite, the Greek goddess of sexual love, beauty, and fertility. In herbal terms, an aphrodisiac is a substance – usually taken in the form of food, drink or drug – that stimulates or increases sexual interest and vigour. Whether aphrodisiacs work or not is a much more difficult question to answer. Some undoubtedly do, but there is little scientific evidence to show how.

The most obvious aphrodisiacs are those that work through the senses. Erotic perfumes, such as musky ambrette (*Abelmoschus moschatus*), foods with sensuous tastes and textures, like okra and oysters, or the suggestive appearance of asparagus and pomegranates, are old favourites. Though powerful substances in their own right, they depend very much on personal taste and associations; what may arouse passion in some people, may be a turn-off for others. Less obviously alluring are aphrodisiacs that work simply through their chemistry, perhaps as relaxants, possibly by influencing hormones or stimulating tissues in the erogenous zones. Scientifically, these are the most interesting, as their effect can be quantified. Having said this, it is as well to remember that there is no limit to the power of suggestion – if you really believe something will have a certain effect, it probably will.

One of the world's top-selling herbs, saw palmetto (*Serenoa repens*) is a small, creeping palm that grows in wetlands in the south-eastern United States. The fruits, which look rather like olives, are gathered from the wild, mainly in Florida. Though best known as a remedy for prostate enlargement, saw palmetto is a hormonal tonic that seems to benefit women as well. Extravagant claims have been made that it increases breast size. More likely, it increases strength and vigour, and can apparently work wonders for impotence and low sex drive associated with ageing or convalescence. In earlier times, settlers made a soft drink called 'metto' from the fruits and noticed it improved digestion and stamina.

In Mexico, leaves from the damiana shrub (*Turnera diffusa*) are made into tea or smoked for their euphoric effects. Damiana liqueurs are popular, too, and are often added to hot cinnamon tea as a tonic for waning powers. This potent herb was unleashed on the American public in 1874 by a druggist in Washington DC, who sold damiana tincture 'to improve the sexual ability of the enfeebled and aged'. No one knows exactly what causes

Aphrodisiacs

damiana's tonic, aphrodisiac effect, but it definitely seems to be anti-depressant, and to increase testosterone levels, while rejuvenating both men and women.

Potency wood or muira puama — an obvious aphrodisiac from its name — is something of a mystery. Three plants have been named as the source of muira puama roots and bark — *Dulacia inopiflora*, *Ptychopetalum olacoides* and *P. uncinatum*. They are small, closely related trees that probably have similar properties, growing in Amazonian rainforests, where they are wild-collected for the herb industry. Muira puama is widely used as a medicinal herb by tribes in Amazonia, and was adopted by herbalists in South America and Europe in the 1920s. Research shows that it has a tonic effect on the nervous system and, in many cases of impotence and loss of interest in sex, may bring dramatic improvements in libido and sexual performance.

Also from South America comes the bark of various trees, known as catuaba. Problems over the identification of catuaba have caused confusion for decades, but in the 1990s, with growing concern about quality and traceability of herbal products, the picture became a little clearer. Basically, the name catuaba refers to several different species that either look alike or have similar properties. They include *Erythroxylum vaccinifolium*, *Anaemopaegma* species and *Trichilia* species. In Brazil, the aphrodisiac effects of catuaba are legendary, and the subject of sayings and songs. It apparently stimulates both brain and the genitals, improving memory as well as sexual prowess.

EURYCOMA LONGIFOLIA

The bark of the yohimbe tree (*Pausinystalia johimbe*) from West Africa contains some very potent alkaloids, the main one being yohimbine, which stimulates the nervous system and genital blood vessels, causing sexual arousal. The bad news is that it raises blood pressure, interacts with a number of prescription drugs and, in excess, causes anxiety, nausea and vomiting, so the risks probably outweigh the benefits. However, correctly prescribed, it is used to treat male impotence.

Most aphrodisiacs have a long history of use in their homelands before entering international trade, so there must be many that have yet to be tried and tested. In Malaysia, for example, everyone smiles knowingly at the mention of tongkat ali (*Eurycoma longifolia*). The Malay name means 'Allah's walking stick' and describes the appearance of this strange rainforest tree, which has a long, skinny trunk, with a tuft of leaves on top. *Tongkat ali* was described to me by a forester who later revealed he had three wives and 14 children. He was in no doubt that it worked.

See also: *Asparagus racemosus*, *Citrus aurantium*, *Myristica fragrans*, *Persicaria odorata* (anaphrodisiac), *Rosa* species, *Sassafras albidum*, *Withania somnifera*.

Allium schoenoprasum
A. tuberosum

CHIVES
GARLIC CHIVES

PORTRAIT

A hardy, clump-forming perennial that resembles a miniature bunch of salad onions, with cylindrical bulbs terminating in hollow leaves and dense, rounded heads of mauve, bell-shaped flowers from spring to early summer. Chives occur wild in damp ground, often beside streams, in parts of Europe, Asia and North America. The related garlic or Chinese chives (*A. tuberosum*) is a south-east Asian species with flat leaves and white flowers in late summer and early autumn.

HISTORY

The chives familiar in most western cuisines are only one of many onion-flavoured members of the *Allium* family (Alliaceae) that are interchangeable as herbs. Local substitutes occur in various

ALLIUM SCHOENOPRASUM

ALLIUM TUBEROSUM

regions. In Britain, John Gerard recorded in 1633 that ramsons (*A. ursinum*) were eaten by 'such as have a strong constitution, and labouring men'. According to the editor of the *West Virginia Hillbilly* in 1986, eating ramps (*A. tricoccum*) was synonymous with spring, like 'changing the oil or your underwear', which were apparently annual events as well. In China, garlic chives are usually blanched, using boxes or long, narrow terracotta pots. A more elaborate method uses layers of different materials, such as sand and straw, to give bands of white, light and dark yellow and green, described as 'five-coloured chives'.

COOKING

Chives' mild onion flavour and bright green leaves are extremely useful in the kitchen, enlivening bland-tasting, pale-coloured foods such as potatoes, eggs, soft cheese, and soups and sauces with a creamy consistency. They are a valuable addition to salads too, and dressings such as *remoulade*, where raw onion is often too overpowering. *Ravigote*, the classic French herb mixture, uses finely chopped chives, chervil, tarragon and shallots as a basis for herb butter or a sauce. For all purposes, chives should be very finely chopped as long pieces of leaf tend to become stringy when cooked or chewed. Lengthy cooking destroys the flavour, so chives are always a last-minute addition. The flowers of both chives and garlic chives are edible and attractive. Add whole buds to salads, or break up a flowering head into individual florets before adding. The flower buds of garlic chives are a delicacy in China, either with a sesame dressing in salads or with a few inches of stem as a stir-fry.

NOTES FOR GARDENERS

Chives and garlic chives tolerate a wide range of soils, including clay, and are not sensitive to pH. They do best in deep, moist but well-drained, fertile soil in sun or partial shade. Both are easily grown from seed sown in spring. Established plants may be propagated by division at the first signs of growth in early spring. These attractive plants merit a place in the border, and to vary the palette there are pink- and white-flowered forms of chives. 'Forescate', with bright pink flowers and a vigorous habit, is one of the best.

ALOE VERA

Aloe vera

ALOE VERA
BARBADOS ALOE, CURAÇAO ALOE

PORTRAIT

Aloe vera occurs widely in tropical and subtropical regions. It is a suckering perennial with a rosette of hard, spine-edged, grey-green leaves that may be spotted in young plants, and a spike of tubular yellow flowers 60–90cm (2–3ft) tall. Some plants in cultivation are the more freely suckering variety *officinalis*, which has softer, greener, more spotted leaves, and orange flowers.

HISTORY

Images of aloe vera are seen in ancient Egyptian wall paintings and Cleopatra used it to beautify her skin. In the Bible it is mentioned as an embalming ingredient, while records of it in ancient Greece begin around 400BC. It was introduced to Britain in the tenth century and was first

The Succotrine Aloe.

Eliz. Blackwell delin. sculp. et Pinx.

1. Flower.
2. Seed Vessel open.
3. Seed.

Aloe Succotrina.

mentioned in Chinese medicine a century later. Aloe vera gel became popular in the West during the 1950s when it was found to heal burns, especially those caused by radiation.

BEAUTY
Aloe vera gel has a soothing effect on sore or irritated skin and is often added to healing creams and after-sun lotions.

HEALING
Aloe vera preparations popular today are made from the gel that drains from the centre of the leaves when they are sliced. An aloe vera pot plant is very useful for first aid – just break off a leaf, slice it lengthwise to allow the gel-like sap to drain out, and then apply directly to the injury. It rapidly soothes stings as well as minor burns, cuts and grazes. The leaves are used externally to heal wounds, burns and skin conditions, or in colonic irrigation, and internally to soothe peptic ulcers and irritable bowel syndrome. Historically, 'aloes' or 'bitter aloes' refers to a purgative drug made from the whole leaves of several species. Curaçao aloe comes from *A. vera*; Cape aloe is from *A. ferox* and related species and hybrids. These are potent laxatives and should not be taken by pregnant women or children under 12 years of age. Excess intake results in griping pains; more seriously, prolonged use disturbs the body's electrolyte balance and ultimately the heart.

NOTES FOR GARDENERS
Aloe vera needs dry, sunny conditions and a minimum temperature of 8°C (46°F). It is easily grown as a garden plant in frost-free areas, or as a houseplant using soil-based compost, such as John Innes No 2, with added sand or grit. As it seldom sets seed, plants must be propagated by separating offsets during the growing season.

Aloysia triphylla — LEMON VERBENA

PORTRAIT
A deciduous shrub, native to Argentina and Chile, with slender oval, pointed leaves, about 10cm (4in) long, and panicles of tiny pale lilac to white flowers in summer. The foliage has a rather rough texture and an intense lemon scent – so much so that in Victorian times this herb was known simply as 'the lemon plant'. Though capable of reaching 3m (10ft) in frost-free conditions, it is often grown as a pot plant in cold areas or planted in the shelter of a wall.

HISTORY
Lemon verbena was introduced to cultivation from Chile in the late eighteenth century. Having probably the strongest, cleanest lemon scent of any non-citrus plant, it rapidly became a favourite. It is grown commercially for oil extraction in Algeria, Tunisia and France. Yields are naturally low, resulting in an expensive product. The essential oil was once popular in perfumery, notably in a citrus-scented cologne known as *eau de verveine*. Its use declined following evidence that it may sensitize the skin to sunlight, and further declined when lemongrass oils (from *Cymbopogon* species) proved a cheaper alternative. Pure essential oil of lemon verbena is often hard to find. 'Verbena oil'

Aloysia citriodora

may be a mixture of lemon, lemongrass, citronella and other lemon-scented herbs, or an oil extracted from the quite different *Thymus hyemalis,* sometimes sold as 'Spanish verbena'. Confusingly, *Verbena officinalis* (vervain) is a related plant that has similar properties, but no aroma.

COOKING
Fresh or dried leaves make a delicious herb tea, either on their own or in a blend; *verveine* tisane is one of the most popular in France. The leaves may also be used to give a lemon flavour to stuffings for fish or poultry. Commercially, the essential oil is an ingredient of liqueurs.

HOME
The dried leaves are very good in pot-pourris.

HEALING
Lemon verbena contains flavonoids and volatile oils that relieve spasms, especially of the digestive tract, and have a mild sedative effect. It is effective for relieving nervous tension and resulting digestive problems, and also helps to reduce fever. As a herb tea it is a good home remedy for indigestion and feverish colds, and is refreshing and reviving, hot or cold, at any time of the day. The essential oil is used by aromatherapists to treat stress-related conditions and to improve liver function. It also has insecticidal effects, and is a useful bactericide for acne and boils.

NOTES FOR GARDENERS
In cold areas lemon verbena is best grown as a container plant in loam-based compost, such as John Innes No 2, but is worth trying outdoors in a sheltered position, such as a dry, sunny border against a wall. If protected by horticultural fleece or a thick layer of mulch, it usually survives – though often looks completely dead until early summer when vigorous new shoots appear from the base. Plants can be propagated by softwood or greenwood cuttings in summer and pot plants should be renewed every few years from cuttings or cut back hard in early spring to keep them within bounds. Pinching them out regularly (use the tips for tea) will encourage compact, bushy growth. Plants can also be grown as standards.

Althaea officinalis   MARSH MALLOW

PORTRAIT
An upright hardy perennial, reaching 2m (6ft) tall, with a fleshy tap root and velvety, broadly ovate leaves with three to five shallow, toothed lobes. Pale pink, hibiscus-like flowers, up to 4cm (1½in) across, appear in summer. As the name suggests, marsh mallow is a plant of wet places, occurring in boggy ground, ditches and brackish marshes in coastal areas throughout Europe and across to central Russia, western Asia and North Africa. It is also naturalized in parts of North America.

HISTORY
The healing properties of marsh mallow were utilized in ancient Greek medicine; Theophrastus (*c*.370–287BC) recorded that the root was soaked in sweet wine as a cordial for coughs. The

53

Althæa officinalis

Published by Dr Woodville Novr 1. 1790.

sweetish roots are rich in mucilage that forms a jelly when infused in water and are famous as the original ingredient of marshmallows. Marshmallow confectionery was developed in France from soft lozenges (*pâté de guimauve*), made from the powdered root, which were sucked to relieve sore throats and coughs. The carrot-shaped dried roots, known as *hochets de guimauves*, were a traditional natural teether for babies. This herb once grew plentifully in marshes of the Thames estuary.

COOKING
Theoretically, the roots could be used to make a kind of soft jelly – or, of course, marshmallows – but marsh mallow is seldom used for culinary purposes today.

HEALING
In contrast, marsh mallow is an important medicinal herb, containing mucilage that soothes and softens tissues, and controls bacterial infection. Its soothing properties are effective against inflammation and ulceration of the digestive tract, as in diverticulitis and irritable bowel syndrome,

ALTHAEA OFFICINALIS

and for urinary tract infections and cystitis. It also has expectorant effects, making it an ideal remedy for irritating coughs and bronchial congestion. Externally, marsh mallow ointment can be used on inflamed skin, boils and abscesses, and to draw out splinters. In the form of a lotion, marsh mallow extracts are useful to bathe inflamed eyes or as a mouthwash. The closely related hollyhock (*Alcea rosea*), musk mallow (*Malva moschata*), common mallow (*M. sylvestris*) and dwarf mallow (*M. neglecta*) have similar properties but are rather less effective.

NOTES FOR GARDENERS
Marsh mallow may prefer marshes in the wild, but is surprisingly adaptable in cultivation. Though ideal for the bog garden, it will thrive and self-sow in borders on most kinds of soil, and even takes heavy clay in its stride. It harmonizes well with classic cottage garden plants, such as lupins, poppies and hardy geraniums. Either grow it from seed sown when ripe in late summer, or by division in autumn or early spring. For enthusiasts there is a white-flowered variety and also a rather better form called 'Romney Marsh'.

Anethum graveolens — DILL

PORTRAIT

An upright, hollow-stalked, hardy annual, 60–90cm (2–3ft) tall, with glaucous, ovate leaves, divided into thread-like segments. Umbels of tiny yellow flowers are produced in summer, followed by flat, oval seeds. Young plants of dill and fennel are easily confused. Dill has more grey-green, matt foliage, and smells more like caraway, while fennel is closer to aniseed. In the wild, dill occurs in warm parts of Europe and Asia. Indian dill is taller, with a pale stem and a different flavour. Once thought to be a different species, *A. sowa* but is now considered a subspecies.

HISTORY

Dill is a traditional Middle Eastern herb that has been important since Biblical times. Its leaves and flowers were found on the mummy of Amenophis II (*c.*1425BC) and both the ancient

ANETHUM GRAVEOLENS

Egyptians and Copts used dill medicinally. It is mentioned as being subject to a tithe in the Talmud (ancient Jewish law), and in Ancient Rome, Pliny (AD23–79) extolled its numerous uses. Classed as a cooling carminative, dill has also been used in Ayurvedic medicine for thousands of years.

COOKING

Both seeds and leaves of dill are used. With its strong, parsley-caraway flavour, it should be added with discretion. It goes very well with fish, seafood, potatoes (especially potato salad), soft cheeses, yogurt, sour cream or crème fraîche, eggs, cucumber, mushrooms and beans. Dill is not easy to combine with other herbs but is a good partner for mustard. Young leaves are known as 'dill weed' and are a favourite flavouring in Scandinavian dishes, such as gravlax (preserved salmon) and pickles. Dill pickles, using small cucumbers or gherkins, a bunch of fresh dill and some dill seeds, are a classic. Dill is popular in Poland too, where the roots and stems are used as well as the leaves and seeds.

HEALING
Extracts of dill have a calming, toning effect on the digestive system and act as a mild diuretic and anti-infective. Their main use is to ease indigestion, colic and wind, notably in the form of gripe water for babies. Dill is reputed to increase milk production in nursing mothers, and as a bonus is passed on to the baby to help prevent colic.

NOTES FOR GARDENERS
Dill is easily grown from seed sown directly in the ground in spring (it does not transplant very well), and then at intervals for a steady supply through the growing season. It thrives in well-drained neutral to slightly acid soil in sun, and where happy will self-sow generously. Plants in dry conditions 'bolt' (run to seed) without having reached their full potential. Over the years, growers have selected strains which are better either for foliage or production, or have a superior flavour, so it is worth buying seed of named varieties, such as 'Dukat', with long-lasting, mellow-flavoured leaves, or 'Long Island Mammoth', which readily produces outsize heads of seeds.

Angelica species   ANGELICA

PORTRAIT
Angelica archangelica (angelica) is a huge hardy biennial that in good conditions can reach 2.5m (8ft) tall. It has stout, hollow stems, long-stalked, bright green, deeply divided leaves, and rounded umbels of tiny yellow-green flowers in late spring and early summer. After flowering, countless flat, oval seeds are formed that in the wild result in imposing colonies. All parts are aromatic and have a liquorice-like taste. Angelica is native to north-east Europe and central Asia, where it grows in damp meadows and beside rivers. Chinese angelica, *dang gui* or *dong quai* (*A. polymorpha* var. *sinensis*) is a hardy perennial and smaller, reaching 1.2m (4ft), with ferny, dull green leaves and flattish umbels of off-white flowers.

HISTORY
Angelica was introduced to Britain from Scandinavia in the sixteenth century and in Parkinson's herbal (*Paradisi in Sole*, 1629) is rated the most important of all medicinal herbs. In earlier times it was regarded as a potent charm against evil spirits, and its extraordinarily beautiful name is connected with a story that its power, especially as an antidote to plague, was revealed to a humble monk by St Michael the Archangel. This northern European legend gave rise to the practice of sucking a piece of angelica root as a protection against all ills. Chinese angelica was first mentioned in Chinese medical texts dating back to about AD200.

COOKING
The young stalks are candied for decorating cakes and desserts. They are particularly good stewed with rhubarb and are worth experimenting with as a flavouring for jam and marmalade. Young flower heads, enclosed in their sheaths, may be eaten raw in salads, braised or added to stir fries, and the tender young leaf stalks are edible in similar ways. Essential oil, extracted from the roots and seeds, is widely used in the food industry, and especially for flavouring vermouth, spirits, and

liqueurs such as Benedictine and Chartreuse. Chinese angelica root is the main ingredient in the tonic *shou wu chih* and, though strongly flavoured, the roots are eaten with meats such as duck and mutton.

HOME
Dried angelica root acts as a perfume fixative and can be used as a substitute for orris (*Iris germanica* var. *florentina*) in pot-pourri. It is effective as soon as it is dried, whereas orris roots take several years to mature.

HEALING
This bitter-sweet herb is a warming tonic with a wide range of applications. It has anti-inflammatory and expectorant effects, relaxes spasms, lowers fever, relieves digestive discomfort, and improves peripheral circulation. Angelica is particularly effective in cases of poor circulation, such as Buerger's disease, which restricts blood flow to the hands and feet. Various parts are used;

ANGELICA ARCHANGELICA

the roots are preferred for respiratory infections. Chinese angelica is also a tonic but acts more on the liver and reproductive system. It is used mainly for menstrual and menopausal complaints, and after childbirth.

NOTES FOR GARDENERS
Angelica seeds have a short viability so should be sown when ripe. For large, lush plants, grow angelica in deep, rich, moisture-retentive soil. Removing the majority of seed heads before they ripen will control excessive self-sowing. Take care when handling angelica plants. They can cause contact dermatitis that may appear soon after touching them or a few days later – or even the following year when angelica is handled again.

VANILLA PLANIFOLIA

Herbal

WHEN WE HEAR THE WORD 'HERB', the first thing that comes to mind is fragrance. Scent in plants is mostly, though not exclusively, produced by volatile oils – delicate, ethereal substances that disperse readily into the air when warmed. Coumarins are another source of fragrance – substances with a vanilla-like aroma that forms when the plant parts are dried or fermented.

Discovering unlikely sources of scents is especially rewarding. The fragrances of vanilla, vetiver, orris, spikenard and coumarin grasses are just as intoxicating as any floral perfume. We may not swoon over the sight of fermented pods, shrivelled roots and blades of grass but our pleasure in their perfume instils a great reverence – not only for the plants, but for those pioneers who long ago discovered their worth and the artisans who to this day are skilled in producing these precious substances.

The word 'coumarin' comes from the Tupi Indian *cumarú*, a tonka bean. These large black seeds are produced by a tropical American tree called *Dipteryx odorata*, which grows wild in Venezuela and is cultivated in Trinidad. The fallen ripe fruits are soaked in rum for a few days and then dried. This process causes the coumarin to crystallize on the surface like a frosting. The beans are added to pot-pourris to make the perfume last longer, and extracts are used in commercial food flavouring and to give a vanilla-like aroma to tobacco and snuff.

HIEROCHLOË ODORATA

Real vanilla comes from the fermented unripe pods of a climbing tropical American orchid, *Vanilla planifolia*. Extraction is a long, complicated process, taking six months, in which the pods are scalded, sweated, then exposed to the sun, dried in the shade, and finally stacked in trunks. In cultivation, the flowers have to be pollinated by hand, so vanilla is a man-made product in more ways than one. Vanilla can be synthesized much more cheaply but is a poor second best to the real thing, which contains more than 35 aromatic compounds. The compounds in vanilla also occur in many balsams and resins (see p.48), which also have very complex aromas. Although vanilla is associated mainly with sweet foods – it has been used to flavour chocolate since Aztec times – it is also used in perfumery and cosmetics.

Coumarins are often likened to the scent of new-mown hay. Among the grasses responsible for this sweet fragrance are vanilla grass (*Hierochloë odorata*) and sweet vernal grass (*Anthoxanthum odoratum*). In Poland, vodka is flavoured by adding a leaf or two of vanilla grass per bottle and leaving it for a few weeks. North American tribes gather vanilla grass and braid the leaves: when dried, they are burnt or hung in lodges to scent the air. The braided grass can also be woven into mats and little baskets that keep their

VETIVERIA ZIZANIOIDES

Aromatics

fragrance for years. Both these grasses can be dried for adding to pot-pourri or dried flower arrangements.

It always comes as a surprise to discover that an otherwise unscented plant has wonderfully aromatic roots. Vetiver or khus khus (*Vetiveria zizanioides*) is a good example. This plain-looking giant grass has nothing to recommend it visually but its roots have a myrrh-like scent with violet overtones. In India, the long roots are woven into screens, which are dampened to waft fragrance into the room. Essential oil of vetiver is calming and uplifting, giving it the name 'oil of tranquillity'. Aromatherapists use it to cleanse the aura, balance the nervous system, and 'ground' those who are stressed or anxious. It is also used in soaps and perfumes with woody notes.

Spikenard is another root extract: a costly essential oil with a musky, patchouli-like perfume that has been traded since the dawn of time. In Ancient Rome it was worth 300 denarii per pound (450g), when a denarius was the daily wage of a labourer. Spikenard was mentioned in the *Song of Songs* (I.12), and in the New Testament as the substance used to anoint the feet of Jesus at the Last Supper. It comes from *Nardostachys grandiflora*, a small plant of the valerian family with pink flowers and aromatic rhizomes, clad in tufts of fibres. Spikenard grows at up to 17,000ft (5,200m) in the Hindu Kush and Himalayas, and it is now endangered in the wild. Having been collected more or less sustainably for thousands of years, in recent decades the combined effects of habitat degradation and over-collection for the expanding demands of the international herb trade, have pushed this aromatic gem to the brink. Alpine plants are usually difficult to cultivate, but spikenard seems more amenable than most and has been cultivated in Britain since Victorian times.

Another root aromatic is orris, from the Dalmatian iris (*Iris pallida*), flag iris (*I. germanica*) and the white-flowered flag iris, var. *florentina*. Traditionally, orris is produced among the vineyards and olive groves surrounding Florence and Siena, turning the stony hillsides lavender-blue or white in the spring. The knobbly rhizomes are harvested from June to August, washed and peeled, then washed again and laid out on straw mats to dry in the sun. Orris has a violet-like scent, used mainly to enhance other perfumes. It comes either as powdered orris, which can be added to pot-pourris as a fixative, or as an essential oil that may be liquid, solid or in the form of an oleoresin. The finest oils are obtained from aged roots – like good wine, orris rhizomes need time to mature.

See also: *Cymbopogan* species, *Inula helenium*, *Juniperus commumis*, *Zingiber officinalis*.

NARDOSTACHYS GRANDIFLORA

IRIS GERMANICA VAR. FLORENTINA

Anthriscus cerefolium CHERVIL

PORTRAIT

A hardy annual about 60cm (2ft) tall in flower, with bright green, fragile, lacy leaves, and umbels of tiny white flowers in early summer. Chervil is native to rocky limestone cliffs in southern Russia, the Caucasus and the Middle East, and is widely naturalized in Europe and the north-eastern United States.

HISTORY

There is little written evidence of chervil in ancient Egyptian times but a basket of chervil seeds was found in the tomb of Tutankhamun. It seems to have been a favourite with the Romans who introduced it to the many regions they occupied. Today it is perhaps more popular in France than anywhere else, and in Arabic is known as *baqdûnis afrangi*, French parsley.

ANTHRISCUS CEREFOLIUM

COOKING

Chervil is the fourth ingredient of *fines herbes* (the others being chives, parsley, and tarragon) and, with chives, shallots and tarragon, is also a vital component of *ravigote* – a finely chopped herb blend that provides the basis for a herb butter or gives piquancy to a sauce. It has an evanescent anise-like aroma that does not stand up to strong flavours or prolonged cooking. Add finely chopped leaves to salads, steamed vegetables, potatoes, and any foods with a bland or subtle taste, such as omelettes, scrambled egg, grilled or poached fish, creamy soups and sauces, soft cheese, or plain grilled chicken. Fresh is best as chervil loses its flavour on drying. For maximum flavour add generous amounts just before serving. The leaves are prettier than parsley as a garnish.

HEALING

Traditionally used as a blood cleanser and spring tonic in central Europe, chervil is a mild diuretic and expectorant that stimulates the metabolism, increases perspiration and lowers blood pressure. Herbalists might use it to treat chronic skin problems, arthritis, rheumatism, gout, fluid retention, and jaundice. It is usually used fresh, the whole plant being cut before flowering and juiced, or infused using a tablespoon of chopped leaves to a cup of boiling water. The crushed leaves can also be applied as a poultice to slow-healing wounds, abscesses and eczema.

NOTES FOR GARDENERS
As chervil resembles so many white-flowered umbelliferous plants, a fair number of which are poisonous, it is better to grow this herb than gather it from the wild. In spite of its long history of cultivation, chervil has undergone little or no selection or breeding, and there is only one cultivar, the curly-leaved 'Crispum'. Sow seed directly in well-drained but moist soil, ideally pH 7–8, in shade or partial shade. Chervil is fast growing: sowing afresh every few weeks will ensure a crop throughout the season. Thin, weed and water plants well as they bolt rapidly in hot dry conditions or when starved and overcrowded. Chervil is extremely useful for a damp, shady spot that few other herbs will tolerate, and is every bit as good as parsley in containers.

Arctostaphylos uva-ursi   BEARBERRY

PORTRAIT
A very hardy, evergreen, prostrate shrub that forms mats about 50cm (20in) across on moors in northern regions worldwide and is increasingly rare in Europe. It bears small, dark green, oval leaves and clusters of waxy, pinkish-white, urn-shaped flowers in summer, followed by relatively large, glossy red berries.

HISTORY
The name *Arctostaphylos* is from the Greek *arkton staphyle*, meaning 'bear's grapes', as the fruits are an important item in the diet of grizzlies and other bears. They were eaten by some native American tribes but not by others. The Chehalis had no time for them, while the Skokomish enjoyed them with salmon eggs. Kinninkinnick, the Klallam name for the plant, was widely adopted by settlers. Ethnobotanists have recorded how various tribes smoked kinninkinnick leaves as an intoxicant, but no hallucinogenic or narcotic compounds have been identified. The foliage has a high tannin content, hence its use for tanning leather in Sweden and Russia. In Iceland a combination of black bog mud and bearberry is used to produce a black dye that retains its colour well.

COOKING
Though similar in appearance and distantly related to cranberry, bearberry fruits are nowhere near as pleasant to eat. They have dry, rather tasteless flesh and large seeds.

HEALING
Bearberry is known as uva-ursi to herbalists, who use it as a urinary antiseptic. It contains arbutin, an irritant but strongly anti-bacterial substance that is effective against *E. coli* and organisms associated with urinary infections. Though toxic in excess and unsuitable for children, pregnant women and anyone with kidney disease, it is an effective remedy for cystitis, especially when the condition is recurrent and resistant to pharmaceutical antibiotics. It works only when the urine is

43

alkaline and should not be taken with medicines that acidify the urine. For this reason, uva-ursi is not recommended for self-medication. In lower doses it is included in numerous over-the-counter remedies for fluid retention and menstrual and menopausal discomfort, presumably for its mild diuretic effect. The leaves can also be made into an infusion for bathing skin inflammations and, in larger quantities, for adding to a sitz bath or bidet after childbirth to soothe and heal tissue.

NOTES FOR GARDENERS

Bearberry needs very acid soil – pH 5 at least – and is difficult to propagate. Dipping seeds in boiling water for 20 seconds before sowing in ericaceous compost can help. Autumn is the best time to sow, leaving trays or pots in a cold frame until germination has taken place. Alternatively, take semi-ripe cuttings in summer, dip in rooting hormone and insert in sand. Best results are obtained with mist propagation at 22°C (72°F), but even then they are slow. Handle the resulting plantlets and seedlings carefully as they dislike disturbance and do not transplant well. The good news is that bearberry thrives in cold, windswept areas at high altitudes, and on the coast. In cool,

ARCTOSTAPHYLOS UVA-URSI

moist conditions it makes good groundcover and can be used to control erosion on steep slopes. 'Vancouver Jade' and 'Wood's Red' have pink flowers; the former has longer, more arching branches than the species, and the latter has a dwarf habit and large fruits.

Armoracia rusticana   HORSERADISH

PORTRAIT

A robust, hardy, clump-forming perennial with a stout tap root that often reaches 60cm (2ft) long and can be 10cm (4in) wide. It produces dock-like leaves up to 50cm (20in) long, and branched, leafy stems of tiny, four-petalled white flowers in summer. Originally found wild from south-east Europe to western Asia, horseradish is now naturalized in many parts of the world, including New Zealand.

HISTORY

Horseradish has been cultivated for some 2,000 years, which is quite a short time compared with many herbs. Its first mention in English was by John Gerard in *The Herball, or Generall Historie of Plantes*, published in 1597. He commented that it was popular in Germany, crushed with vinegar, as a sauce with fish and meat. By the seventeenth century, horseradish sauce had become popular in both Britain and France, from where it has spread worldwide.

COOKING

The young leaves have a mild, pleasant flavour and are good in salads and sandwiches, especially with smoked or oily fish. The fresh root can be grated alone, or with apple, as a condiment for fish, or with vinegar and cream or oil to accompany roast beef, cold meats or hard-boiled eggs. Creamed horseradish is good mixed with English or French mustard, too. Horseradish sauce is usually served cold as heating destroys the volatile oils responsible for the pungency.

ARMORACIA RUSTICANA

HEALING

The essential oil in horseradish is almost identical to mustard oil and is similarly very pungent, irritant and stimulating. Used with care, or as part of the diet, horseradish has many beneficial effects. It improves the circulation and digestion, and is antibacterial, helping to prevent food poisoning. Medicinally, horseradish acts as a diuretic and expectorant, and cools the body by increasing perspiration. It speeds the excretion of toxins in conditions such as arthritis and gout, and is good for colds, flu and feverish chills. Excess causes gastric irritation, and it should be avoided by anyone with digestive disorders. It also depresses thyroid function. Horseradish poultices are used for infected wounds, pleurisy and arthritis, but again care is needed to avoid excessive use, which may cause blistering.

NOTES FOR GARDENERS

Horseradish is rampant and ineradicable, so think carefully before planting. Unless you use large quantities, one solution might be to grow some in a large pot, harvesting and repotting as required.

Young roots from second-year plants taste best so there is little point in having huge old clumps. Keep the plants evenly moist for tender, well-flavoured roots. Horseradish is rarely grown from seed as it is so easy to propagate from root cuttings. Every little bit will sprout, which is why it is so difficult to get rid of once planted. Pieces the size of your little finger make ideal cuttings. Plant them well below the surface in winter, or in trays in a cold frame. In cold areas roots can be harvested in late autumn and stored in damp sand for winter use. The variegated form is less vigorous and more ornamental.

Arnica species ARNICA

PORTRAIT
There are 32 species of *Arnica* in northern temperate regions and the Arctic. In general they grow in mountainous areas, usually in colonies, and have yellow daisy flowers in summer, and rather sticky or downy, aromatic, opposite leaves. Most species reach about 60cm (2ft). The best known is *A. montana*, a rhizomatous perennial that grows on poor, acid soils in European alpine pastures, but there are a number of North American species, including *A. chamissonis,* which are equally effective and often more easily cultivated. *Arnica montana* is a protected species, having declined through over-collection and changes in land management.

HISTORY
Arnica has long been a popular remedy in Germany and Austria for bruises and sprains, and also internally for heart complaints. In old age, Goethe (1749–1832) took arnica tea for angina.

COOKING
In Europe arnica is listed as a natural source of food flavouring but in the USA it is considered unsafe in all foods, apart from alcoholic beverages.

HEALING
Arnica preparations are made from the flowers of *A. montana* or *A. chamissonis* subsp. *foliosa.* Extracts take the form of tinctures, ointments, oils and homeopathic preparations for external application to sprains, bruises, swellings due to dislocation or fracture, chilblains, rheumatic muscles and joints, and boils. Arnica should never be applied to broken skin. The tincture may also be used in a gargle or mouthwash for throat and mouth inflammations. It is no longer considered safe to take arnica internally, unless in homeopathic doses; excess can be seriously toxic. Allergic reactions to arnica are common, so a test patch is a good idea, and even then, avoid prolonged use.

NOTES FOR GARDENERS
Arnica montana is challenging to grow at low elevations. It likes cool, moist, well-drained, acid soil in sun, and dislikes winter wet – in the wild the ground would be frozen solid through the coldest months. European arnica is also very sensitive to artificial fertilizers and in the wild has refused to recolonize land that was fertilized 60 years ago. *Arnica chamissonis* is much more tolerant, thriving in most well-drained garden soils. Sow seed in autumn in a cold frame to allow stratification or divide plants in spring.

Arnica *montana*

Published as the Act directs by Dr Woodville Jany 1. 1790.

Herbal Balsams,

Trees and shrubs protect their vital organs — wood, bark and buds — by exuding sticky gums, resins and balsams. These substances are highly astringent and aromatic, containing tannins and oils that protect plant tissues from pests, diseases and herbivores. They ooze freely from the bark in some species, in others appearing only when the plant is stressed. Resins are insoluble in water and flammable, and are a feature of woody plants growing in areas subject to fires. They encourage the flames to pass quickly, consuming little more than the resin itself, peeling bark and leaves, all of which are dispensable. Gums harden on drying but are soluble in water, while balsams or oleoresins are a gooey mixture of resin and oils. Other combinations occur, blurring distinctions between the various secretions.

Some gum resins are extremely astringent, making them important in medicine for contracting tissues and drying secretions. They bind with proteins, detoxify the digestive system, control bleeding, diarrhoea, discharges and mucus, so are commonly used in remedies for digestive and respiratory complaints, healing sore tissues and wounds, and arresting haemorrhage. Gum resins from Australian eucalypts are known as kinos, after the very astringent sap extracted from kino or bastard teak (*Pterocarpus marsupium*).

The most famous gum resins are frankincense (*Boswellia sacra*) and myrrh (*Commiphora myrrha*) from the deserts of Arabia. Ancient literature is full of references to these hallowed substances, which were brought as gifts to the newborn Jesus. Frankincense, which comes mainly from the Dhofar region of Oman, has innumerable uses in medicine, hygiene, perfumery and skin care, and is a major component of incense burned in religious services. Extracts are even used in anti-wrinkle creams: frankincense is associated with longevity and considered rejuvenative in Ayurvedic medicine, as is myrrh (*Commiphora myrrha*). Myrrh relieves pain; it was offered to Jesus before the crucifixion and symbolizes suffering. It was well known as a perfume fixative in ancient Egypt: a recipe for oil of lilies called for 5oz (140g) of myrrh in scented wine and one thousand lilies. Less familiar is guggul (*C. wightii* syn. *C. mukul*), which has long been used in Ayurvedic medicine for bone, joint and nerve pain.

South-east Asia is home to Borneo camphor or borneol (*Dryobalanops aromatica*), a pungent, stimulant crystalline substance that exudes as oil or crystallizes in cavities in the trunk. It is used medicinally and in pine-like fragrances. *Styrax benzoin*, a Sumatran tree, yields benzoin or gum Benjamin, which was first described by Ibn Batuta, an Arab traveller who reached the

Boswellia sacra

Liquidambar styraciflua

48

Gums & Resins

East Indies in 1325. He called it *luban jawi*, meaning 'frankincense of Java', which over time became Benjamin or benzoin. Benzoin gives body and lasting qualities to almost any kind of perfume and is a useful anti-oxidant in cosmetics; it is also the main ingredient in friar's balsam and other cold remedies.

Balsam from the tropical American tree *Myroxylon balsamum* has also been in use for centuries. Tolu balsam is a brownish crystalline substance collected by making V-shaped incisions in the bark; Peru balsam is an oily fluid, extracted by beating and scorching the bark of the variety *pereirae*. Tolu balsam has a long-lasting cinnamon-vanilla aroma and is used as a fixative in floral perfumes, such as champac (see p.109), mimosa and honeysuckle. Peru balsam lacks the vanilla note; it blends well with perfumes containing heliotrope or limeflower (see p.279).

ACACIA FARNESIANA

North America has its balsam trees too. Balm of gilead or balsam fir, *Abies balsamea*, is used medicinally, and as a fragrance and fixative. Sweet gum, *Liquidambar styraciflua*, is used in cough and cold remedies, and as an antiseptic for skin diseases. Balsam from the Asian *L. orientalis* has an even stronger fragrance. Known as storax, it is an excellent fixative for the scents of cassie (*Acacia farnesiana*), lavender (see p.155), and lemon verbena (see p.31).

Though most of these plant secretions are wonderfully aromatic, there is a notorious exception. Gum resin from *Ferula assa-foetida* has a most objectionable odour, as suggested by the name 'devil's dung'. How then, can its alternative name be 'food-of-the-gods'? The answer is because, in minute quantities, its foul-smelling sulphur compounds, just like those of garlic, enhance the flavour of many foods. It is an essential ingredient of many Indian recipes. Ferulas are large perennials from the Mediterranean and Middle East, commonly known as giant fennel. The resin is collected by making incisions in the stems or by cutting down the plant and scraping it from the stump.

FERULA ASSA-FOETIDA

Gums from various plants are chewed in different parts of the world as a traditional way to clean teeth, strengthen gums and sweeten the breath. Examples include *chicle* from *Manilkara zapota*, the chewing gum of the Aztecs; frankincense and gum arabic (*Acacia senegal*) in the Middle East; cutch (*A. catechu*) in India; and mastic (*Pistacia lentiscus*) in the Mediterranean. Gum arabic and gum tragacanth (*Astragalus gummifer*) also have a long history of use in thickening foods and enhancing flavours. They may sound archaic but they are as important now as they were thousands of years ago; only now the food industry has renamed them E413 and E414.

See also: *Cinnamomum camphora*, *Eucalyptus* species, *Pinus* species.

PISTACIA LENTISCUS

Artemisia abrotanum

SOUTHERNWOOD
LAD'S LOVE

PORTRAIT

A hardy, deciduous or semi-evergreen shrub with erect stems, reaching 1m (3ft) tall, and grey-green leaves, finely divided into thread-like segments. Panicles of tiny dull yellow flowers appear in warm summers only. Southernwood is probably native to southern Europe, but has been cultivated for so long that its origins are uncertain.

HISTORY

Used since ancient times as an insect repellent and anti-infective, southernwood was a key component of nosegays or tussie-mussies – posies of sweet-scented herbs that were carried to keep away bad odours and disease in Elizabethan England. Until the nineteenth century, a bunch of southernwood and rue was placed in court to protect against jail fever.

ARTEMISIA ABROTANUM

HOME

Dried southernwood can be made into sachets to repel moths and fleas and scattered in animals' bedding for the same reason.

HEALING

In common with other artemisias, southernwood is a bitter herb that acts as a tonic for the liver and digestive system. It stimulates the uterus so is not recommended during pregnancy, though it may help some kinds of period pains. In the right dose it can be used to expel threadworms in children. Externally, it may relieve frostbite and sciatica, and aid the removal of splinters. Rumour has it that it does indeed stimulate hair growth.

NOTES FOR GARDENERS

Southernwood is essential in the herb garden as a foil for other plants or as a low, informal hedge. A trouble-free plant, it always remains neatly upright and needs only a trim in spring to maintain health and vigour. It tolerates most soils and prefers sun, but is otherwise undemanding. Plants can be propagated by semi-ripe cuttings in summer.

Artemisia absinthium

A. pontica

WORMWOOD
ROMAN WORMWOOD

PORTRAIT
Artemisia absinthium (wormwood) is a hardy, shrubby perennial, reaching 60–90cm (2–3ft) in height and breadth, with more or less evergreen, finely divided, silvery foliage and panicles of tiny yellowish bobble-like flowers in summer. It grows wild in waste ground, often in stony soil, from Europe to Siberia, and is naturalized in north-eastern and central United States, parts of South America and New Zealand. Roman wormwood or small absinthe (*A. pontica*) is smaller, with finer, upright, unbranched stems arising from creeping rhizomes. It is similar to wormwood in flavour and uses, but milder.

HISTORY
The scientific name *absinthium* means 'without sweetness', referring to the intense bitterness of wormwood; the common name comes from the German *Wermut*, 'preserver of the mind', as the herb was reputed to enhance mental functions. A household remedy since Biblical times, wormwood is notorious as the flavouring of absinthe, an alcoholic aperitif first made by Henri Pernod in 1797. The drink was such a success that by the nineteenth century, absinthe drinking had become a social institution, much like afternoon tea. Following the discovery that thujone – a major constituent of wormwood's essential oil – is addictive and causes irreversible damage to the nervous system, one country after another, beginning with Switzerland in 1908, banned the use of wormwood oil as a flavouring.

COOKING
Extracts of *A. absinthium* are not permitted as flavourings in many countries, but Roman wormwood (*A. pontica*) is still used to flavour wine and vermouth.

HEALING
The bitterness of wormwood (*A. absinthium*) kick-starts the liver and gall bladder, stimulating the appetite and priming the digestive system so that digestion, especially of fatty foods, is improved. It is therefore an excellent remedy for loss of appetite, dyspepsia, and gall bladder complaints. The dried leaves and flowering tops, harvested mainly in eastern Europe, are made into infusions and tinctures, or powdered as a digestive tonic. The essential oil is too toxic for internal use. Wormwood stimulates the uterus so should not be taken during pregnancy.

NOTES FOR GARDENERS
The silver-green foliage of wormwood looks good with roses, hardy geraniums and other cottage garden flowers, and also makes an elegant companion for white flowers. The cultivar 'Lambrook Silver' has finer, more silvery foliage and reaches only 75cm (30in). Wormwood enjoys neutral to

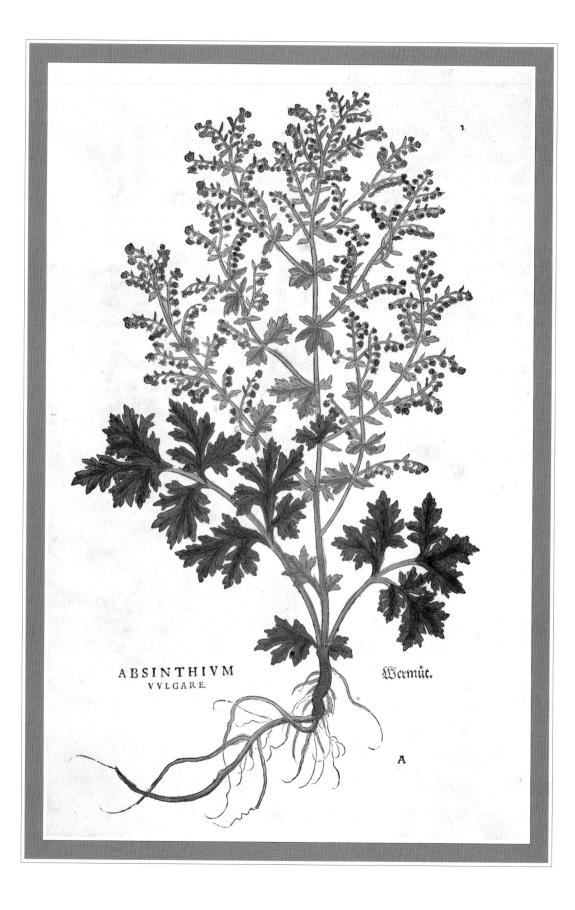

ABSINTHIVM
VVLGARE.

Wermůt.

A

alkaline, well-drained soil and full sun. Propagate by seed, sown on the surface at 21°C (70°F), or by heel cuttings of side shoots in early summer. Prune hard in spring to maintain a neat, bushy habit. The leaves secrete a substance that inhibits the growth of other plants and the germination of seeds within a metre (yard) radius. Soak the prunings in water to make a natural herbicide.

Artemisia annua

SWEET WORMWOOD
SWEET ANNIE

PORTRAIT
A fast-growing, sweet-scented, frost-hardy annual with stiffly upright, often reddish stems, and bright green, shiny, feathery leaves. Tiny yellow flowers are produced in panicles in summer. Found wild on cultivated and waste ground from south-east Europe across to Iran, this giant annual reaches 1.5–3m (5–10ft) tall.

ARTEMISIA ANNUA

HISTORY
Sweet wormwood was first recorded in Chinese medicine in *Shen Nong's Canon of Herbs (Shen Nong Ben Cao Jing)*, which dates back to about AD200. Modern research in Thailand has now shown that *A. annua*, in the form of Artesunate, is effective against drug-resistant strains of malaria and the synthetic analogues, arteflene and artemether, have been produced as front-line anti-malarials.

HEALING
Known as *qing hao* in Chinese medicine, sweet wormwood was traditionally used to treat feverish illnesses, notably malaria, and heat stroke. It can also be used externally to control bleeding.

NOTES FOR GARDENERS
Easily grown from fresh seed sown in warmth in early spring, sweet wormwood is a superb plant for filling in gaps in the back of the border or creating a short-lived, aromatic green screen. In spite of its effectiveness as a drug against malaria, sadly there is no indication that the plant will repel mosquitoes.

Artemisia dracunculus TARRAGON

PORTRAIT

A shrubby perennial, about 1m (3ft) tall, with narrow, pointed leaves and tiny yellow-green flowers that do not produce viable seed in cool summers. Tarragon grows wild in southern Russia and in parts of central and eastern Europe, in scrub and rocky areas. It is not reliably hardy in cold wet winters or on heavy soils. Russian tarragon, *A. dracunculus* subsp. *dracunculoides*, is hardier but has a poor flavour.

HISTORY

Tarragon was known as a 'dragon herb', a cure for venomous stings and snake bites, hence the name *dracunculus*, little dragon. In his *Herball* of 1597, Gerard recorded a strange story about the origin of tarragon, telling how it was produced by inseminating a radish root or sea onion with flax seed.

ARTEMISIA DRACUNCULUS

COOKING

Tarragon gives a penetrating but subtle anise-like flavour to many different foods. It is a classic herb with chicken, but equally good with salmon and other fish, soups and any dish *à l'estragon*. Its flavour enhances white wine vinegar and mustard too, and these in turn lend a tarragon flavour to sauces and dressings. Tarragon is an essential ingredient of Béarnaise sauce and *fines herbes*.

HEALING

Tarragon is not much used medicinally today. Up to 70 per cent of the volatile oil consists of methyl chavicol, which is toxic in excess and potentially carcinogenic. It was once used to improve the digestion and bring on menstruation, and the root was considered a cure for toothache.

NOTES FOR GARDENERS

Tarragon thrives in warm summers, mild winters and well-drained, slightly acid (pH 6.2) soil. Sandy, stony and gravelly soils with low fertility suit it fine. Tarragon will not stand shade, waterlogging, or heavy frost. In cold areas it needs a sheltered spot or the protection of a thick mulch in winter. Propagation is only successful by taking semi-ripe cuttings in summer: try using sections 5–7cm (2–3in) long from a supermarket pack of fresh tarragon. Home-grown tarragon is best frozen for winter use as it is tricky to dry without loss of flavour.

Artemisia vulgaris   MUGWORT

PORTRAIT

A hardy perennial, reaching 60cm–1.2m (2–4ft), with reddish stems and irregularly toothed, deeply divided, dark green leaves that have grey-white undersides. Panicles of inconspicuous, red-brown flowers appear in late summer. Mugwort is a common weed throughout temperate regions of the northern hemisphere, thriving alongside busy roads and other polluted places.

ARTEMISIA VULGARIS

HISTORY

Mugwort was one of nine sacred Druidic herbs that were believed to protect against evil and poisons. In the Middle Ages it was known as *Mater Herbarum*, Mother of Herbs, in reverence of its magical and healing powers. It is still an important plant in the Isle of Man, where is it called bollan bane ('white herb'). The tradition of wearing sprigs of mugwort on 4 July at the annual Manx parliament dates back to the Norse kingdom of Man. In China, where it is known as *ai*, mugwort plays a major role in exorcizing demons on the fifth day of the fifth moon during the summer solstice. Fashioned into human images, it is hung over doorways to drive away misfortune, evil and death. Mugwort is also used to burn three rows of scars on the shaved heads of Buddhist novices.

COOKING

Mugwort is bitter but decidedly more palatable than most other artemisias. It is a traditional flavouring for eels and carp, especially in Germany, Spain, and Britain, and is worth trying in stuffings for game, goose, duck or pork.

Healing

A tonic herb with many different uses, acting mainly on the nervous and digestive systems. It also has diuretic effects, increases perspiration and, in the right dose, expels tape worms. Western and Chinese herbalists differ in their usage of mugwort, the former recognizing it as a uterine stimulant that brings on delayed or difficult menstruation, while the latter use it to prevent miscarriage and control haemorrhage of various kinds. It is given as a tincture for abdominal pains and labour, and also applied as a poultice to relieve pain. In Chinese medicine mugwort is the main herb used in *moxa*, a technique for stimulating acupuncture points in cases of internal cold. The dried leaves are compressed into a wick that is burnt briefly close to the skin. White mugwort (*A. lactiflora*) is a traditional Chinese remedy for both menstrual and liver problems.

Notes for Gardeners

Mugwort may be a weed but is not weedy in appearance or invasive in behaviour. Very easily grown from seed or division in spring or autumn, it is fine for the back of the herb border or tucked away near a fence or hedge. For a more prominent position, there are several variegated and golden-leaved forms. 'Oriental Limelight' is both. White mugwort has a magnificent dark form, known as 'Guizhou', in which the foliage is purple-flushed.

Asparagus officinalis   ASPARAGUS

Portrait

A hardy perennial, reaching 1–1.5m (3–5ft) tall, with creeping rhizomes and upright stems that appear in spring as stout, succulent shoots. The foliage consists of short, fine, soft, leaf-like structures called cladodes; the true leaves are reduced to tiny triangular scales. Small, pale green, bell-shaped flowers appear in summer, followed by poisonous red berries. Wild asparagus can be found in coastal areas over most of Europe.

History

Asparagus has been cultivated since ancient Egyptian times as a vegetable and, as the name *officinalis* suggests, as a medicinal herb too. The word *officinalis*, meaning a storeroom for herbs, is medieval Latin, from the Latin *officina*, a workshop. As a consequence, key herbs in the pharmacopoeia became known as officinals.

Cooking

Young shoots or 'spears' are steamed and served hot or cold as a vegetable, or chopped and added to soups and savoury tarts. Slender shoots, known as sprue, are especially good in salads.

Healing

Asparagus contains asparagine, a strong diuretic that in most gives the urine a characteristic odour. It also contains asparagusic acid that kills roundworms, threadworms, and the parasitic flatworms that cause bilharzia. Herbalists regard asparagus as a cleansing herb that acts on the liver, bowels

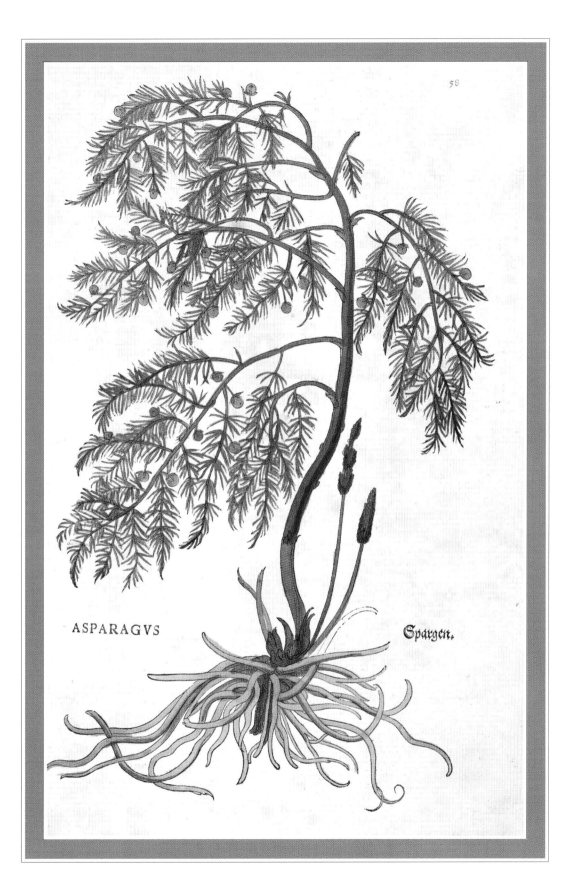

ASPARAGVS   Spargen.

and kidneys. It is used mainly to treat cystitis, kidney problems, fluid retention, and to help flush out toxins in rheumatic joints. *Shatavari (A. racemosus)* is the most important herb for women in Ayurvedic medicine. It is a soothing tonic that acts on the female reproductive organs, helping to treat a wide range of problems, from infertility and loss of libido to threatened miscarriage and menopausal syndrome.

NOTES FOR GARDENERS
Asparagus needs rich, light, well-drained soil in full sun. For culinary use it is usually grown from one-year-old 'crowns' which are planted 1m (3ft) apart in spring. Varieties such as 'Thielim' and the all-male 'Jersey Knight' quickly develop into large, high-yielding plants. Asparagus can also be grown from seed but resulting plants are less uniform. Again, for culinary use it is best to choose a fast-growing, heavy cropping variety. All asparagus plants are ornamental and make a good background in the border. 'Purple Jumbo' has especially attractive purple shoots and purple-flushed foliage.

ASTRAGALUS MEMBRANACEUS

Astragalus membranaceus

MILK VETCH

PORTRAIT
A hardy perennial, reaching 60cm (3ft) tall, with sprawling stems and symmetrical leaves divided into 12 to 18 pairs of leaflets. In summer it produces small, pale yellow pea flowers, followed by papery pods about 2.5cm (1in) long, containing dark brown, kidney-shaped seeds. Milk vetch grows wild in open, rather dry, wooded areas, and in grass at the edges of forest in northern China, typically with pine trees on sandy soil. *Astragalus membranaceus* var. *mongolicus* is similar in appearance and use but prefers damper sites in mountainous regions of north-eastern China.

HISTORY
Known in Chinese medicine as *huang qi*, milk vetch has been an important herb for more than 2,000 years. *Huang* is the Chinese word for yellow, referring to the flesh of the root – the useful part of

the plant — and *qi* means 'leader', indicating that it is a key herb in the pharmacopoeia. The plant was first described in botanical terms by Dr Alexander von Bunge, a Russian physician with a keen interest in east Asian plants who wrote a monograph on the genus *Astragalus* in 1868.

HEALING

Chinese milk vetch is a sweet tonic herb that stimulates the immune system and benefits the spleen, stomach, lungs, liver, circulation and urinary tract. In China it is as popular as ginseng, and regarded as a better tonic for younger people. It appears in numerous patent medicines, primarily for lack of energy, poor appetite, impaired circulation and recurrent infections. Milk vetch is one of several herbs used in *fu zheng* therapy, which strengthens the immune system in cancer patients while they are undergoing chemotherapy and radiation.

NOTES FOR GARDENERS

Milk vetch prefers deep, well-drained, sandy, neutral to alkaline soil and can be propagated by seed sown in spring or autumn. Germination may be slow because the seeds have a hard seed coat. It can be speeded up by nicking or filing the seeds so that they take up water more quickly, or by soaking them in warm water overnight. As a garden plant, it is neither especially attractive nor unattractive, but is prized because of its relative rarity in collections of herbs in the West. As a crop it is a long-term project: the roots are not harvested until they are four or five years old.

Belamcanda chinensis

LEOPARD LILY
BLACKBERRY LILY

PORTRAIT

A short-lived evergreen perennial, 30–90cm (1–3ft) tall, with a fan of iris-like leaves and branched heads of yellow to orange, spotted, six-petalled flowers that open in succession in summer, each lasting only a day. The flowers are followed by three-chambered pods that split open to reveal shiny black seeds — hence the name blackberry lily. *Belamcanda chinensis* has a wide distribution in China, Japan, northern India and eastern Russia, and is naturalized in eastern and southern areas of the United States. It grows in dry, often sandy grassland, sometimes in partial shade and frequently near streams or in coastal meadows.

HISTORY

Known in Chinese medicine as *she gan*, the leopard lily was first mentioned in medical literature in the *Shen Nong Ben Cao Jing*, an ancient and revered herbal that dates from AD25–220 and was written by the legendary emperor Shen Nong. Jesuit missionaries in China sent seed to Europe in the 1730s and the plant was first described botanically by Linnaeus in the eighteenth century as *Ixia chinensis*. This name was superseded by *Belamcanda chinensis* in 1802. Leopard lilies were grown in English gardens by 1759 and reached the United States in 1825.

HEALING

The rhizomes are used in Chinese medicine as an expectorant and an anti-inflammatory. Leopard lily also lowers fever and has antibacterial, antifungal and antiviral effects. Traditionally it was a

Belamcanda chinensis

remedy for breast cancer and, according to Shen Nong, for laryngeal tumours. Farm labourers value it for relieving 'rice field dermatitis', a frequent complaint when working in paddy fields; while herbalists prescribe it mainly for throat infections and 'wet' coughs. In common with many members of the iris family (Iridaceae), the leopard lily is a poisonous plant and is not recommended for amateur use. It is contraindicated during pregnancy.

NOTES FOR GARDENERS

Easily grown in well-drained soil in sun or part shade, leopard lilies thrive in poor, dry conditions but make larger specimens in humus-rich soil. Propagate them by dividing rhizomes in the spring, making sure that each section has at least one 'eye' or bud, and leave to dry off before planting so that the cut surfaces do not succumb to fungal infection. Plants are easily raised from seed sown in spring. Though described as frost hardy in gardening manuals, *B. chinensis* often survives hard frosts but dislikes winter wet. The clusters of berries are an attractive feature that last into winter.

BELAMCANDA CHINENSIS

Borago officinalis

BORAGE
STAR FLOWER

PORTRAIT

A hardy annual with hollow stems, oval leaves and five-petalled, star-shaped, bright blue flowers that have black, pointed centres formed by the projecting stamens. The foliage is juicy but covered with coarse, rather bristly hairs. It wilts almost instantly when picked, so is no good for garnishing or selling as a cut herb. Borage is native to Mediterranean regions, growing on waste and cultivated ground. In average conditions it reaches about 60cm (2ft) but in rich soil it may grow to twice this size.

HISTORY

Borage has a reputation for bestowing courage and uplifting the spirits. In the first century AD, Pliny referred to it as *Euphrosinum* because of its euphoric effect.

Borago officinalis

COOKING

The leaves have a cucumber-like flavour and are an essential garnishing for Pimms No I, a gin-based drink that originated in Pimm's restaurant in London. The flowers can be frozen in ice cubes as a pretty addition to summer drinks, or crystallized for cake decoration. They are also decorative in salads, though turn pink on contact with lemon juice or vinegar. The leaves are edible, finely chopped because of their bristly texture, in salads, sandwiches and soups. They do, however, contain pyrrolizidine alkaloids that may cause liver damage in excess.

HEALING

A soothing, cooling herb with diuretic effects, borage may help in the form of fresh juice or an infusion for feverish respiratory infections, kidney problems, rheumatic and skin complaints. It is ,however, seldom used by herbalists today. More important now is the oil extracted from the seeds which, like evening primrose oil, is a rich source of gamma-linolenic acid (GLA) – an essential fatty acid (EFA) that underpins the body's hormonal systems and is often deficient in modern diets.

BORAGO OFFICINALIS

Deficiencies of EFAs are associated with various conditions, ranging from pre-menstrual syndrome to eczema.

NOTES FOR GARDENERS

Borage is easily grown from seed sown in spring in almost any soil, even clay, and where happy will self-sow freely. Given the choice, it prefers well-drained to dry conditions in sun, but tolerates partial shade and both acid and alkaline soils. Plants form a tap root and do not transplant well when larger, though seedlings usually move successfully. Large specimens tend to sprawl and may need staking to prevent wind damage. Borage has succulent foliage and delicate flowers that are difficult to dry. It is a herb to use fresh and enjoy in the border for its blue, bee-loved blooms. The white-flowered form is pretty too.

Calendula officinalis

MARIGOLD
POT MARIGOLD

PORTRAIT

An aromatic, long-lived, bushy annual with bright green leaves and vivid yellow-orange daisies – not to be confused with French marigolds, *Tagetes patula*. The plants reach about 30cm (12in) high and flower almost all year. Originating in Mediterranean regions, the wild pot marigold has single flowers. Double-flowered orange, apricot or cream forms make more of a splash in the garden.

HISTORY

Marigolds have been valued as a medicinal herb and colourant for fabrics, foods and cosmetics since the ancient Greek, Roman and Arabic empires. In the Middle Ages, the flowers were also dedicated to the Virgin Mary, the word marigold originally being 'Mary's gold'. 'Somme use it to make theyr here [hair] yelow . . . not being content with the colour . . .' wrote William Turner in *A New Herball*

CALENDULA OFFICINALIS

(published between 1551 and 1568). In the seventeenth century, Culpeper referred to the marigold as a herb of the sun, the strong shape and colour of the flowers linking it to the astrological sign Leo.

COOKING

Cheaper and more easily grown than saffron, marigold petals give a hint of yellow to rice and soups if added when cooking. If you make your own cheese, try adding a strong infusion of petals to the curds to produce an appetizing shade of golden yellow. Petals from the central disc can be scattered on salads: they brighten up the greenery and make the salad healthier still.

BEAUTY

Marigold is good for soothing and healing dry, cracked skin, spots and enlarged pores. You can buy readymade marigold cream or lotion or make your own lotion by simply steeping flowers in boiling water for 20 minutes. When cool, strain and dab directly on the affected area, or add to rose water and glycerin, available from any pharmacy.

HEALING
Herbalists refer to marigold as calendula. It is considered an excellent antiseptic healing herb for eczema, ulcers, nappy (diaper) rash, fungal infections and varicose veins, as well as minor wounds, burns and sunburn. Though primarily a remedy for inflamed, sore skin, calendula can also be taken internally as an infusion or tincture to heal inflammatory conditions of the digestive system, such as ulcers, gastritis and colitis, and has mild oestrogenic effects which may help menopausal and menstrual problems. Calendula stimulates the liver and gall bladder, flushing out toxins that often underlie skin problems, so working well from the inside too.

NOTES FOR GARDENERS
Marigolds like well-drained soil and sun but are remarkably tolerant. They self-sow readily and are simplicity from seed – ideal for beginners and children to grow – with large, easy-to-handle seeds that germinate quickly. Sow in autumn or early spring where you want them to flower, thinning to 30cm (12in) apart, or in seed trays or pots to plant out later. In frosty areas, protect young plants in winter. As plants develop, pinch out the main flower bud to encourage side shoots. The only other care required is deadheading to encourage more flowers. Leave a few heads in late summer and there will be plenty of seed for next year. Remember that named varieties do not reliably come true from home-grown seed, generally producing smaller, less double flowers in successive generations.

Camellia sinensis   TEA

PORTRAIT
A small, frost hardy to hardy, evergreen shrub, reaching 6m (20ft) but normally pruned to 1m (3ft) in height, and bearing leathery, elliptic leaves. White flowers, about 2.5cm (1in) across, with a boss of yellow stamens, appear in winter, followed by capsules containing large, oily seeds. Tea is native to China but is now cultivated in many parts of the world. There are more than 350 cultivars varying in habit, flavour and cultural requirements.

HISTORY
Tea has been drunk in China for 3,000 years or more and, after water, is the most widely consumed beverage in the world. In every language in the world, the word for tea is derived from the Chinese words *t'e* or *ch'a*. According to Chinese legend tea was discovered by the Emperor Shen Nong in about 2700BC when a gust of wind blew some leaves into a pot of boiling water. An Indian version tells how Buddha fell asleep while meditating and, dismayed at his weakness, tore off his eyelids which rooted in the ground and grew into tea plants, producing eyelid-shaped leaves with the power to induce wakefulness. Tea was introduced to Europe by the Dutch and the Portuguese in the seventeenth century. In Japan, the tea ceremony is still an important social ceremony today but it began in China as a Buddhist ritual during the Song Dynasty (AD960–1279).

COOKING
Tea is occasionally used to flavour foods – dried fruits and ham, for example – by soaking them in an infusion.

HEALING

Green (unfermented) tea has proven beneficial effects when drunk in normal daily quantities. It contains polyphenols or catechins that are better antioxidants than vitamin C or E. Drinking green tea may therefore strengthen the immune system and help to prevent heart disease, strokes, cancer, and dental caries. It also has diuretic and stimulant properties, containing 50mg of caffeine per cup (compared with 85mg in coffee).

NOTES FOR GARDENERS

Growing your own tea is perfectly possible and there are clones that are hardy to -23°C (-9°F). Where conditions outdoors are unsuitable, grow it as a pot plant with protection in winter. For optimum growth, provide rich soil in sun or partial shade, ample water and humidity, and a daytime temperature range of 20–30°C (68–86°F). Regular pinching out ensures compact growth – and a cup of green tea. Propagate plants either by seed sown as soon as it is ripe, or by semi-ripe cuttings in summer at 18°C (64°F).

CAMELLIA SINENSIS

Capsicum species   PEPPERS

PORTRAIT

Capsicum annuum is a tender annual or short-lived perennial with oval leaves reaching 12cm (5in) long, and small, bell-shaped white flowers, followed by pendent, conical fruits up to 15cm (6in) long. Plants approach 1.5m (5ft) tall in good conditions. Peppers originated in tropical parts of South America. Today more than 1,700 varieties are grown worldwide, derived from *C. annuum*, and also from *C. baccatum*, *C. chinense*, *C. frutescens*, and *C. pubescens*. There are five main groups: Cerasiforme Group (cherry pepper) with small, hot, spherical fruits that ripen to red, yellow or purple; Conioides Group (cone pepper) with hot, conical, upright fruits that ripen to scarlet, crimson or purple; Fasciculatum Group (red cone pepper) with hot, conical, upright fruits, bright red in colour and up to 7cm (3in) long; Grossum Group (bell pepper) with large, sweet, goblet-shaped fruits that ripen to yellow, red or purple; and Longum Group (cayenne or chilli

733

SILIQVASTRVM
TERTIVM.

Langer Indianischer Pfeffer.

qq

pepper) with very hot, tapered green fruits, 15–30cm (6–12in) long, that ripen to red or dark purple. Within these groups there are pod types associated with different regions, e.g. New Mexico.

HISTORY

Peppers were described botanically in 1493 by Dr Chauca, physician to Christopher Columbus's expedition. Colombus was searching for a source of black pepper (*Piper nigrum*) but discovered 'red pepper' among the Arawak tribe instead and brought it back to Spain. Chilli peppers were introduced to India and Africa during the sixteeenth century by the Portuguese, and during the 17th century reached almost every other part of the world. They remain major crops throughout South and Central America, but today's main commercial producers are China and Turkey.

COOKING

Chilli powder and cayenne come from the ripe, dried, ground fruits of *C. annuum* and tabasco from *C. frutescens.* Their pungency is dependent on capsaicin, a compound that is absent in sweet (bell)

CAPSICUM FRUTESCENS 'TABASCO'

CAPSICUM CHINENSE 'SCOTCH BONNET'

peppers, from which mild-flavoured paprika is made. Peppers of all kinds are used fresh or dried, unripe or ripe, as flavourings or as vegetables, raw or cooked, in pickles, chutneys and countless savoury dishes, especially in South and Central America, Mexico, India and south-east Asia. Pungent (or hot) peppers are an important food preservative in the tropics. Peppers of all kinds are nutritious, especially when ripe; the vitamin C content doubles as the fruits turn red.

HEALING

The medicinal uses of cayenne were promoted by Samuel Thomson in the early nineteenth century. Though extremely irritant in excess, in therapeutic doses it stimulates the metabolism, cooling and detoxifying the body as the perspiration rate increases. Herbalists use it as a warming stimulant for colds, flu, poor circulation and digestive problems. Applied externally, usually in the form of capsaicin-based creams, cayenne has warming, pain-relieving effects, which may be helpful in neuralgia, rheumatism, arthritis and chilblains. Eating chillies and 'hot' food when visiting the tropics is a good way of preventing or minimizing gastric infections.

NOTES FOR GARDENERS
Chilli peppers are attractive plants when fruiting and varieties such as 'Purple Tiger' have the bonus of variegated leaves. They thrive in rich, light soil, full sun, high humidity and a daytime temperature of 21–25°C (70–77°F). Unlike certain varieties of sweet peppers, they do not crop well outdoors in cool areas. Pinch out young plants to encourage bushiness and stake them as fruits develop and plants become heavier. Under glass, plants may need misting to encourage fruit to set if there is limited access for pollinating insects. Wear gloves when harvesting or preparing chilli peppers: juice from the cut surfaces may cause painful inflammation in contact with eyes or broken skin.

Carthamus tinctorius
SAFFLOWER
SAFFRON THISTLE

PORTRAIT
A hardy annual with stiffly upright stems 60cm (2ft) tall and oval to linear, wavy-edged or lobed, often spiny-toothed leaves. The thistle-like flowers are 3.5cm (1½in) across and may be yellow, orange or red. Safflower grows wild on rocky hillsides and beside paths in Iran and north-west India. It is cultivated commercially in Africa, Australia, China, India, parts of the Mediterranean and south-east Asia.

HISTORY
Safflower was introduced to Egypt during the New Kingdom (1567–1085BC) or possibly earlier, and remains were found in the tomb of Tutankhamun. It was used as a source of oil and dyes, and the colourful flowers were included in garlands for the dead. Safflower was first mentioned as a medicinal herb in China in AD1061. Traditionally, the robes of Buddhist monks were dyed with saffron thistle flowers. In the eighteenth century, British government papers were tied with cotton tape, dyed red with safflower, giving rise to the expression 'red tape'. In nineteenth-century Europe, it was widely used as a red dye for silk and feathers, and the pigment was also sold as a cosmetic known as *rouge végétal*, replacing toxic lead-based rouges.

COOKING
The large white seeds are a source of oil that is rich in unsaturated fatty acids, used in cooking and in cholesterol-reducing diets. Known also as false or bastard saffron, the dried petals are used to adulterate expensive genuine saffron or passed off as saffron in tourist centres in countries where true saffron is an unlikely crop, such as Sri Lanka.

HOME
Safflower florets yield a yellow, water-soluble dye, and also red shades, which are extracted by an alkali such as washing soda.

HEALING
Both the oil and flowers lower cholesterol and reduce coronary artery disease. In Chinese medicine they are known as *hong hua* and used as a uterine stimulant for menstrual problems and following childbirth. Externally, the flowers relieve sprains, bruises, and painful or paralysed joints.

CARTAMVS   Wilder gartensaffran.

m

Notes for Gardeners

Safflower is easily grown in light, well-drained soil in sun and is reasonably drought-tolerant. Sow seed in spring at 10–15°C (50–59°F). Saffron thistles are popular as cut flowers, both fresh or dried. There are several named varieties, such as 'Lasting White', 'Orange Ball', and 'Summer Sun', which have cream, orange and yellow flowers respectively. For drying, cut long stems when the flowers first open and hang upside down in bundles to dry in a cool, well-ventilated place, out of direct sun.

Carum Carvi

Carum carvi   CARAWAY

Portrait

A hardy biennial, up to 75cm (2½ft) tall, with hollow stems and dark green, deeply divided leaves that resemble those of carrots. Umbels of tiny white to pink flowers appear in the summer of the second year, followed by crescent-shaped seeds. Caraway is native to various parts of Europe and western Asia, where it favours damp grassland and disturbed ground.

History

Caraway was an important spice in Arab cooking before it became popular in Europe during the thirteenth century. Comfits or 'sugar plums', made from the seeds were a favourite snack in Elizabethan England. Confusingly, in several European languages, words for caraway and cumin (see p.96) are the same, though the two species differ in flavour and uses.

AROMATIC USES
The essential oil is used in soap and dental hygiene products.

COOKING
Caraway leaves give a pleasant parsley-dill flavour to soups and salads, and the parsnip-like roots make an interesting vegetable. The pungent seeds are popular in Jewish cuisine, and are an essential flavouring of rye bread, goulash, and seed cake. Other well-known uses are with cabbage (especially sauerkraut), cooked apples, cheese, and as a basis for alcoholic drinks such as *kümmel* and schnapps.

HEALING
Caraway seeds are an excellent remedy for indigestion and wind, and may simply be chewed to give relief. As they relax spasms in the digestive tract, caraway extracts are added to various products for digestive problems, and to laxatives to reduce griping. The seeds have expectorant effects too and may help bronchitis and pleurisy.

NOTES FOR GARDENERS
Caraway is happiest in rich, well-drained, neutral to slightly acid soil in full sun, but tolerates clay. Sow seed from late spring to late summer where plants are to flower, as they do not transplant well after the first seedling stage. To catch the seeds before they fall, and to prevent excessive self-sowing, cut the seed heads before they are quite ripe and hang them upside down in paper bags. They will finish ripening and all you need to do is shake the bag to release them.

Caulophyllum thalictroides   BLUE COHOSH

PORTRAIT
A hardy perennial, about 75cm (30in) tall, with a matted, rhizomatous rootstock. It produces a solitary leaf, or occasionally a pair of leaves, with three main divisions that are subdivided into bluntly ovate, three-lobed leaflets. The new foliage is glaucous and purple-brown, turning green as it matures. A cluster of similarly coloured, star-shaped flowers appears as the new foliage emerges. These are followed by spherical, deep blue berries. Blue cohosh is widely distributed in rich damp woods in eastern North America, but is vulnerable to over-collecting when plants are uprooted in large quantities for the herb trade.

HISTORY
Also known as squaw root, it was an important women's herb to native Americans, especially to the Menominee, Meskwaki, Potawatomi and Ojibwa. Its uses were first published in *The Indian Doctor's Dispensary* by Peter Smith in 1813, and some 75 years later it was introduced to western medicine by J. U. and C. G. Lloyd, authors of *Drugs and Medicines of North America*. Blue cohosh was one of many native American herbs adopted by Samuel Thomson, founder of Physiomedicalism (an early form of naturopathy), in the nineteenth century. Late twentieth-century research showed that blue cohosh can both inhibit ovulation and prevent the fertilized egg from implanting in the uterus, giving potential as a contraceptive.

HEALING

Blue cohosh is primarily a uterine stimulant, used to treat pelvic inflammatory disease, endometriosis, difficult menstruation, and complications during childbirth. It should not be taken by anyone with hypertension or heart disease, or during pregnancy unless prescribed by a qualified medical practitioner. It also has anti-inflammatory effects and may help relieve rheumatism, arthritis and gout. The closely related *C. robustum*, an oriental species, is used in similar ways in traditional Chinese medicine.

NOTES FOR GARDENERS

This woodland herb needs moist, humus-rich, neutral to acid soil in shade. If you can grow trilliums, it is worth trying to grow blue cohosh, perhaps alongside those other famed North American woodland herbs, goldenseal (*Hydrastis canadensis*) and ginseng (*Panax quinquefolius*). These four aristocrats of the eastern woodlands would make a splendid show together, each having different and very distinctive foliage. Blue cohosh is propagated mainly by division as it is slow and erratic from seed.

CENTELLA ASIATICA

Centella asiatica

GOTU KOLA

PORTRAIT

A tender creeping perennial, rooting at the nodes, with clusters of kidney-shaped leaves, up to 5cm (2in) across, that have indented margins. In summer, tiny pink flowers are borne at ground level, hidden beneath the foliage. Gotu kola is a variable and adaptable weed throughout the tropics, growing mainly in wet places, such as paddy fields.

HISTORY

Gotu kola is a key herb in Ayurvedic medicine and was traditionally used in both India and Africa to treat leprosy. Known as *brahmi*, it was also taken to aid meditation and bring knowledge of the Brahman, the Supreme Reality. Through traditional uses in Madagascar, gotu kola entered the French pharmacopoeia in 1884 and came to the notice of western medicine.

75

COOKING

Grown with ample moisture and shade, the leaves are edible in salads (in sunny dry conditions they become tough and bitter). In south-east Asia there are better tasting varieties with frilly, bright green leaves that are more palatable for eating raw or adding to curries. Dried leaves may be added to herb teas.

BEAUTY

Gotu kola stimulates the production of collagen and improves the tone of veins near the surface of the skin, making it a valuable ingredient of anti-wrinkle, skin-firming creams and face masks.

HEALING

Gotu kola is a rejuvenating, diuretic herb that clears toxins, reduces inflammation, aids healing and regeneration, and has a balancing effect on the nervous system. It contains brahmoside, a mild tranquillizer that improves memory and concentration, and substances that improve circulation. When applied externally, its great strength lies in healing wounds and minimizing scar tissue after accidents, surgery or burns. Other uses are to ease rheumatism and rheumatoid arthritis, and to treat varicose veins and ulcers. Excessive amounts – taken internally or externally – cause itching, headaches, and even transient unconsciousness.

NOTES FOR GARDENERS

Being a weed, gotu kola is extremely easy to grow. All it needs is moist to wet soil and ample warmth. Though tropical, it copes with temperatures as low as 10°C (50°F), when it may lose its leaves but resprouts when warmer weather returns. Propagation is simply by division, either of a whole chunk, or by separating lengths or runners that already have roots. It can be grown in pots on the kitchen windowsill, as a marginal beside a tropical pool, or as a trailing plant in a hanging basket somewhere shady.

Chamaemelum nobile ROMAN CHAMOMILE
Matricaria recutita GERMAN CHAMOMILE

PORTRAIT

Chamaemelum nobile (Roman chamomile) is a hardy, mat-forming, evergreen perennial with strongly aromatic, divided leaves up to 5cm (2in) long, and long-stalked, daisy-like flowers in summer. Chamomile grows wild on sandy grassland in western Europe, North America and the Azores. German chamomile (*Matricaria recutita*) is an annual or biennial, also with finely divided foliage and similarly scented daisy-like flowers, which reaches 30cm (12in) tall. It is native to Europe and western Asia. Flowers of the two kinds are used in the same ways. As a garden plant, Roman chamomile wins outright, having the bonus of evergreen, aromatic foliage.

HISTORY

Roman chamomile has been used medicinally in Europe for more than 2,000 years. In Saxon times it was known as *maythen* and was one of nine sacred herbs. It became a favourite strewing herb in

Camemille

Europe before the days of carpets and was sometimes burnt to sweeten the air. The earliest record of its cultivation in England is in 1265 and in Tudor times it became popular for making lawns, seats and fragrant banks. *Chamaemelum* comes from the Greek *chamai*, ground, and *melon*, apple, referring to its low habit and apple-scented foliage. The Spanish *manzanilla* means 'little apple'.

COOKING

Chamomile tea is one of the most popular herb teas and was immortalized in Beatrix Potter's *Tale of Peter Rabbit*. German chamomile is best for this purpose as it is less bitter than Roman. Chamomile is a flavouring in vermouth, but in spite of its name, is not an ingredient of the dry sherry known as Manzanilla, which is named after a place, not the plant.

BEAUTY

Chamomile is added to after-sun lotions and to hair products as a conditioner and lightener, especially for fair hair. The essential oil is used to scent soaps, cosmetics, and perfumes.

MATRICARIA RECUTITA

HEALING

Chamomile is a sedative herb that acts mainly on the digestive system. The two species are used interchangeably to relieve insomnia, digestive disorders and upsets (especially when stress-related), travel sickness, nausea and vomiting during pregnancy, anorexia, colic and hyperactivity in children. Excessive use is not recommended during pregnancy and lactation. Applied externally, chamomile soothes sunburn, minor burns, haemorrhoids, mastitis and leg ulcers. In addition, German chamomile is used for asthma, hay fever, and catarrh. Chamomile may cause a reaction in anyone who is prone to allergies, especially if sensitive to members of the daisy family.

NOTES FOR GARDENERS

Roman chamomile needs neutral to acid, light soil in full sun, and a modicum of moisture and warmth. It dislikes extremes, whether hot dry summers or cold wet winters. Its modest size gives scope for edging borders or growing between paving slabs. For larger areas – lawns, seats, and the like – plant the non-flowering form 'Treneague', which has all the fragrance but remains neatly ground-hugging, rather than straggling upward to flower. Set plants 10cm (4in) apart in spring and keep well weeded until individual plantlets have grown together to form a mat. The species can be grown from seed, but double and non-flowering forms must be propagated by division. German chamomile is easily grown from seed sown in autumn or spring on well-drained, neutral to slightly acid soil in sun.

Cinnamomum camphora   CAMPHOR TREE

PORTRAIT

A large, tender, evergreen tree, with narrowly oval, pointed, glossy leaves up to 10cm (4in) long, which are flushed red when young. Small, bowl-shaped, pale yellow-green flowers are produced in spring and summer, followed by black fruits. This majestic, fast-growing member of the laurel family (Lauraceae) grows wild in east and south-east Asia, reaching 30m (100ft) tall, with a spread

CINNAMOMUM CAMPHORA

of 12m (40ft). The foliage is aromatic and can be used medicinally but camphor, a crystalline compound, is mostly extracted from the wood of trees that are at least 50 years old.

HISTORY

Camphor was mentioned in ancient Chinese herbals but was unknown in the West before the seventeenth century. Samuel Hahnemann, the founder of homeopathy, prescribed camphor for the early stages of cholera when an epidemic struck Europe in 1831. Then in the late nineteenth century it was used in the manufacture of celluloid, a transparent plastic made in sheets from camphor and nitrocellulose, formerly used for cinematographic film. Celluloid became synonymous with development of the movies in their early years. These days, camphor is mainly synthesized.

HOME

Camphor is best known as the ingredient of mothballs, which are placed among clothing and fabrics to deter moths.

HEALING

Camphorated oil, a blend of camphor and peanut (groundnut) oil, is used in liniments for joint and muscle pain, balm for chilblains, lip salves and inhalants for colds and catarrh. It is absorbed through the skin and mucous membranes, relieving pain, reducing inflammation, warming the tissues and clearing congestion. Camphor has long been used in both Chinese medicine, mainly for skin diseases and wounds, and in Ayurvedic medicine for bronchial complaints, rheumatism, and gout. As camphor stimulates the circulation and central nervous system, it can be extremely toxic if overused.

NOTES FOR GARDENERS

In frost-free areas, camphor can be grown outdoors in moist, well-drained soil as a specimen tree. There are some fine examples around the herb garden in the Royal Botanic Gardens in Melbourne, Australia. It tolerates occasional low temperatures, to 0°C (32°F), but is happiest at a minimum 10°C (50°F). In cold areas, young plants may be grown in pots, using John Innes No 3 loam-based compost. Plants can be propagated by seed sown when ripe at 18°C (64°F), or by semi-ripe cuttings in summer. Prune if required after flowering or in spring.

Cinnamomum zeylanicum   CINNAMON

PORTRAIT

A tender evergreen tree, reaching 10–15m (30–50ft), with light brown, furrowed bark, smelling and tasting of cinnamon, and leathery, narrowly oval leaves, up to 18cm (7in) long, which have three pale main veins and are pink when young. Clusters of inconspicuous yellow-white flowers appear in summer, followed by egg-shaped purple-black berries. Cinnamon trees grow wild in southern India and Sri Lanka, and are widely planted as coppiced shrubs for commercial crops. Stems 1–5cm (½–2in) in diameter and 2–3m (6–10ft) long are harvested in the rainy season. The bark is removed in strips that dry into the familiar quills. Both bark and leaves are distilled for oil.

HISTORY

Cinnamon is literally a spice to die for. Attempts to gain a monopoly over supplies were a major factor in colonial expansion and cost many lives. When Portugal invaded Ceylon in 1536, the annual tribute demanded from the Sinhalese was 250,000lb (113.4 tonnes) of cinnamon.

AROMATIC USES

Essential oil from the leaves has a delicate, carnation-like scent that is used in perfumery. Oil from the bark has the typical cinnamon aroma and is used in food flavouring and oral hygiene products.

COOKING

Though *C. zeylanicum* is the most popular kind of cinnamon in the world, there are a number of other species that are used locally. These include *C. burmannii* (Indonesian cassia), *C. cassia* (cassia, Chinese cinnamon), *C. iners* (wild cinnamon), *C. loureiri* (Saigon cinnamon), and *C. tamala* (Indian cassia, *tejpat*). All are used to flavour curries, chutneys, puddings and a wide variety of bakery products. Cinnamon sugar is a popular topping for toast, desserts, and cappuccino. *Cinnamomum cassia* is one of the Chinese 'five spices', the others being anise, cloves, fennel seeds and star anise.

HEALING
Cinnamon is a stimulating, warming herb that has antibacterial, antifungal and antiviral properties. It improves the circulation and digestion, and is particularly good for 'cold' people. A good home remedy for colds, flu and digestive upsets involves simply adding some ground cinnamon to a hot drink. The essential oil should not be taken internally and can be very irritating if applied to the skin.

NOTES FOR GARDENERS
Cinnamon thrives in moist, well-drained acid soil in sun or partial shade and in high humidity, where the temperature does not fall below 15°C (59°F). It is usually grown from seed though this is difficult to obtain, even in the tropics, as the ripe fruits are popular with birds. Cuttings can also be taken from young shoots with three leaves.

CINNAMOMUM ZEYLANICUM

Citrus aurantiifolia — LIME

PORTRAIT
A small, tender, evergreen tree, 3–5m (10–15ft) tall, with spiny branches and light green, oval leaves that have winged stalks. Clusters of small, fragrant white flowers appear in spring and summer, followed by rounded to egg-shaped green fruits, which turn yellow-green when ripe. They are rather smaller than lemons and have smoother, thinner peel that is difficult to remove. Limes are native to tropical Asia.

HISTORY
Although most citrus species reached Mediterranean regions at a very early date (by at least 400BC), limes do not thrive in Mediterranean-type climates and therefore spread more readily to various parts of the tropics, such as the West Indies. Arab traders brought limes to Europe in the thirteenth century and from there the Spanish introduced them to the Americas in the 1500s.

AROMATIC USES
The essential oil is a source of citral, used in perfumery.

COOKING
Limes are used in similar ways to lemons – in marmalades, jellies, confectionery and drinks. Key limes, which are also known as Mexican or West Indian limes, are small, greenish-yellow fruits with thin rind and a particularly good flavour and aroma. They are excellent for drinks and, of course, Key lime pies. In India lime juice is used to coagulate milk to make fresh cheese, such as *paneer*. The kaffir lime or makrut (*C. hystrix*), native to the Philippines, has aromatic leaves that are widely used in south-east Asian cuisines, notably as the flavouring of Thai curries and the Indonesian sauce *kecap*.

HEALING
Lime juice is often added to medicines in south-east Asia and Guyana, especially for diarrhoea. An infusion of lime leaves is said to relieve a bilious headache.

CITRUS AURANTIIFOLIA

NOTES FOR GARDENERS
Limes need well-drained soil, ample warmth, moisture and humidity, and a minimum temperature of 13°C (55°F). They will not grow in waterlogged soil. If grown in pots in a hard water area, make sure to use rainwater as, like all citruses, limes dislike alkaline water. There are several varieties that are less thorny, relatively seedless or hardier. Look out for 'Tahiti', with a good flavour and few, if any seeds, and 'Thornless Key', which is hardier than the usual Key lime. 'La Valette' is a cross between lime and lemon: it crops prolifically and is easy to grow.

Citrus aurantium

C. bergamia

SEVILLE ORANGE
BITTER ORANGE

BERGAMOT ORANGE

PORTRAIT

Citrus aurantium is a rounded, tender tree, reaching 10m (30ft) tall and 6m (20ft) wide, with spiny branches and oval leaves. Large, white, very fragrant flowers are borne in spring and summer, followed by spherical orange fruits. Although Seville oranges sound quintessentially Mediterranean, like other citruses they originally came from south-east Asia. *Citrus bergamia*, the bergamot orange, was once considered a variety of the Seville orange and is similar in appearance but with much larger leaves and paler, more aromatic rind. In Morocco, bergamot orange flowers are preferred for orange flower water.

CITRUS SPECIES

HISTORY

The medicinal uses of *C. aurantium* were mentioned in Chinese medical literature dating back to around AD200. It was probably brought to Europe from the East Indies by Portuguese sailors in the twelfth century and first cultivated in Italy. Neroli oil, distilled from the flowers, was reputedly named after an Italian princess, Anne-Marie of Nerola, in the sixteenth century, who used it to scent gloves.

AROMATIC USES

Neroli oil and petitgrain (distilled from the foliage) are important in perfumery. Orange flower water, a by-product of neroli, is used in perfumery and cosmetics. Bergamot oil from *C. bergamia* is an important ingredient of eau-de-Cologne and toilet water.

COOKING

Aromatic Seville oranges are considered the best for making marmalade. Essential oil extracted from the unripe fruits is the key flavour in Grand Marnier, Cointreau, Triple Sec, and Curaçao.

Plate 349.

The Orange=Tree.

Eliz. Blackwell delin. sculp. et Pinx.

1. Flower.
2. Fruit.
3. Seed.

Aurantia.

The dried peel is used in *bouquet garni* and for flavouring certain Belgian beers, while the delicately scented orange flower water is used in desserts. Bergamot oil is used to flavour Earl Grey tea.

BEAUTY
Bergamot oil, or bergapten extracted from the oil, sensitizes the skin to sunlight and was once added to tanning preparations, but discontinued as a possible allergen or carcinogen. Use of the essential oil directly on the skin, whether neat or diluted, is not recommended. Citrus extracts are used as antioxidants and exfoliants in skin creams.

HEALING
In Chinese medicine the ripe fruits of *C. aurantium*, with pips and peel removed, are known as *zhi ke*, and whole unripe fruits are *zhi shi*. Both are used for indigestion, stubborn coughs, and prolapse. *Zhi shi*, the stronger of the two, is also used for shock. Neroli oil is often used by aromatherapists. It has antidepressant and tonic effects, is reputedly aphrodisiac, and benefits skin and digestion. Orange flower water is gentle enough to relieve colic in babies. Bergamot oil is used in douches for vaginal infections.

NOTES FOR GARDENERS
Seville orange thrives in well-drained, neutral to acid soil in full sun, with a minimum temperature of 3–5°C (41°F). It can be grown in pots, using loam-based John Innes No 2 compost. A number of varieties are offered by specialist nurseries, such as: 'Bouquet de Fleurs', a thornless, floriferous, very scented plant that is ideal for hedging; 'Bouquet de Nice' with double, gardenia-like flowers; and 'Chinotto', which has tiny dark green leaves, a compact habit, and tiny fruits that are prized for candying and preserving whole. The bergamot orange needs similar conditions.

Citrus limon   LEMON

PORTRAIT
A large, tender, evergreen shrub or small tree, anywhere between 2–7m (6–22ft) tall, with spiny branches and narrowly oval, toothed leaves, up to 10cm (4in) long. Fragrant white flowers, purple-tinged in bud and about 4cm (1½in) across, appear in spring and summer, followed by ovoid, bright yellow fruits, 7–15cm (3–6in) long. Like other citruses, lemon trees originated in Asia.

HISTORY
Lemons were introduced to Europe by the Arabs, who had obtained stocks from northern India in the tenth century. Lemons were unknown to the ancient Greeks and Romans, and were not recorded in Italy until the mid-fifteenth century.

AROMATIC USES
Lemon oil, and citral extracted from it, are used in perfumery, and to scent soaps, gels, cleansers, and household cleaning products. Dried lemon peel is often added to pot-pourris.

COOKING

Lemon juice is indispensable in the kitchen in sauces, salad dressings and marinades. It helps set jam, and commercial pectin is made from the inner peel and pulp. Lemon peel or zest also has numerous uses as a flavouring in both sweet and savoury foods, and as the key ingredient of lemonade and many other soft drinks. Its acidity coagulates protein and can be used to make soft cheese and to prepare raw fish in the South American dish *ceviche*. Preserved lemons are characteristic of Moroccan cooking. *Limonato* is Italian lemon-flavoured olive oil, made by pressing lemons with the olives.

HEALING

Lemon has tonic, refreshing and cooling effects. It acts as a diuretic, reduces inflammation, improves the circulation and increases resistance to infection. Hot lemon juice with honey is a traditional remedy for colds and sore throats, and a dab of lemon juice is a handy treatment for poisonous stings and bites. Though highly acidic, lemon is alkaline when digested and therefore

CITRUS LIMON

beneficial in rheumatic and arthritic complaints. It is rich in bioflavonoids that strengthen blood vessels, helping varicose veins, thread veins, bleeding gums and bruising.

NOTES FOR GARDENERS

Lemons need well-drained, neutral to acid soil in sun, and a minimum temperature of 7°C (45°F). In cold areas they make excellent pot plants and the occasional home-grown lemon is perhaps a more realistic proposition than growing enough Seville oranges to make marmalade. One of the best for pot culture is 'Meyer', a compact variety discovered in China in the early 1900s. It flowers and fruits almost all year round. As with all citruses, allow the compost to almost dry out before watering, as they dislike constant moisture. You can grow lemons and other citruses from seed but some varieties may not come true. However, many are apomictic, producing seed without being pollinated and therefore retaining the genetic constitution of the mother plant – so there is a chance your seedlings may be identical to the parent. Commercially, most citruses are propagated by grafting.

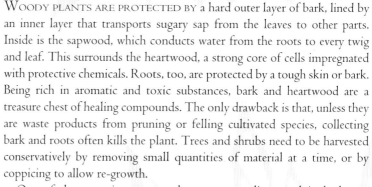

Herbal Barks

CINCHONA PUBESCENS

WOODY PLANTS ARE PROTECTED BY a hard outer layer of bark, lined by an inner layer that transports sugary sap from the leaves to other parts. Inside is the sapwood, which conducts water from the roots to every twig and leaf. This surrounds the heartwood, a strong core of cells impregnated with protective chemicals. Roots, too, are protected by a tough skin or bark. Being rich in aromatic and toxic substances, bark and heartwood are a treasure chest of healing compounds. The only drawback is that, unless they are waste products from pruning or felling cultivated species, collecting bark and roots often kills the plant. Trees and shrubs need to be harvested conservatively by removing small quantities of material at a time, or by coppicing to allow re-growth.

One of the most important substances ever discovered in bark was quinine, an alkaloid from tropical American *Cinchona* trees. Jesuits in the Lima area learnt the use of Peruvian bark as an anti-malarial from native people in about 1630. Its use spread rapidly among colonial powers, enabling them to conquer territories in regions that would otherwise have proved fatal to Europeans. So great was demand that by the early nineteenth century wild *Cinchona* plants were almost extinct and the Dutch established plantations in Java. The taking of a daily dose of quinine led to the invention of gin and tonic. Quinine is extremely bitter: diluting it in soda water and adding gin disguised the flavour. Quinine also goes down in history as the substance that led Samuel Hahnemann (1755–1843) to formulate the Law of Similars ('like cures like'), so laying the foundation for homeopathy.

The wood of lignum vitae (*Guaiacum officinale*), a beautiful West Indian tree with sky-blue flowers, is one of the hardest known. It also contains about 20 per cent resin. The Spanish began exporting lignum vitae to Europe in 1503 for its fine timber and medicinal by-products. Wild populations dwindled rapidly and in 1701 Martinique banned further exploitation, making it the first plant species to be protected by law. Sir Hans Sloane (1660–1753), benefactor of the Chelsea Physic Garden, who practised medicine in Jamaica, found local people used lignum vitae to treat syphilis, which had been introduced by colonists. Through his influence it was adopted in Europe and for the next 200 years was the best anti-syphilitic known.

Belonging to the same family as lignum vitae, the creosote bush or chapparal (*Larrea tridentata*) is also rich in resins. Creosote bushes cover vast areas of desert in the south-western United States and Mexico, and desert tribes once drank 'chapparal tea' as a cure-all. The branches contain a potent

GUAIACUM OFFICINALE

& Woods

antioxidant that until the late 1960s was used by the food industry to prevent rancidity in fats and oils. It also has antibiotic, antifungal and anti-tumour effects.

Rather different properties are found in the bark of *Rhamnus* species. These shrubs contain anthraquinone glycosides that are powerful laxatives. The main species used are the European alder buckthorn (*R. frangula*) and American cascara sagrada (*R. purshiana*).

More soothing effects come from the powdered inner bark of slippery elm (*Ulmus rubra*), which is pinkish-brown, sweet and mucilaginous, with a fenugreek-like aroma. It lubricates tissues, reducing irritation and drawing out toxins, giving damaged areas a chance to heal. Taken as a runny porridge, it coats the lining of the digestive system, easing gastric and bowel disorders.

Fragrant woods are rich in volatile oils that have been put to use since earliest times, whether to smoke or barbecue food, burn as incense, or distil for oil. Sandalwood (*Santalum album*) reached Europe in the 1880s and has been in demand for perfumery ever since. The essential oil is also used by aromatherapists for its relaxing, purifying effects. Sandalwood trees are twenty to forty years old before they develop sufficient heartwood for oil extraction. Eaglewood (*Aquilaria malaccensis*) is similar in perfume to sandalwood and even more valuable. Heartwood from trees more than fifty years old contains a resin that is an ingredient of incense. Gnarled pieces are displayed as treasures in Japanese incense shops.

LARREA TRIDENTATA

Fragrant, durable cedar wood (*Cedrus atlantica*) is insect-repellent, making it ideal for blanket chests and floors in oriental carpet shops. Cedar oil, distilled from the wood, was used for embalming in ancient Egypt. Today, the warmed oil can be inhaled to ease bronchial congestion and soothe tension, and is added to products for skin and scalp problems.

Curare is a resinous arrow poison, used by South American tribes for hunting. It kills instantly by paralysing the animal, leaving the flesh untainted. One ingredient is the woody stem of a giant liana called pareira (*Chondrodendron tomentosum*). In 1812, intrigued by reports of early explorers who witnessed its effects, Charles Waterton paralysed a donkey using curare and kept it alive by inflating its lungs with bellows – an experiment that led to the development of surgical anaesthesia. Peruvian cat's claw (*Uncaria tomentosa*) is another tropical American liana: it is now a source of alkaloids for treating cancer and AIDS, but for 2,000 years has been used by Amazonian tribes as a contraceptive, and to restore health.

CEDRUS LIBANI

See also: *Cinnamomum* species, *Salix* species, *Tabebuia* species.

Codonopsis pilosula

DANG SHEN

PORTRAIT

A hardy perennial, herbaceous climber with twining stems reaching about 2m (6ft) long, and downy, oval leaves up to 3.5cm (1½in) long. In summer it produces bell-shaped, pale green, purple-tinged flowers. In the wild it is found scrambling among shrubs in parts of north-east Asia.

HISTORY

As Chinese herbs go, *dang shen* is a recent addition to the pharmacopoeia, having first been mentioned as one of the four ingredients of *Soup of the Four Gentlemen*, a famous energy tonic, which dates back to the Song Dynasty (around AD1200). The other ingredients are Chinese thistle daisy or *bai zhu* (*Atractylodes macrocephala*), Chinese liquorice (*Glycyrrhiza uralensis*), and a fungus known as Indian bread or *fu ling* (*Wolfiporia cocos*).

CODONOPSIS PILOSULA

HEALING

In China *dang shen* is on a par with ginseng and often preferred because it is milder. It is also more easily grown and therefore cheaper. *Dang shen* is a sweet, warming, soothing herb that stimulates the immune and nervous systems, increases secretion of body fluids, and strengthens the spleen, stomach and lungs. Chinese herbalists prescribe it for poor appetite, low energy, convalescence, and anaemia. The tubers are often cooked with rice as a nourishing *congee* (porridge or soup), rather than taken as a medicine. Several other species are used interchangeably, including *C. tangshen* from western China.

NOTES FOR GARDENERS

Codonopsis need light, well-drained soil in partial shade – humus-rich, sandy, acid soil is ideal. Give them the shelter of shrubs through which they can scramble, or support them with a wigwam of fine birch twigs. Though not showy plants, they repay close attention as their bell-shaped flowers are often beautifully patterned inside. Plants can be propagated by seed sown in autumn or spring.

Coriandrum sativum

CORIANDER
CILANTRO, CHINESE PARSLEY

PORTRAIT
This hardy annual starts off with lobed, dark green leaves which become more finely divided as stems elongate to about 60cm (2ft) and form flower buds. They have a warm, oily smell that tastes much nicer than it sounds. The tiny white, often mauve-tinged flowers are borne in flat-topped clusters known as umbels. They are followed by spherical fruits, which are pale brown and have a sweet, almost citrus scent when ripe. Coriander is native to southern Europe and western Asia.

HISTORY
Coriander is one of the world's oldest herbs. Seeds were found in ancient Egyptian tombs and though introduced to China in about AD600, coriander is still known as *hu*, 'foreign'. It is also mentioned several times in the Old Testament and is included among bitter Passover herbs.

CORIANDRUM SATIVUM

COOKING
With coriander you get two herbs in one as the leaves and seeds have quite different aromas and uses. The flavour of coriander leaves is characteristic of many dishes originating in south-east Asia, India, Mexico and the West Indies, and production has increased worldwide to satisfy demand. It is a perfect match for spicy blends of green chilli, coconut, lemon or lemon grass, and lime or kaffir lime, and is thus a vital ingredient of many curries, spicy soups and chutneys. The strongly flavoured roots can be finely chopped and added too. In some regions the similar tasting culantro (*Eryngium foetidum*), rau ram (*Persicaria odorata*, formerly known as *Polygonum odoratum*) and papaloquelite (*Porophyllum ruderale*) are used instead, because they are easier to grow in hot climates where true coriander runs quickly to seed. Coriander seeds are used in curries as well – ground coriander is one of the main spices in *garam masala* – and are an essential ingredient of pickling spices and dishes *à la grecque*. In contrast, they flavour gin, liqueurs, vermouth, bread and cakes, and go very well with apples. Try the crushed seeds in the topping for apple crumble to give an age-old dessert new life.

HEALING

The essential oil, extracted from the seeds, has uses in flavouring, perfumery and medicine. Aromatherapists regard it as anti-rheumatic. Seed extracts are added to laxatives to reduce griping and are an ingredient of gripe water for babies. A tea made from bruised seeds relieves indigestion and wind, and chewing the seeds sweetens the breath after eating garlic.

NOTES FOR GARDENERS

Coriander is one of those herbs, like chervil (see p.42) and rocket (see p.202), that is best sown at intervals because it grows quickly and tends to bolt (elongate for flowering) in warm dry spells or if plants are too close together. For harvesting seeds, you don't have to worry – just collect ripening heads as they start to turn brown and hang to dry. But for a continuous supply of leaves, sow every three to four weeks from spring to early autumn, spacing seeds about 10cm (4in) apart to give large, leafy, productive plants. Better still, sow a variety bred specially for leaf production, such as 'Cilantro'. Coriander leaves freeze better than they dry: there is no need to chop them first – they crumble easily when frozen.

Crataegus laevigata
C. monogyna

HAWTHORN
MAY

PORTRAIT

The two kinds of hawthorn are very similar, both being hardy deciduous, densely branched shrubs or small trees, up to 8m (25ft) tall and wide, with glossy, dark green, lobed leaves, about 5cm (2in) long. In late spring they produce flattish clusters of heavily scented white to pink flowers, each 1.5cm (½in) across, followed by globose to egg-shaped dark red fruits. *Crataegus monogyna* differs from *C. laevigata* in having more deeply lobed leaves, and fruits with one stony seed rather than two. It is less often found in woods, preferring a more open position, and has a wider distribution, from Europe to Afghanistan, whereas *C. laevigata* is confined to Europe, especially in northern parts. To confuse matters further, hybrids are quite common in the wild, producing plants intermediate between the two, which not surprisingly are known as *C. x media.*

HISTORY

The custom of going 'a-Maying' – cutting branches of may blossom to deck doorways – and choosing a May queen goes back to pagan times when, as part of a fertility ritual, the queen of the May was fêted in the spring and put to death at the end of the growing season. Though hawthorn is rarely in flower on 1 May in northern Europe, it would have been flowering on the old May Day which, before 1732, was 13 days later. Its traditional role in the festival was to protect against evil spirits that were thought to be especially active at this time. Bringing may blossom into the house is considered bad luck, and even to cause death or illness. This may be because its sickly scent contains trimethylene, an odour given off as a corpse starts to decay. According to old records, the scent of May blossom is reminiscent of the smell that permeated the city of London between 1664 and 1665, when it was stricken by the Great Plague. Some 68,000 people – over a sixth of the population – died within the space of a year.

COOKING

The leaf buds and newly opened leaves are known as 'bread and cheese', and are a traditional spring treat in rural areas of Britain. The flowers – heads only, without stalks – make a country liqueur if packed into a jar with a little sugar and covered with brandy. Hawthorn berries (haws) are rather dry but can be used to make jelly to accompany meat and cheese.

HEALING

Hawthorn fruits and flowers improve the circulation and regulate heart beat, blood pressure and coronary blood flow. They have been described as a tonic for the ageing heart. Unlike most medicinal plants that act on the heart, hawthorn is non-toxic and is included in a number of over-the-counter remedies for strengthening the circulatory system. (Such remedies are not intended to treat serious heart or circulatory problems, which do of course require professional medical attention.) Fruits of the Chinese haw (*C. pinnatifida*) are similarly used for circulatory problems in Chinese medicine.

CRATAEGUS LAEVIGATA

CRATAEGUS LAEVIGATA

NOTES FOR GARDENERS

Hawthorns are undemanding, coping with shallow alkaline soils and disliking only really wet conditions. The common hawthorn is unbeatable as a dense, thorny, stock-proof hedge, and the deep pink ornamental varieties of *C. laevigata*, such as 'Crimson Cloud' and the double 'Paul's Scarlet' are rightly popular as specimen trees. Propagation is tedious. Seeds may take 18 months to germinate, and cultivars must be budded or grafted. With this in mind, the modest price of hedging plants or a young tree is a bargain.

Crataegu

NATURAL COLOURINGS ARE FOUND in various parts of plants – flowers, fruits, berries, husks, leaves, bark, roots and rhizomes. Their presence is often indicated in the scientific name *tinctor* (*-ius, -ia, -um*), 'for dyeing'. The most important pigments are: carotenoids, such as bixin from annatto and crocin from saffron; flavonoids, which can give either reds, purples and blues or yellows, depending on the type; and tannins, which again can give reds or yellows, according to their chemistry. Many of these compounds have aromatic, health-giving or healing properties too, so it is no coincidence that dye-rich plants are often also herbs.

In the dim and distant past, human beings learnt that natural colourings could be manipulated to make daily domestic life as visually interesting as the world around us. They dyed clothes, textiles, hair, skin and food, developing skills in handling pigments that led to more sophisticated forms of art. The colours in some plant parts – such as walnuts and onion skins – give long-lasting colours, while the majority fade or 'bleed'. By trial and error, our ancestors learnt that by mixing the colouring with other natural substances, such as urine, wood ash or metal salts, dyes could resist the effects of sunlight and water.

JUGLANS REGIA

Henna (*Lawsonia inermis*) is a Middle Eastern shrub that looks rather like privet. It bears lilac-scented flowers, which are used in perfumery, and small evergreen leaves that yield an orange-red dye. Powdered henna leaves were used to colour skin and nails, and to both dye and condition hair as long ago as 3200BC. The elaborate use of henna has been known since earliest times and still characterizes many cultures in Asia. Ancient Egyptian mummies had their nails, finger tips, palms and soles dyed with henna. It was also used to dye men's beards and moustaches, and the manes and tails of favourite horses. Mehndi (painting semi-permanent designs on the body with henna), and bindi (the wearing of a henna spot between the brows to indicate that a woman is married) are ritual art forms, widely practised in India, Africa and the Middle East.

Walnut was recorded by Pliny in the first century AD as a source of brown colourings for hair, and is still used in hair tints and conditioners for dark hair. Both common walnut (*Juglans nigra*) and black walnut (*J. regia*) yield long-lasting black and brown dyes. Butternut (*J. cinerea*) produces browns and yellows; it was used by the native American Menominee tribe to dye deerskin shirts, and later by settlers, which is why Confederate soldiers were known as 'butternuts'.

The colour red is perennially popular. The roots of madder (*Rubia tinctorum*) and munjeet (*R. cordifolia*) have been used for 5,000 years to

ALKANNA TINCTORIA

Colourings

brighten up the world. The former was immensely important in ancient cultures of the Nile Valley and Mediterranean. Processing madder roots involved unsavoury ingredients such as animal dung, blood and rancid fat, so madder dyeing took place in villages inhabited only by dyers. Production once centred on Turkey, which is why for centuries the distinctive colour was known as 'Turkey red'. Munjeet or Indian madder also yields glorious shades of red and, with indigo, produces 'Egyptian purple'. Dyer's alkanet (*Alkanna tinctoria*) gives purples too. It was used in cosmetics by the ancient Greeks and Romans, and for centuries was a permitted colouring in wine and medicines.

No one knows when annatto (*Bixa orellana*) was first used. This handsome shrub with bright red spiny capsules and oily orange-brown seeds was a familiar colouring, often with ritual significance, to the Incas of Peru, the Aztecs and Mayas of Mexico, and many Amazonian tribes. Its use as body paint may have helped protect the skin from infection, insect bites and parasites. Annatto reached Europe in the sixteenth century and commercial plantations were established in India in 1787. The carotenoids in annatto seeds give shades of orange and yellow. Being virtually tasteless, they are of major importance in the food industry as a colourant (known as E106b) for products such as butter, margarine, cheese and smoked fish. Annatto is also used in cosmetics, hence the name 'lipstick tree'.

True saffron (*Crocus sativus*) is unusual among herbs in that the part used is a very small component of the flower – the style, which is a thread-like appendage that connects the stigma to the ovary. It takes 150,000 flowers – and 400 hours labour – to produce 1kg (2.2lb) of saffron. Though used for millennia as a food colouring and fabric dye in the Near East, saffron was unknown in Europe until the Crusades. Now it is most familiar as the essential flavouring and colouring in dishes such as risotto, paella, biryani and bouillabaisse. It is prohibitively expensive to use saffron as a dye: so-called 'saffron robes' of Buddhist monks were dyed with the much cheaper and more readily available turmeric (*Curcuma longa*, see p.97).

Julius Caesar described how the ancient Britons intimidated their enemies by painting their bodies with a blue dye made from woad (*Isatis tinctoria*). Woad remained the single most important source of blue dyes until the 1630s when it was superseded by indigo from the tropics. It was a major item of European trade throughout the Middle Ages, and woad mills were a common sight – and smell – in many areas; Elizabeth I forbade the fermenting of woad within five miles of her palaces.

See also: *Carthamus tinctorius, Curcuma longa, Sambucus nigra*.

BIXA ORELLANA

ISATIS TINCTORIA

95

Cuminum cyminum

CUMIN

Portrait
A small, slender, half-hardy annual reaching only about 30cm (12in) tall, with blue-green leaves that are divided into thread-like segments. It produces umbels of tiny white to mauve flowers, followed by ribbed, grey-green fruits, 13mm (½in) long, containing pungently aromatic, brown seeds, similar in appearance to caraway. Cumin is found wild on disturbed or cultivated land in eastern Mediterranean regions. It has nothing in common with black cumin, *Nigella sativa*, a kind of love-in-the-mist with black seeds that have a quite different peppery, fruity flavour.

History
Cumin was a major herb in ancient Egypt, both for culinary and medicinal purposes. According to the Roman writer Pliny (AD23–79), cumin oil lightens the skin and was used by scholars to make

CUMINUM CYMINUM

their teachers think they were pale from overwork. Though once popular in Europe, today cumin is used mainly in the Middle East and Asia, as it has been since biblical times. In Greek culture cumin symbolizes avarice and a mean person is said to have eaten cumin.

Cooking
Cumin seeds are an ingredient of spice mixtures such as *garam masala* and characteristic of Middle Eastern couscous (a spicy dish made from a granular kind of semolina, cooked with meat, vegetables and fruit). They have a pungent, rather bitter flavour that marries well with other spices (as in curries) and with lamb. Cumin is also good with cucumber and yogurt. The essential oil is used in commercial food flavouring.

Healing
Cumin aids digestion and may help relieve migraine of digestive origin. It is widely used in Ayurvedic medicine to improve liver function and to help assimilation of other herbs in a prescription.

Cuminum

NOTES FOR GARDENERS

As cumin is not a very fetching plant and is a fiddle to grow and harvest, it may be better to buy it than grow it. Growing your own cumin has three main requirements – well-drained, light soil in full sun, a warm climate with three to four months of guaranteed hot weather and, lastly, sufficient space to grow enough to make it worthwhile – say a row or a square metre or two. Sow seed at 13–18°C (55–64°F) in spring, preferably *in situ*, or in cold areas in seed trays and plant outside at the same time as bedding plants. Harvest before the seeds are fully ripe and hang upside down over paper to catch the seeds as they ripen.

CURCUMA LONGA

Curcuma longa

TURMERIC

PORTRAIT

A tender perennial, about 1m (3ft) tall, with a large, golden-fleshed rhizome and pointed, elliptic leaves up to 50cm (20in) long. Small yellow flowers, almost hidden by pale green, white-tipped lower bracts, appear in a pineapple-shaped flower head beneath the foliage in summer. Turmeric is native to India, where it occurs in seasonally dry forest.

HISTORY

Turmeric has been cultivated in Asia for more than 2,000 years. It is also known as Indian saffron from its use as a food colouring and source of yellow and orange dyes for fabrics. In Ayurvedic medicine it has long been valued for its beneficial effects on the digestive system. Turmeric was first mentioned as a medicinal herb in China in the *Tang Materia Medica* by Su Jing in AD659.

Cooking

Turmeric is the most widely used flavouring and colouring in Asian cooking, giving a characteristic yellow hue to curries, chutneys, pickles (such as piccalilli) and rice dishes. It is also an ingredient of Thai *kra ry* powder, and of the Indonesian dish *rendang*. Though turmeric is the equivalent of saffron in the Middle East and Europe, and of annatto in South America, it has a strong flavour so cannot be used as a substitute for either.

Healing

Turmeric extracts stimulate the digestion, circulation and uterus, and help normalize energy flow. Research has shown that they have anti-inflammatory and antibiotic effects, and significantly improve liver function. Turmeric is added to several over-the-counter remedies for the liver and gall bladder, and is often combined with *Berberis* or *Mahonia* in herbal prescriptions to treat liver disease. Improving liver function makes it a useful remedy for skin diseases, which may be due to toxins. Externally, turmeric helps heal minor injuries, sores and ringworm, and is an ingredient of massage oils and liniments.

Notes for Gardeners

Given sufficient warmth – above 16°C (60°F) – and moisture, turmeric is easy to grow. In cold areas, fresh rhizomes bought from Asian greengrocers can be planted in pots of compost and put in a propagator or airing cupboard to start them off in late winter or early spring. When shoots appear, move pots to a warm, humid, sunny place. By the end of the growing season, when temperatures fall and the leaves start to yellow and die down, you should have rather more rhizome than you first planted – either for using in the kitchen, or for replanting into a larger pot the following spring. As turmeric virtually never produces seeds, propagation is by division of the rhizome into small sections, each with a dormant bud or eye.

Cymbopogon citratus   LEMON GRASS

Portrait

A robust, clump-forming, tender perennial with almost cane-like stems and linear leaves up to 1m (3ft) long. This giant lemon-scented grass, reaching more than 1.5m (5ft) tall, grows wild on savannah in southern India and Sri Lanka, and is widely naturalized in East Asia. It seldom flowers in cultivation.

History

Traditionally, during religious festivals in Greece and Turkey, lemon grass infusion replaces yogurt in *nistisemos trahanas*, a fermented dairy/cereal food that must be milk-free for periods of fasting. Lemon grass oil is among the top ten essential oils in world trade, and India and Guatemala are currently the largest producers.

Aromatic Uses

Lemon grass oil is of major importance in the perfume and flavouring industries. It contains 75–85 per cent citral, and is either used directly or as a source of citral from which many kinds of lemon scents and iones – synthetic violet scents – are made. It is also used in the manufacture of vitamin A. Oil distilled from *C. citratus* is known as West Indian lemon grass oil and is produced in Australia, the Far East, Central Africa, Brazil, Guatemala, and Haiti. So-called East Indian or Cochin lemon grass comes from *C. flexuosus*, a similarly lemon-flavoured grass that is grown commercially in the Madras area and in Kerala, southern India. East Indian lemon grass oil is used mainly in food flavouring.

COOKING

The base of the stem is bulbous and relatively tender. Finely chopped, it gives a characteristic lemon-like tang to curries and soups, especially in Thai and Vietnamese cooking. It is particularly good with chicken, fish, and seafood dishes. The outer layers, upper parts, and leaf blades are too fibrous to eat but may be added to dishes for flavouring and removed before serving. Fresh lemon grass is readily available but dried and ground products, such as *sereh* powder, are handy for the store cupboard. Lemon grass makes a refreshing herb tea and is an ingredient of many herb tea blends.

CYMBOPOGON CITRATUS

HEALING

Lemon grass contains citronellal, the insect-repellent substance that predominates in *C. nardus* (citronella). It can help to keep bugs away, and its anti-fungal and anti-bacterial effects make the oil a useful remedy for insect bites, and for problems such as ringworm, lice, scabies and athlete's foot. Taken internally, lemon grass is a cooling herb that eases digestive upsets and minor feverish illnesses, and is gentle enough for children.

NOTES FOR GARDENERS

Lemon grass and its kin are large, not very pretty plants. In areas where the temperature never falls much below 10°C (50°F), it can be grown at the back of a border. All it needs is hot wet summers and dry warm winters. Soil is immaterial – it takes anything from clay to sand in its stride. In cold areas it can be grown in a pot, but may need a larger pot and more space than is practicable for the amount you can harvest. Rather than growing it as a lone specimen, treat it as an annual instead, planting up a youngster as a fountain-like centrepiece in a large container of other herbs or baby vegetables.

Cynara cardunculus (Scolymus group)

Cynara cardunculus (SCOLYMUS GROUP) GLOBE ARTICHOKE

PORTRAIT

A huge, hardy perennial, reaching 2m (6ft) tall and 1.2m (4ft) wide, with deeply cut leaves, up to 80cm (32in) long and 40cm (16in) across, which are covered with a grey-white bloom. In summer, large purple, thistle-like blooms appear, 10-12cm (4–5in) across, clad in stout, usually blunt spines. These are followed by seeds that have a tuft of fine hairs to parachute them away on the wind. Globe artichokes are unknown in the wild.

HISTORY

Globe artichokes were cultivated by the Romans and may have been first grown in England during the Roman occupation. Then they seem to have been forgotten about and were apparently reintroduced in 1548. There have been differences of opinion in botanical circles over whether the

CYNARA CARDUNCULUS SCOLYMUS GROUP

globe artichoke is a separate species, *C. scolymus*, but evidence now suggests that it was derived from cultivated plants of *C. cardunculus* (cardoon), a smaller, spinier species from Mediterranean regions.

COOKING

The edible part is the flower head, when in bud. Only the base of each bract is eaten. The heads are boiled and eaten bract by bract, either hot with hollandaise sauce or melted butter, or cold with vinaigrette. Where the stalk joins the flower head there is a fleshy heart that is also eaten as a vegetable. Both artichoke hearts and baby artichokes (buds of side shoots) can be pickled or preserved in brine or oil. Young leaf stalks may be blanched and eaten like cardoon. Artichokes are the basis of a liqueur known as *cyna*, and yield an enzyme with rennet-like properties.

HEALING

Artichoke leaves, stems and roots contain bitter substances that detoxify and regenerate the liver and stimulate the gall bladder. They also help to reduce cholesterol and blood sugar. The levels of bitter compounds are highest in the leaves just before flowering. Extracts are added to digestive tonics and taken to alleviate liver and gall bladder problems, jaundice, hepatitis, diabetes and arteriosclerosis.

NOTES FOR GARDENERS
This is a splendid architectural plant for the border or *en bloc* in the vegetable garden. It also makes a fine background plant for the white garden if flower heads are religiously removed. As well as providing *hors d'oeuvres*, the removal of flowering stems keeps the foliage in good condition for longer. Artichokes like well-drained soil in sun and reach impressive dimensions when well fed. In cold areas, where temperatures fall below −15°F (5°F), mulch dormant plants with straw, dry bracken or the like. Propagate them by seed or by removal of side shoots in spring, or by root cuttings in winter. Set out the resulting plants 1m (3ft) apart.

Daucus carota　　　　　WILD CARROT

PORTRAIT
A hardy biennial, 30–90cm (1–3ft) tall, with a brownish-white, spindle-shaped tap root, ridged stems, fern-like leaves and tiny white flowers in summer, followed by flat, spiny fruits. The flowers are produced in umbels up to 7cm (3in) across, which are often purplish in the centre and have conspicuous bracts. This is the wild carrot from which cultivated carrots, subspecies *sativus*, were derived. It is a common wild flower in grassland throughout Europe, temperate Asia and North Africa, especially near the sea, and is naturalized in North America and elsewhere.

HISTORY
Carrots have been an important vegetable and fodder crop in Europe, North Africa and many parts of Asia since at least classical times, but were not widely grown in Britain until the sixteenth century. Orange-rooted carrots are the most popular, but they may be anything from white to yellow, dark red or purple, depending on the variety. A decoction of wild carrot seeds was a traditional hangover cure, perhaps because of its detoxifying effect. It was also a 'morning-after' contraceptive: research shows it contains a substance that inhibits implantation in mice, so it might have worked.

AROMATIC USES
Wild carrot oil extracted from the seeds has an orris-like scent and is used in perfumery.

COOKING
The roots of wild carrots are strongly aromatic and decidedly unpalatable. Cultivated carrots are extremely nutritious, especially raw or juiced, and are often included in special naturopath diets such as liquid-only diets to detoxify and revitalize the body.

BEAUTY
Stabilized extracts from the oil are used in anti-wrinkle creams to restore elasticity of the skin and help keep it soft and smooth.

Daucus Carota L.

HEALING

Extracts of the whole wild carrot plant are used to treat urinary stones and cystitis. The seeds stimulate the uterus and help menstrual problems; they should not be taken during pregnancy. A tea made from the root helps relieve gout as it encourages the excretion of uric acid. All parts have a diuretic and tonic effect. In addition, the leaves contain substances that act on the pituitary gland, increasing the production of sex hormones. The roots of cultivated carrots are a rich source of beta carotene, which improves eyesight and skin health, and has anti-cancer effects. Excess is toxic, causing the skin to turn yellow – the normal adult daily requirement of vitamin A, which includes beta carotene, is 750mcg.

NOTES FOR GARDENERS

Being a grassland species, wild carrot is well-suited to the wild flower meadow. It is in its element on dry, sandy, neutral to alkaline soil in full sun but thrives in most well-drained garden soils. Sow seed *in situ* in spring, summer or autumn. With its ruff of finely divided bracts beneath the umbel, wild carrot is one of the easier white-flowered umbellifers to identify should you wish to use it medicinally. Many of the rest are poisonous.

Dioscorea batatas — WILD YAM
CHINESE YAM, CINNAMON YAM,

PORTRAIT

A half-hardy perennial climber with vertical, spindle-shaped tubers up to 1m (3ft) long and heart-shaped, deeply veined leaves, 4–8cm (1½–3in) long. The stems twine anticlockwise, reaching 3m (10ft) or more. Spikes of tiny, white, cinnamon-scented flowers appear in summer, followed by three-angled capsules. Bulbils are also produced in the leaf axils, falling to the ground as the vine dies down in winter. Chinese or cinnamon yams (*Dioscorea batatas* syn. *D. opposita*) are found in woods and along field boundaries in China, Korea, Taiwan and Japan. The North American wild yam (*D. villosa*) occurs in similar situations and is similar in appearance, but with slender rhizomes and yellow-green flowers.

HISTORY

Known as *shan yao*, 'mountain medicine', Chinese yam has been used medicinally in China for more than 2,000 years. The rihizomes of many yams contain hormonal substances that are used in the manufacture of steroids and contraceptive pills, notably the Mexican yam (*D. macrostachya*), an ancient Aztec herb, which is now being promoted as a natural form of hormone replacement therapy (HRT). In Ayurvedic medicine yams, known as *aluka*, are used to treat sexual and hormonal problems and hysteria. In homeopathy, *D. villosa* is used for colic, especially in babies – hence the common name, colic root. Long before, it was used by the native American Meskwaki tribe to relieve labour pains, and by the black population in the southern states of the USA for rheumatism.

COOKING

In common with many yams, the roots of Chinese yam are edible as a vegetable.

HEALING

Chinese yam is a gentle tonic herb that improves appetite and digestion, and benefits the respiratory and urinary systems. It is prescribed for poor appetite, chronic diarrhoea, asthma, dry coughs, night sweats, frequent urination and incontinence. Its hormonal effects are also suggested by its use for problems of the reproductive organs, such as involuntary ejaculation. Yam is a component of 'the pill of eight ingredients', a traditional Chinese remedy for under-active thyroid, kidney disease and diabetes. The North American wild yam or colic root (*D. villosa*) is an acrid, anti-inflammatory herb that stimulates bile flow, dilates blood vessels, and controls spasms. It is used for arthritis, inflammatory conditions of the digestive tract, gall bladder complaints, morning sickness, ovarian, menstrual and labour pains, cramp, bronchial infections, asthma and catarrh.

NOTES FOR GARDENERS

Chinese yam is easily grown from seed or from the numerous little bulbils it produces. All it needs is reasonably fertile, well-drained soil in sun or partial shade. The North American yam is hardier

DIOSCOREA SPECIES

and just as easy to grow. Both make attractive climbers for a fence or in amongst shrubs, or perhaps grown up a wigwam as a feature in the herb garden.

Echinacea species

ECHINACEA
PURPLE CONE FLOWER

PORTRAIT

Echinacea purpurea is a hardy perennial with deep-veined, slender oval leaves and stiff stems of large purple-pink daisies in summer. The flowers are about 12cm (5in) across and have a spiky golden-brown central cone, surrounded by broad petals that tend to droop as the flower ages. Plants reach 1.5m (5ft) tall and are magnificent when in bloom. There are nine species of *Echinacea* in the prairies of central and eastern North America, three of which (*E. purpurea*, *E. pallida* and *E. angustifolia*) are used medicinally for similar purposes. Some are increasingly rare due to over-collection.

History

Echinaceas were important medicinal herbs to native Americans, especially among tribes who lived on the plains where the plants grow. They were regarded as a cure-all and the first line of defence for infected wounds or poisonous bites and stings. Use of the herb was adopted by settlers in the eighteenth century and by 1895 homeopaths in Germany were prescribing echinacea remedies. Commercial cultivation of *E. purpurea* and research into its properties began in Germany in the late 1930s. The name *Echinacea* comes from the Greek *echinos*, hedgehog or sea urchin, referring to the spiky seedhead.

Healing

Echinacea is an immune-system stimulant. It increases the activity of various cells in the body whose job is to eliminate germs and toxins, and inhibits the growth of viruses. This explains why echinacea is so effective in preventing colds and flu or reducing their severity. Echinacea can also be used externally to treat minor wounds and burns, and various skin conditions. The

ECHINACEA PURPUREA

best way to take echinacea is in the form of fresh juice, pressed from the flowering plant in summer, but a wide range of products, including tinctures, capsules and ointment, are available to treat problems that occur at other times of the year. Root extracts are also used. Chewed fresh, the root causes a tingling, slightly anaesthetic effect and was a traditional remedy for toothache and snake bite.

Notes for Gardeners

With its long-lasting, colourful flowers, echinacea is a must for the herbaceous border and readily available (among the ornamentals, not the herbs) at most garden centres. Plants can be raised from seed, sown when ripe or in spring at 13°C (55°F), or from root cuttings taken from late autumn to early winter. There are a number of named varieties of *E. purpurea*, some with pure white petals, others with deep magenta, and several that reach only 80cm (2½ft) tall. Pale purple coneflower (*E. pallida*) is also worth growing and easy to come by. It reaches about 1m (3ft) and has more graceful flowers with paler, narrower petals.

Herbal Flowers

JASMINUM OFFICINALE

GARDENIA AUGUSTA

CANANGA ODORATA

Images of flowers are deep in our subconscious and woven into the fabric of everyday life through art, design, religion and folklore. Over the centuries, certain flowers, such as lilies and roses, have taken on mystical significance, having colours, shapes, scents and healing properties that have inspired generations. Flowers may look fragile but their chemistry is as complex as any other plant part. Scented flowers are rich in volatile oils and other substances that improve health and vitality. Obvious uses are in aromatherapy, perfumery, skin care and fragrant delights such as pot-pourri and tussie-mussies. More subtle still, they are key ingredients in flower remedies, in which the healing energy of plants is transferred to water through the power of sunlight, and in homeopathy. Some are edible too, in salads, preserves, floral waters and vinegars, or to flavour tea and Eastern spice mixes.

The scent of jasmine is deeply sensual and relaxing, a floral aphrodisiac with a special affinity for female energy. Jasmine flowers symbolize femininity; their perfume is eternally popular in fragrances for women. The exquisite essential oil comes mainly from the hardy climbing jasmine, *Jasminum officinale* and from royal jasmine (*J. grandiflorum*), which has larger flowers. It takes eight million flowers to produce 1kg (2.2lb) of oil, which was traditionally extracted by enfleurage – placing individual flowers on a layer of odourless fat to absorb their oils. Aromatherapists use jasmine oil to calm and lift the spirit, and clear congestion. The tropical Arabian jasmine (*J. sambac*) is the main species used to scent tea.

Gardenia or Cape jasmine (*Gardenia augusta*) is a handsome shrub from warm parts of East Asia, easily grown as a houseplant as it flowers more freely when young. The waxy white flowers have a sumptuous fragrance and, though often synthesized, the essential oil is a component of exotic oriental perfumes. Gardenia is known as 'the happiness herb' in the East and the fruits are used to improve liver function.

Nothing – not even jasmine or gardenia – is as exotic as ylang-ylang (*Cananga odorata*), a tropical Asian tree with pale yellow-green flowers that exude an intense fragrance at night. When mature, a single tree produces about 120kg (265lb) of flowers a year, yielding 350g (12oz) of essential cananga oil. Ylang-ylang is a favourite ingredient for perfumes, soaps and skin lotions, and is often used in hair products. In Victorian times, ylang-ylang was blended with coconut oil to make a hair dressing known as Macassar oil, and the backs of chairs were covered with antimacassars to protect the upholstery. The essential oil is also used in aromatherapy to relieve anxiety and depression, high blood pressure and sexual neuroses.

CONVALLARIA MAJALIS

Champac (*Michelia champaca*), also from tropical Asia, produces yellow, magnolia-like flowers with a delicious fragrance, similar to ylang-ylang but with a fruity note. They are prescribed in Ayurvedic medicine in infusions for fevers and digestive upsets, and macerated in oil for rheumatism and gout.

Known by perfumers as muguet, the exquisite scent of lily-of-the-valley (*Convallaria majalis*) is a favourite in snuff, fragrances and skin-care products. The dainty flowers are also in great demand for bridal bouquets. There is, however, another side to this modest plant: it contains cardiac glycosides, similar to those in foxglove (*Digitalis* species), but less cumulative and generally preferred by herbalists for treating cardiovascular disorders.

Flowers of clove pink or wild carnation (*Dianthus caryophyllus*) have a warm, spicy scent, reminiscent of cloves and, like the spice, they contain eugenol. The essential oil, known as oeillet, is extracted for perfumery, and the flowers, with bitter white bases removed, can be added to salads, crystallized, pickled in vinegar, made into syrup or dried for pot-pourri.

VIOLA ODORATA

Sweet violets (*Viola odorata*) were grown commercially in classical times and were great favourites with the Romans, who drank violet-flavoured wine. Napoleon adored them; he was nicknamed Caporal Violette and died wearing a locket of violets from Josephine's grave. Violets enjoyed cult status again in Victorian England and many fine varieties, now lost to cultivation, were grown for posies and perfumery. Essential oil from the flowers is still used in perfumes and violet leaf oil is an ingredient of skin-refining products. Fresh flowers are edible and can be used in similar ways to clove pinks.

Though very different in appearance, the bright yellow, mimosa-like flowers of cassie (*Acacia farnesiana*) are similar in fragrance to violets, with a touch of orange blossom. The solid extract of the flowers, known as 'cassie absolute', is important in perfumery and the shrubs were once grown on a large scale in the south of France and Lebanon.

The sacred lotus (*Nelumbo nucifera*) is revered in many Eastern cultures and sacred to Hindus and Buddhists alike. The Hindu mantra, *om mani padma hum*, means 'jewel in the lotus', referring to the deity Brahma. Various parts of the plant, including the stamens, are used in Chinese medicine, while Ayurvedic medicine favours rhizomes and seeds. Most parts are edible too; tea scented with lotus stamens and pollen is heavenly.

See also: *Calendula officinalis*, *Citrus* species, *Lavandula species*, *Myrtus communis*, *Primula veris* and *P. vulgaris*, *Rosa* species, *Salvia* species, *Sambucus nigra*, *Tilia* species.

NELUMBO NUCIFERA

Elettaria cardamomum   CARDAMOM

PORTRAIT

A tender evergreen perennial, reaching 3m (10ft) tall in the wild, with thick, gnarled rhizomes and stout, cane-like stems bearing two rows of smooth, narrow, pointed leaves up to 60cm (2ft) long. Flower spikes are produced at the base of the stem. They are semi-prostrate, about 60cm (2ft) long, and clad in dark green bracts, from which emerge white orchid-like flowers, with a lip striped in purple-pink. These are followed by pale green pods, each containing 15–20 aromatic brown seeds. Cardamom is native to tropical rainforests in India and Sri Lanka, which produce the finest pods, though much of today's market is supplied by Guatemala.

HISTORY

Cardamom was exported from the East along caravan routes since ancient times and was introduced to Europe by the Romans. It was an ingredient of the ancient Egyptian ointment *metopion*, which was used both as a perfume and a medicine. Being native to India, cardamom has a long history of use in Ayurvedic medicine. The first mention of it as a Chinese medicinal herb was made in about AD721.

COOKING

Cardamom is a multi-purpose spice, used to flavour a wide range of food and drinks, from dairy desserts, cakes and pastries, mulled wine and baked or stewed fruit, to pickles, chutneys and pilaus. Use the pods whole or crushed, or remove the seeds, which are hard and sticky, and quite difficult to grind. Cardamom is an important ingredient of curry powder and of the Ethiopian hot spice blend known as *mit'mit'a*. In the Middle East, it is added to coffee, and in India the seeds are chewed to sweeten the breath. Grains of paradise or melegueta pepper (*Afromomum melegueta*) has a similar aroma to cardamom but a more peppery flavour.

HEALING

Cardamom is primarily a digestive tonic and expectorant. It has a pleasant flavour and combines well with other herbs, especially with fennel to calm nervous digestive upsets in children. According to Ayurvedic medicine, it controls mucus formation associated with eating dairy products, and detoxifies caffeine. In Chinese medicine it is similarly used for digestive and bronchial complaints, and also for symptoms of weak kidney energy, such as bed-wetting.

NOTES FOR GARDENERS

Cardamom is a fine foliage plant, resembling hedychiums and gingers, which in warm areas can be grown among shrubs or at the back of a border. It needs a minimum temperature of 10°C (50°F) and rich soil in partial shade, as the leaves tend to yellow in full sun. In cold areas, grow it in pots, using loam-based compost, such as John Innes No 2, with additional well-rotted leaf mould, compost or manure, though containerized plants are unlikely to flower. Commercial propagation is mainly by seed to avoid mosaic virus, but for garden ornamentals the best method is to divide the rhizomes in spring. Seed can be sown as soon as it is ripe at about 24°C (75°F), but seed-raised plants take five years to flower, while those from division take only three.

Plate 385

Eliz. Blackwell delin. sculp. et Pinx.

The greater & lesser
Cardamoms & Grains
of Paradyce.

1. Flower of y lesser Cardamoms. 4. Fruit of y Grains of Paradyce
2. Fruit of y great Cardamoms.   5. Fruit of all Three open.
3. Fruit of y lesser Cardamoms.   6. Seed of all Three.

Cardamomum majus,
minus et maximum,
vel Grana Paradisi.

Eleutherococcus senticosus

SIBERIAN GINSENG
Eleuthero

Portrait

A hardy, suckering, deciduous shrub that can reach 7m (22ft) tall but is often much smaller. It has thick roots, prickly stems and dark green leaves divided into five leaflets, resembling those of a horse chestnut. Rounded clusters of tiny flowers are produced in summer – males purplish and females green – followed by blue-black berries. Siberian ginseng forms dense thickets in mountainous areas of south-eastern Russia, north-eastern China, Korea and northern Japan.

History

Siberian ginseng was among the 100 or so most important herbs listed in the 2,000-year-old Chinese herbal, *Shen Nong Ben Cao Jing*, in which it is called *ci-wu-jia*. Although it does not feature in traditional Russian medicine, in the 1960s it was investigated by Russian scientists Brekhman and

ELEUTHEROCOCCUS SENTICOSUS

Dardymov, as part of a study of adaptogenic herbs that might be useful to astronauts and athletes. (The term adaptogen was in fact coined by Russian researchers and refers to a herb that has a tonic effect on all organs and systems, thus adapting the body to stress and improving resistance to infection.) Since then it has been marketed as a kind of ginseng, and indeed it belongs to the same family as the true ginsengs (*Panax* species, see p.193).

Healing

Siberian ginseng stimulates the immune and circulatory systems, regulates blood pressure, lowers blood sugar and reduces inflammation. It has proved useful in the background treatment of cancer and exposure to toxic chemicals and radiation. More generally, it is taken during convalescence and periods of physical and mental stress, and by the weak and elderly. Studies have shown that it increases physical and mental performance, improving alertness and stamina. It is not suitable for children or anyone on hormone medication, and is not recommended during pregnancy. The best way of taking Siberian ginseng is for a few weeks at a time, in the run-up to a stressful period. It is gentler than Korean ginseng (*Panax ginseng*) but likewise is contraindicated with caffeine and other stimulants.

NOTES FOR GARDENERS

It is a mystery why this important medicinal herb is not more widely grown in the West, as it is a tough, hardy plant that would not look out of place among other shrubs or in the woodland garden. All it needs is moist, rich soil in sun or partial shade. The easiest method of propagation is by removing suckers before growth starts in early spring. Hardwood cuttings, root cuttings or stratified seed are other options. To harvest the roots, excavate and remove sections in the autumn without disturbing the stems.

ERYNGIUM FOETIDUM

Eryngium foetidum

CULANTRO
FIT WEED, FALSE CORIANDER

PORTRAIT

A tender, evergreen perennial, reaching 30–40cm (12–16in), with a rosette of elongated leaves up to 25cm (10in) long, which have spine-toothed margins. A branched flowering stem emerges from the rosette in summer, bearing star-shaped flower heads, each consisting of a cylindrical umbel of tiny greenish-white flowers, surrounded by five or six green, spine-edged bracts. Culantro grows wild in seasonally dry grassland and waste ground in Central and South America, southern Mexico and the West Indies, and is naturalized in West Africa and Uganda.

HISTORY

The rather unpleasant scent of culantro is supposed to repel snakes if planted near doorways. This strong-smelling herb is also known as *chardon étoile* (star thistle) in Central America, *cilantron* or

Plate XXVI

2.

Fitch del et lith.

Vincent Brooks Imp.

Eucalyptus urnigera, H.f.

cilantrillo in Mexico, *chadon benée* (blessed thistle) in Dominica, and other variations such as shadow bennie, elsewhere in the Caribbean. In various places it is called false, spiny or thorny coriander too.

COOKING
Culantro is similar to coriander in flavour, but stronger. The roots are used to flavour soups, and the less pungent flower heads are used in Mexican *mole* (a highly spiced, savoury sauce based on chilli peppers and chocolate). The Caribbean seasoning mix known as *sofrito* includes culantro, cilantro (coriander) and chillis as the key ingredients. Increasingly popular in south-east Asian cooking, young culantro leaves are steamed with rice and added to many vegetable, meat and seafood dishes.

HEALING
Culantro improves digestion, lowers fever and relaxes spasms. In Carib medicine, it is regarded as a cure-all, and is especially used for epilepsy and fits (hence the name fitweed in Tobago), high blood pressure, fevers and chills in children.

NOTES FOR GARDENERS
Culantro is easier to grow in hot climates than cilantro or coriander (*Coriandrum sativum*), which goes to seed quickly in warm dry conditions. It also has the advantage of being perennial, though can be grown as an annual in areas with cold winters, and is a manageable size for containers. Ideal growing conditions are moist, reasonably fertile, heavy soil, in sun or partial shade, and a minimum temperature of 15–18°C (59–64°F). The leaves are best before flowering and retain their flavour better than coriander when dried. The roots – preferably of two-year-old plants – are lifted at the end of the growing season and used fresh, or dried. Propagate plants by seed sown in spring or by root cuttings when a plant is not in active growth.

Eucalyptus species

EUCALYPTUS
GUM TREE

PORTRAIT
There are more than 600 species and varieties of *Eucalyptus,* which occur in a range of habitats, from desert to swamp, mainly in Australia. Their hardiness depends on species and provenance, ranging from fully hardy to tender. They are evergreen trees and shrubs, often with valuable timber, elegant foliage and interesting bark. The leaves, which are aromatic and rich in oils, commonly change shape as the plant ages: young plants have opposite leaves that are often rounded, while mature plants have alternate, generally longer leaves. The flowers are composed of numerous stamens, which in most species are white or cream, and in some are pink, red or orange. The shapes of the flower buds and fruits are important for identification, as many species have similar foliage and flowers.

HISTORY
Aboriginal people used numerous species in a host of different ways for food, medicine and materials, but only a handful are commercially exploited today. Apart from timber, the main

product is essential oil. The first sample of essential oil sent back to England by the early colonists was from a peppermint tree (*E. piperita*) in 1788. Commercial production of eucalyptus oil was started in Dandenong, Victoria, in 1852 by Joseph Bosisto, an emigrant from Yorkshire, England.

AROMATIC USES

Lemon-scented gum (*E. citriodora*) is the richest known source of citronellal for the perfumery industry. The lesser known *E. macarthurii* yields geranyl acetate, which has a lavender-like scent. The leaves are lovely in pot-pourris and for herbal flower arrangements.

HEALING

Eucalyptus oils are strongly antiseptic, expectorant and anti-inflammatory. They are used in inhalants, remedies for coughs and colds, dental hygiene products, liniments, ointments and soaps. The main constituent is cineole, which makes up 60–90 per cent of the oil and has the typical eucalyptus scent. The main cineole-rich species are *E. dives* (broad-leaved peppermint), *E. globulus* (blue gum), *E. polybractea*, *E. radiata*, *E. smithii* and *E. viridis*. Other constituents include phellandrene, which is used in disinfectants and germicidal products, and piperitone, from which synthetic menthol and thymol are made. Gum trees also produce an oleo-resin known as kino, which contains antiseptic, astringent compounds that are useful in controlling diarrhoea and urinary tract infections.

NOTES FOR GARDENERS

Two of the most easily and widely grown eucalypts are the lemon-scented *E. citriodora* and the blue gum, *E. globulus,* which make excellent pot plants when young. The former is tender, needing minimum 5–7°C (41–45°F), and likes rather dry conditions; the latter thrives in moist, even wet soils and is hardy to a minimum -15°C (5°F), but often re-sprouts if cut down by frost. Young blue gum plants are often available in garden centres in the spring for use as feature plants in bedding schemes and containers. To grow your own, sow seed in spring at about 18°C (64°F). Outdoors, plant them in neutral to slightly acid soil in full sun. In containers use loam-based compost, such as John Innes No 3, with extra sand or grit. To control size and shape, prune eucalypts in spring.

Eupatorium species

BONESET
JOE PYE WEED

PORTRAIT

Eupatorium perfoliatum (boneset) is a hardy, upright perennial, reaching 1.5m (5ft) tall, with thick rhizomes and narrow, pointed, deeply veined leaves that are joined together around the stem. Dense, flat-topped clusters of long-stamened white flowers appear in late summer. Boneset is a common wildflower of wet places in eastern North America. The closely related Joe Pye weed (*E. purpureum*) is a giant perennial with lilac-pink flowers, similarly eastern North American in distribution, but in open woods, often on alkaline soil.

History

Boneset was used medicinally by many North American tribes for various ailments before being adopted by settlers. Despite its name, it was not used to mend broken bones, but to relieve the severe aching and fever associated with the early stages of a virulent strain of flu that in the late eighteenth century was known as breakbone fever – a term now applied to dengue fever. Boneset was extremely important as a household remedy in the nineteenth century. According to Charles Millspaugh in *Medicinal Plants* (1892): 'There is probably no plant in American domestic practice that has more extensive or frequent use than this.' Research has shown that boneset is as effective as aspirin in relieving symptoms of the common cold.

Healing

Boneset lowers fever, relieves bronchial congestion and stimulates the immune system. It is an excellent, if very bitter remedy for colds, flu, catarrh and acute bronchitis. In over-the-counter medicines it is often combined with yarrow, elderflower and ginger or chilli. European hemp

EUPATORIUM PERFOLIATUM

EUPATORIUM PURPUREUM

agrimony (*E. cannabinum*) is similarly used to treat flu, especially in homeopathic remedies. Joe Pye weed has different effects, acting on the genito-urinary organs and uterus, and being used to treat urinary tract infections, prostate problems, and difficulties with menstruation and labour.

Notes for Gardeners

Eupatoriums are ornamental plants for the border or woodland garden. There are few more impressive sights than a clump of Joe Pye weed, 3m (10ft) tall, in flower against a blue sky and alive with bees and butterflies. Hemp agrimony and boneset are slightly smaller and prefer a damper position, perhaps beside a pond. Propagate them by seed or division in spring.

![Pelargonium fragrans](PELARGONIUM FRAGRANS)

PELARGONIUM FRAGRANS

![Pelargonium crispum](PELARGONIUM CRISPUM)

PELARGONIUM CRISPUM

MYRRHIS ODORATA

Herbal

MOST PEOPLE THINK OF HERBS as undistinguished green plants with leaves that are used for flavouring. Leaves may be the commonest plant part with culinary, medicinal, or cosmetic uses but, far from being boring, they are endlessly varied in shape, size, texture, aroma and even colour.

Leaves vary enormously in chemical constituents too. Many are rich in oils that make them highly aromatic, while others contain deadly alkaloids, astringent tannins or slimy mucilages. Generally speaking, whether deciduous or evergreen, leaves are a renewable resource. Unless ruthlessly harvested or unless a plant naturally has only scant foliage, the loss of a few leaves is not likely to damage a plant as much as depriving it of roots, bark or reproductive parts. Careful harvesting by pinching out or pruning can even benefit plants by stimulating new growth.

For a perfume as exotic as patchouli, the plant is rather disappointing. The velvety leaves, though wonderfully scented, are unremarkable, and the flowers are pretty weedy too. Patchouli oil is obtained from the dried leaves of several species, the best coming from *Pogostemon cablin*. In India, dried patchouli leaves were traditionally placed among clothes and their lingering scent in imported shawls entranced the Victorians; in the 1860s patchouli was the height of fashion. A century later, during the hippy era, it enjoyed a resurgence. Used in minute amounts with other perfume oils, patchouli is a valuable ingredient in perfumery. It is also used to heal skin problems, and in aromatherapy for depression, exhaustion and low libido.

Geranium oils are distilled from the leaves of *Pelargonium* species, which produce large quantities of foliage and oil quite cheaply, so are in great demand by the perfume industry. Scented pelargoniums come from South Africa but are grown commercially in many parts of the world. Rose-scented kinds, such as *P. capitatum*, 'Graveolens' and 'Attar of Roses' yield the classic geranium oil, which is a fragrance in its own right, though often used to adulterate rose oil. Other kinds have fragrances resembling lemon, orange, peppermint, nutmeg or eucalyptus.

Many different herbal leaves are used to make alternatives to Indian or China tea. Rooibos tea is made from a broom-like South African shrub, *Aspalathus linearis*. It tastes similar to ordinary tea, but has a lower tannin content and no caffeine. Buchu tea made from intensely scented *Agathosma* species, is so popular in South Africa that some species are seriously over-collected. They vary in flavour but all benefit digestive problems, rheumatism, bronchial and urinary tract infections. Also South African, honeybush tea is made from fermented foliage of *Cyclopia* species.

Foliage

The leaves of some herbs are so sweet that they can be used as low-calorie sweeteners. The ferny foliage of sweet cicely (*Myrrhis odorata*) has an anise-like flavour that takes the edge off sour fruits such as rhubarb and gooseberries. Stevia (*Stevia rebaudiana*) contains stevioside, which is 300 times sweeter than sugar. Though not permitted as a sweetener in some countries, it has been used in the Japanese food industry since the 1970s. Aztec sweet herb (*Phyla scaberrima*) is a South American shrub with sweet-tasting leaves, though their camphor aroma overpowers subtle flavours.

Maidenhair ferns are familiar houseplants seldom thought of as herbs. Their delicate fronds have been used since classical times to make soothing syrups for coughs and bronchial congestion. Extracts are also a traditional ingredient of hair tonics, and of the flavouring 'capillaire', once used in soft drinks. Most commonly used is *Adiantum capillus-veneris*.

Another unlikely herb is the carnivorous sundew (*Drosera rotundifolia*), whose sticky little spoon-shaped leaves are used in cough mixtures. In the seventeenth century, a sundew liqueur called *Rosa Solis* was popular as a tonic and aphrodisiac. Sundews are tiny plants that grow in nutrient-poor, waterlogged soils. Some 25 million plants are collected annually from bogs in Finland – a harvest that may not be sustainable.

Oakmoss (*Evernia prunastri*) is an extremely slow-growing, aromatic lichen that grows on trees. It was used in ancient Egypt for packing embalmed mummies and, many centuries later, in Europe for powdering wigs. Oakmoss resin is actually essential oil, evaporated to form a sticky solid. It is an exceptional fixative, used especially in 'mossy' perfumes such as *chypre* and *fougère*. Oakmoss cannot be cultivated. Around 9,100 tonnes (9,000 tons) are gathered annually, mainly from cork oak plantations and orchards in France, the Balkans and Morocco.

Sphagnum or peat moss, from *Sphagnum* species, is quite different. It is a lush moss that grows in acid bogs worldwide and is ecologically important as the basis of peat. There are now restrictions on harvesting it from the wild to prevent the irreversible decline of peat bogs. When dried, sphagnum is twice as absorbent as cotton wool, as well as being naturally antiseptic. Before the days of feminine hygiene products and babies' nappies (diapers), pads of sphagnum were used for sanitary purposes in many parts of the world. Peat extracts, such as peat tar and sphagnol are used to treat skin diseases and irritations. They are astringent, antibiotic and control itching.

See also: *Aloe vera, Aloysia triphylla, Artemisia* species, *Camellia sinensis, Centella asatica, Eucalyptus* species, *Galium odoratum, Gingko biloba, Perilla frutescens, Plectranthus amboinicus, Sassafras albidum.*

AGATHOSMA OVATA

PHYLA SCABERRIMA

SPHAGNUM SPECIES

Fallopia multiflora

FO TI
FLOWERY KNOTWEED

PORTRAIT

A herbaceous climbing perennial, reaching 7–10m (22–30ft) and hardy to –15°C (5°F). It has tuberous rhizomes weighing up to 6lb (2.7kg) and reddish stems bearing slender, heart-shaped, bright green leaves about 10cm (4in) long. It blooms profusely in autumn, bearing panicles, 20–24cm (8–10in) long, of tiny white flowers. Flowery knotweed is a common vine throughout most of China except colder north-eastern parts.

HISTORY

An important Taoist longevity remedy, *fo ti* (also known as *he shou wu*) was first described as a medicinal herb in China in AD713. *He shou wu* means 'black-haired mister', alluding to its reputation for restoring colour to grey hair.

FALLOPIA MULTIFLORA

HEALING

The tubers are used in remedies to counteract symptoms of ageing, such as premature greying, impotence or early menopause. They have a tonic, rejuvenating effect on the liver and reproductive, urinary and circulatory systems, clearing toxins, and lowering both blood sugar and cholesterol levels. Used externally, *fo ti* is applied to wounds, boils and sores, as it has antibacterial effects.

NOTES FOR GARDENERS

Though looking rather like the dreaded Russian vine (*Fallopia baldschuanica*), flowery knotweed is better behaved – at least in cultivation in Britain – and has more attractive foliage which is almost luminous green when young. It likes well-drained, moist, sandy soil in sun and needs protection in very cold winter weather. In areas with cool summers it may flower very late or not at all. Propagation is easy, as it roots easily from cuttings, even in water. When the plant is dormant, you can remove the numerous small tubers that are produced each year, either for medicinal purposes or as propagules. New plants can be grown from root cuttings, layering or seed.

Filipendula ulmaria   MEADOWSWEET

Portrait
A hardy perennial, some 60cm–1.2m (2–4ft) tall, with dark green, deeply veined leaves that have pale, downy undersides and are divided into two to five pairs of uneven-sized, pointed, oval, toothed leaflets. The foliage smells like wintergreen when crushed. In summer, large heads of fluffy, creamy-white, almond-scented flowers appear, making a fine sight in marshes and damp meadows throughout Europe and temperate Asia, and also in parts of North America where it is naturalized.

History
The common name was probably derived from the earlier 'meadwort', meaning a herb used to flavour mead and beer, rather than from the plant's natural habitat. According to Mrs Grieve,

FILIPENDULA ULMARIA

author of *A Modern Herbal* (1931), meadowsweet was one of three sacred herbs of the Druids, the others being water mint (*Mentha aquatica*) and vervain (*Verbena officinalis*). On a more practical note, it was important in medieval times as a strewing herb for earthen floors. More recently, it is famed as the plant from which salicylic acid was first isolated in 1838. This substance was later synthesized as aspirin – a term derived from the plant's former scientific name, *Spiraea ulmaria.*

Healing
Though meadowsweet contains compounds akin to aspirin, it does no damage to the digestive tract as the corrosive salicylic acid is buffered by soothing, healing compounds. It is in fact a highly effective remedy for acidosis, heartburn, gastritis and ulcers of the digestive tract. Being astringent, it also controls diarrhoea and eases griping. Having similar effects – but not side-effects – to aspirin, it relieves pain and is a useful herb for aching joints and flu. However, anyone who is sensitive to salicylates (aspirin) should not take meadowsweet for whatever reason.

NOTES FOR GARDENERS

Meadowsweet luxuriates in rich, wet, neutral to alkaline soil in sun or partial shade, but unlike most bog plants can do surprisingly well in a border, as long as the soil is reasonably moisture-retentive. If conditions are too dry, it is prone to mildew. There are ornamental forms with golden leaves and yellow-variegated foliage that are especially attractive in spring, and one with double flowers that last rather longer than the singles. Propagation is by seed sown in spring, but varieties can be increased by division only, in autumn or early spring.

Foeniculum vulgare   FENNEL

PORTRAIT

A tall perennial, reaching 2m (6ft), with hollow, upright stems, and glossy, aromatic leaves that are divided into thread-like segments. Umbels of tiny, dull yellow flowers are produced in summer, followed by grey-brown seeds. Fennel originated in southern Europe and the Mediterranean but is naturalized in coastal areas and waste ground in most temperate countries. In Mediterranean regions, sweet or Roman (Florence) fennel (*Foeniculum vulgare* var. *dulce*) predominates, while in central Europe and Russia, the bitter or wild fennel (*F. vulgare*) is more common. The essential oil from these strains is quite different.

HISTORY

The use of fennel as a culinary and medicinal herb dates back to at least ancient Egyptian times. Egyptian herbals recommended it as a remedy for eye problems, and in ancient Greece it was taken as an aid to slimming. Throughout history it has also been regarded as an antidote to poisons, especially to snake venom. In medieval times the seeds were eaten during Lent to allay hunger, and put in keyholes to bar the entry of ghosts.

AROMATIC USES

Essential oil from sweet fennel seeds is used in aromatherapy, perfumery, soaps and toiletries.

COOKING

The anise-flavoured leaves are particularly good with fish, olives and snails, and may be added, finely chopped, to salads, sauces and soups. Fennel stems make a good base for barbecuing fish. The seeds have a more intense flavour that complements Italian salami, stuffings, bread, biscuits and suchlike. They also make a very pleasant herb tea. The young flower heads are edible too, and may be added to herb vinegars. Fennel oil is the principal flavouring of liqueurs such as *fenouillette* and *Sambuca*. Florence fennel (*F. vulgare* var. *dulce*) develops a bulbous base and is eaten as a vegetable, though the leaves can also be used for flavouring. The tender, crunchy leaf bases of young side shoots can also be eaten in salads.

HEALING

Fennel relieves indigestion, wind and colic, and improves appetite. It is an ingredient of 'gripe water' for babies, and is sometimes added to laxatives and colon-cleansing preparations to reduce

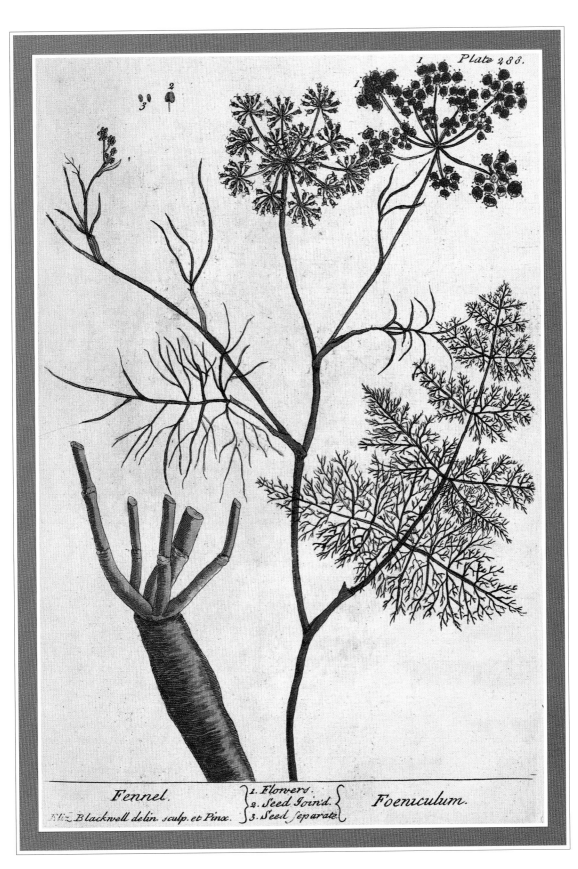

Plate 288.

Fennel.

1. Flowers.
2. Seed joind.
3. Seed separate.

Foeniculum.

Eliz. Blackwell delin. sculp. et Pinx.

griping. In addition, fennel increases lactation and might be a good herb tea for nursing mothers. The other main area of use is in dental hygiene products and massage rubs, as it has anti-inflammatory properties too.

NOTES FOR GARDENERS

Fennel is an asset to any garden. The flowers attract beneficial insects, such as hoverflies and ladybirds, which prey on pests. Its stiffly upright stems, which seldom need staking, and dense, feathery foliage are both a fine feature and a good background for other plants. The bronze version, *F. vulgare* 'Purpureum' is particularly handsome. Fennel is pretty tolerant of soils and conditions, drawing the line only at shade and getting wet feet for any length of time. Florence fennel is much more fussy, requiring rich, moist but light soil if it is to build up large, succulent bulbs. Plants that are dry or starved will try to flower instead, leaving a puny, elongated, fibrous base that is almost inedible. Where happy, fennel self-sows freely. Elsewhere, or as a start, sow seed in autumn or spring (the bronze form comes true from seed). Clumps can be transplanted or divided in early

FOENICULUM VULGARE

spring, taking care to dig deeply so that as much root as possible is retained, otherwise they can suffer a serious setback. Don't plant fennel near dill as the two plants hybridize, producing seedlings that are neither one thing nor the other.

Galium aparine

GOOSEGRASS
CLEAVERS

PORTRAIT

A scrambling annual with stems up to 3m (10ft) long, which climbs by means of the hooked bristles that cover the entire plant. It bears whorls of between six and nine narrow, pointed leaves, and tiny greenish-white flowers in spring and summer, followed by globose green-purple fruits that stick fast to passing fur and fabric. Goosegrass is a common weed that is found throughout Europe.

HISTORY

This is a herb with some very descriptive names, such as sticky Willy, stick-a-back, claggy Meggies, Robin-run-the-hedge, and sweethearts (because of its tendency to cling). The name goosegrass comes from its use as a food for geese and chickens. The perfectly spherical fruits were once used by Bedfordshire lace-makers to cover the heads of pins to protect their fingers.

COOKING

Though unpleasant to handle, young stems are surprisingly edible when cooked as the bristles disintegrate. As a vegetable, goosegrass is supposed to help slimming. The seeds have been roasted as a coffee substitute in times of need.

HEALING

Goosegrass has astringent, diuretic and laxative effects, and is an alterative – a herb that strengthens the immune system and improves the metabolism as a whole. In particular, it has a

GALIUM APARINE

tonic effect on the lymphatic system. Herbalists use it for conditions such as glandular fever (mononucleosis), tonsillitis and recurrent throat infections, cystitis and other kidney or bladder complaints, ME (myalgic encephalomyelitis or chronic fatigue syndrome), benign breast tumours and cysts, eczema and psoriasis. It can be taken internally or used externally but in all cases is best used fresh, cut before flowering and either juiced, frozen or, for external use, packed into jars and covered with oil. As it does not have a strong taste, it can be added to carrots, apples, tomatoes, celery and other ingredients for juice extraction.

NOTES FOR GARDENERS

Though invaluable as a herb, goosegrass is a bit of a menace, sticking to everything, clogging up strimmers and capable of considerable spread in the space of a season. The only place you are likely to want this in the garden is in a native hedgerow or woodland area, or perhaps along fencing somewhere behind the scenes. It likes moist, well-drained, neutral to alkaline soil in shade, and is only too easy to propagate from seed in spring and summer.

Herbal Fruits

Ananas comosus

Carica papaya

FRUITS ARE NATURE'S WAY OF TEMPTING US. When ripe they have enticing shapes and colours, and flavours and textures that are hard to resist – we are being duped by a plant into dispersing its seeds. Fruits also protect the developing seeds, which is why unripe specimens are often green to camouflage them, and hard, bitter or sour to prevent them being eaten before the seeds are ripe.

As well as being good to eat, fruits are rich in vitamins, minerals, sugars and sometimes proteins. In hot countries they are a source of liquid refreshment too. Herbal fruits are those with constituents that have therapeutic properties over and above their food value. Some of these substances are extracted and used separately to concentrate their benefits. Examples are the essential oils in citruses, which are used in aromatherapy, fragrances and flavourings, and fruit acids (AHAs) which are added to revitalizing skin creams. Some fruits are poisonous to human beings even when ripe (see Herbal Poisons, p.146), though often eaten by other creatures without harm. Correct identification is important – deadly nightshade berries might look like blackberries or blueberries but just a few would cause serious poisoning.

Pineapples, of course, are beneficial. The juice is anti-inflammatory and makes a nice-tasting gargle for a sore throat. The inner peel is a folk remedy for removing corns. Bromelain, an enzyme extracted from the pineapple plant (*Ananas comosus*), is an ingredient of food supplements that aid digestion of proteins. It also protects against *E. coli* infections and is an effective anti-inflammatory and blood coagulant, used in preparations to heal burns, ulcers and surgical wounds.

Papaya or pawpaw (*Carica papaya*) contains another enzyme, papain, which is similar to the digestive enzyme pepsin and breaks down protein and wheat gluten. Papain has wide applications, from digestive supplements and products for treating deep or slow-healing wounds, to use as a meat tenderizer and a shrink-proofing for wool and silk. It also interferes with the hormone progesterone, which explains why women in some parts of the world eat papayas to prevent conception.

Many fruits have laxative effects, perhaps to ensure that seed dispersal takes place before the seeds are damaged by the gut. Figs (*Ficus carica*) are mildly laxative and more so when concentrated in remedies such as syrup of figs or compound fig elixir. They also soothe irritated tissues, so extracts are added to remedies for throat infections and coughs.

Prunes are a type of plum (*Prunus domestica*) with a high fibre and sugar content, enabling them to dry without fermenting or turning mouldy. They are traditionally eaten at breakfast for their stimulating effect on the digestive system, and extracts are added to laxative preparations, such as confection of senna, to improve their taste.

Fruits of the wild strawberry (*Fragaria vesca*) are cooling and mildly astringent. Crushed or juiced, they soothe sunburn and reduce skin blemishes. They are much more aromatic than the large hybrid strawberries. Though not sweet tasting, cucumbers (*Cucumis sativus*) are technically fruits. Their cooling effect is proverbial. Whether sliced straight from the fridge or incorporated in skin lotions, cucumber refreshes and calms reddened skin and tired, sore eyes.

Extracts of avocado (*Persea americana*) are soothing in a different kind of way: they are emollient and replenishing for dry skin, scalp and hair. Avocados have the highest protein content of any fruit (about 25 per cent) and contain 18–27 per cent oil.

Blackcurrants (*Ribes nigrum*) were not always as popular as they are today; the sixteenth-century herbalist John Gerard described them as 'of a stinking and somewhat loathing savour'. As everyone knows, the fruits are high in vitamin C, but less well known is their effectiveness in relieving sore throats, which gave them the common name 'quinsy berry' (quinsy being an old-fashioned term for a serious throat inflammation).

FRAGARIA VESCA

The tamarind (*Tamarindus indica*) is an African tree that spread to other parts of the tropics in the seventeenth century. Its name is from the Arabic tamar-Hindi, 'date of India'. Tamarind fruits are like brown bean pods and contain sticky pulp. Some varieties are very tart, and are used as a souring agent in curries, satay dishes, chutneys and sauces; others are sweet and can be eaten like dates. The fruits have laxative effects and are used in Ayurvedic preparations, especially for constipation associated with fever or sun stroke.

Jujubes or Chinese dates come from *Ziziphus jujuba*, a spiny Asian shrub that is known in China as da zao, 'big date'. They have been used as a tonic in Chinese medicine since the later Han dynasty (AD25–220) and are often added to prescriptions to balance other ingredients and improve the flavour. Though grown by the ancient Greeks and Romans, and naturalized in Spain, they are much commoner in the East. The shiny, mahogany-red fruits have a sweet-and-sour taste and complex constituents that soothe irritated or damaged tissues, control coughing, protect the liver, moderate allergic responses, and strengthen the immune system. They help relieve chronic fatigue and stress-related disorders, and prevent the formation of digestive ulcers.

ZIZIPHUS JUJUBA

See also: chillies (*Capsicum annuum*), citruses (*Citrus* species), olive (*Olea europaea*), pomegranate (*Punica granatum*), blackberry (*Rubus fruticosus*), raspberry (*R. idaeus*), elderberry (*Sambucus nigra*), bilberry, blueberry and cranberry (*Vaccinium* species), grape (*Vitis vinifera*).

CITRUS BERGAMIA

Galium odoratum
G. verum

SWEET WOODRUFF
LADY'S BEDSTRAW

PORTRAIT

A creeping, rhizomatous perennial, up to 45cm (18in) tall, with four-angled stems and whorls of between six to nine bright green, narrow, pointed leaves. In spring and summer it produces clusters of pure white, star-shaped, scented flowers. Sweet woodruff occurs mainly in damp, ancient woodlands on chalk, from Europe as far east as Siberia, and in North Africa. The related lady's bedstraw, *G. verum*, prefers dry grassland and bears masses of tiny, bright yellow, honey-scented flowers in summer. Its close relative, lady's bedstraw (*G. verum*), is a taller, more straggly plant, reaching 15–90cm (6–36in). It prefers an open sunny position in dry grassland on neutral to alkaline soil, and occurs in Europe, western Asia, and North America.

GALIUM ODORATUM

HISTORY

Woodruff's earlier name was woodrove, alluding to the way it spreads through woods. When growing, woodruff has no fragrance, but in the drying process coumarins are developed that produce a scent like new-mown hay. In the past, this was much appreciated, and sprigs or bunches of dried woodruff were used to scent clothes, pot-pourris, herb pillows and snuff. Lady's bedstraw dries similarly and was once used to stuff mattresses, especially for women in labour (hence its name).

COOKING

The aroma of dried woodruff disperses readily in acidic liquids, which is why it is traditionally added to wine and fruit cups. The practice began in Alsace, where the aromatic tonic drink is known as *Maitrank* or *Maibowle*. In Germany it is also added to wheat beer. Lady's bedstraw was apparently once used in cheese-making, as indicated by another common name, 'cheese rennet'. It also yields a yellow dye that has been used to colour butter and cheese.

HEALING

Sweet woodruff improves liver function and strengthens capillaries, making it a useful remedy for hepatitis, jaundice and vein problems, such as varicose veins and phlebitis. It also has diuretic, sedative and anti-inflammatory effects. Lady's bedstraw has similar diuretic effects, which could prove useful in treating gout, and kidney and bladder complaints, such as cystitus and stones.

NOTES FOR GARDENERS

Woodruff makes ideal deciduous groundcover under trees and shrubs, or as a background and 'splash guard' for bulbs that flower in late spring. It works well beneath hostas too. Given moist, fertile soil in shade, it romps away in alkaline conditions but tolerates anything – even clay – in the region of pH 6–8. Lady's bedstraw tends to flop in a border and is best in wildflower meadows on well-drained, neutral to alkaline soil where dry, sunny conditions prevail. It looks lovely with grasses that serve the practical purpose of supporting its fragile stems. Propagate both plants by seed sown when ripe, or by division in autumn or early spring.

Gaultheria procumbens　　　　WINTERGREEN

PORTRAIT

A hardy evergreen, creeping shrublet, 7–15cm (3–6in) high, with glossy, pointed, dark green, oval leaves up to 5cm (2in) long and waxy, pink-white, urn-shaped flowers in summer. These are followed by relatively large, spherical red fruits that often remain all winter. The foliage is strongly aromatic when crushed. Wintergreen or checkerberry occurs in dry woods and clearings in eastern North America.

HISTORY

Wintergreen was long used by native North American tribes to ease aches and pains, and to help breathing when hunting or carrying heavy loads. The essential oil contains 98 per cent methyl salicylate, an anti-inflammatory similar in effect to aspirin. For many years wintergreen was the main source of methyl salicylate, though it can also be obtained from the birches *Betula lenta* and *B. nigra*. Production was centred in Monroe County, Pennsylvania, where some 60 stills processed the leaves between April and September. Most methyl salicylate is now synthesized, though some products that help breathing, such as Olbas Oil and Olbas Pastilles, contain the real thing.

AROMATIC USES
Oil of wintergreen is used in woody fragrances, soaps and toothpastes.

COOKING
In the states of Kentucky, Ohio and Pennsylvania, the leaves are used for a tea, known locally as 'mountain tea'. The aromatic fruits can be added to fruit pies, or made into jam, jelly and syrup. As a flavouring wintergreen is used in the food industry, mainly in root beer, cola-type soft drinks, candy and chewing gum.

HEALING
Wintergreen has diuretic and expectorant properties and is a good antiseptic. It reduces inflammation and, applied externally, increases blood flow to the area, thus improving excretion of toxins and promoting healing. Products containing wintergreen oil are used to treat rheumatism, arthritis, sciatica, myalgia, sprains, neuralgia and catarrh. The oil is not suitable for anyone who is sensitive to salicylates (aspirin) and in excess is very toxic, causing liver and kidney damage. It should never be applied directly to the skin.

NOTES FOR GARDENERS
Wintergreen forms attractive ground cover under tall conifers, among heathers or dwarf conifers, or in the rock garden, perhaps above small bulbs. It needs acid soil in partial shade but is otherwise undemanding. Propagate by seed sown on the surface of peat, or by semi-ripe cuttings in summer – or easiest of all, by rooted runners or suckers in spring, or division in autumn.

Gentiana lutea — YELLOW GENTIAN

PORTRAIT
An upright hardy perennial, reaching 1.5m (5ft) tall, with fleshy roots and broadly oval, pleated, blue-green basal leaves up to 30cm (12in) long. Tall, leafy spikes of star-shaped yellow flowers, 2.5cm (1in) across, appear in summer. Yellow gentian is a plant of mountain meadows in the Alps, Appenines, Carpathians and Pyrenees. It has been over-collected for medicinal use in many areas.

HISTORY
The genus *Gentiana* was named after King Gentius of Illyria (*c*.500BC), who is credited with discovering the medicinal uses of *G. lutea*. Gentians of various kinds contain some of the most bitter compounds known, and are used as a scientific standard to measure bitterness. Yellow gentian, which is also known as bitterwort, is so bitter that its taste can still be detected when diluted to 1 in 12,000 parts. Bitter herbs improve digestion by 'kick-starting' the liver and gall bladder, priming

the digestive system to break down and assimilate food – hence the traditional bitter aperitif, such as gin and tonic.

COOKING

Used to flavour Angostura Bitters and various liqueurs, such as gentian brandy and Enzian schnapps, for which purpose the roots are left to ferment so that they become more aromatic and rather less bitter.

HEALING

Though often used in the past to treat malaria and other feverish illnesses – and still used for this purpose in Ayurvedic medicine – yellow gentian is now mainly a digestive herb. It is particularly useful for stimulating the appetite in chronic illness, convalescence, depression and eating disorders such as anorexia. More generally, it is added to remedies for digestive upsets, and tonics to improve liver function in jaundice, hepatitis and liver disease. In Chinese medicine *G. burseri* var. *villarsii*, formerly known as *G. macrophylla* (large-leafed gentian, *qin jiao*) and *G. scabra* (ryntem root, *long dan cao*) are used for liver disorders and imbalances.

NOTES FOR GARDENERS

Yellow gentian is a long-lived plant but can be difficult to establish in lowland or warm areas where summers are too dry and winters are wet rather than frozen. It needs deep, moist, rich, neutral to alkaline soil in sun or partial shade. Propagate by seed sown when ripe in trays in a cold frame, which should germinate the following spring if subjected to periods of freezing. In mild winters, stratify seed before sowing by keeping it in the freezer for several weeks.

Geranium species

WILD GERANIUM
CRANESBILL

PORTRAIT

Geranium maculatum (American cranesbill, wild geranium) is a clump-forming hardy perennial, up to 75cm (30in) tall, with palmate leaves, 10–20cm (4–8in) across, which are divided into five to seven main lobes. Clusters of lilac-pink or light to deep pink, saucer-shaped flowers, about 3cm (1½in) across, are produced from spring to early summer, followed by beaked fruits that forcibly eject the black seed when ripe. American cranesbill grows wild in woodland and grassland in eastern United States. Herb Robert (*G. robertianum*) is a hardy annual or biennial, widely distributed in Europe, western Asia and eastern North America, with reddish stems, highly divided palmate leaves, and small deep pink flowers.

HISTORY

Wild geranium was in widespread use among native American tribes and early settlers who found it an excellent astringent for sore or damaged tissues of all kinds. It was also used to treat venereal diseases. Unlike most astringent herbs, it does not have a particularly unpleasant taste. Herb Robert has a foetid, mousy smell and may have been named after Robin Goodfellow, the house goblin of European folklore.

Geranium maculatum

BEAUTY

Extracts of American cranesbill are used in products to minimize wrinkles and enlarged pores.

HEALING

Though still important as a first-aid herb, cranesbill's astringent effects are now more often utilized to control diarrhoea (especially in children and the elderly), discharges, excess mucus production, profuse sweating, and both internal and external bleeding. Herb Robert has similar uses.

NOTES FOR GARDENERS

American cranesbill is one of the first hardy geraniums to flower, and as such is a valuable addition to the border or woodland garden. It thrives in most soils in sun or part-shade, and enjoys damp, even wet conditions. There is a white-flowered form, *albiflorum*, which is less robust but especially lovely for places lit by early or late sun. Propagate plants by seed sown in autumn or spring, or by division in early spring. Fresh seed germinates readily, and established plants usually self-sow – in which case keep them away from other hardy geraniums as hybrids are no use for medicinal purposes. Herb Robert may need some restraint, as it tends to self-sow prolifically, but is a pretty and long-flowering plant for woodland walks, walls, and other nooks and crannies. The white form 'Celtic White' has bright green foliage that is devoid of any red pigmentation, whereas 'Album' has pale pink to white flowers and the usual red-flushed foliage.

Ginkgo biloba

GINKGO
MAIDENHAIR TREE

PORTRAIT

A hardy deciduous tree, reaching 30m (100ft) tall, with bright green, fan-shaped, lobed leaves, up to 12cm (5in) across, resembling those of maidenhair ferns. The leaves turn butter yellow before falling. Trees are either male or female, and fruiting occurs only when they are grown close together, and in warm summers. The fleshy, yellow, plum-shaped fruits smell unpleasant when ripe, but contain large, edible nuts. Ginkgos are native to remote areas of Zhejiang and Guizhou provinces in central China.

HISTORY

The ginkgo tree is a botanical dinosaur. Plants alive today are unchanged from ancestors which grew 200 million years ago. Though common in cultivation, ginkgos were thought to be extinct in the wild until populations were discovered in the late twentieth century. Ginkgos are sacred in China and Japan, and often found near temples. In China the fruits symbolize longevity and are eaten at weddings with other auspicious plants such as mushrooms and seaweed. The oldest ginkgo in Britain dates back to 1754 and is in the Royal Botanic Gardens, Kew. Western research into ginkgo began in the 1960s, establishing new and different uses for this ancient Chinese herb.

COOKING

Ginkgo nuts are slightly larger than peanuts but milder in flavour. They are served roasted in Japanese bars to accompany drinks, and used fresh, canned or dried and pre-soaked in soups such as bird's nest soup, casseroles and stir-fries. Ginkgo nuts are a traditional garnish for Korean dishes, such as *shinsollo*. The nuts yield an edible oil.

HEALING

In Chinese medicine ginkgo nuts are prescribed for asthma, bronchial congestion, coughs and incontinence. In western medicine the leaves are used. They contain ginkgolides, substances unknown elsewhere in the plant world, which improve the blood supply to the brain, eyes, ears and extremities. This results in improved memory and learning capacity, and may ease a variety of other conditions, such as tinnitus, vertigo, deteriorating sight and hearing, vein disorders and cramps in the legs due to poor circulation. Ginkgolides may also reduce the risk of a stroke and reduce allergic reactions. While the medical profession regards ginkgo mainly as a useful treatment for senile dementia, it has become the best-selling herbal supplement of all in Germany and France, where millions take ginkgo regularly to maintain brain function and circulation.

GINKGO BILOBA

NOTES FOR GARDENERS

Not surprisingly, ginkgos are tough – perfectly hardy, tolerant of pollution and about the only tree able to survive the wind tunnels created by buildings. Given a reasonably sunny spot and any well-drained soil, ginkgos are superb garden and street trees that take hard pruning and are virtually pest- and disease-free – every garden should have one. Though naturally fairly columnar when young, there are very narrow forms for confined spaces and several other interesting cultivars, including a variegated one. Most trees reach about 5m (15ft) after 10 years but young saplings make beautiful container plants. Patient gardeners can propagate gingkos by sowing ripe nuts, or by semi-ripe cuttings in summer.

Glycyrrhiza glabra   LIQUORICE

PORTRAIT

A hardy perennial, 1–1.5m (3–5ft) tall, with stout roots and pinnate leaves, up to 20cm (8in) long, composed of anything between nine and seventeen oval leaflets. Pale lavender-tinged, off-white pea flowers are produced in loose spikes in summer, followed by oblong pods, about 3cm (1½in) long. Liquorice grows wild in scrub and ditches in Mediterranean regions and south-west Asia. Chinese liquorice (*G. uralensis*), which is native to central Asia, China and Japan, is smaller, with dense spikes of violet flowers and curved pods.

HISTORY

Liquorice is mentioned in Assyrian medical texts dating back to the late second millennium BC, and its uses were described by both Theophrastus (*c*.372–*c*.287BC) – who called it Scythian root – and

GLYCYRRHIZA GLABRA

Pliny (AD23–79). Its cultivation spread to northern parts of Europe during the Middle Ages. In 1305 Edward I taxed liquorice imports to pay for repairs to London Bridge. Liquorice was introduced to Pontefract, Yorkshire by Dominican friars, though legend also relates how 'twigs' were washed ashore from a shipwrecked Spanish galleon, which is why liquorice is known locally as 'Spanish'. Pontefract became the centre of a thriving liquorice industry and to this day is famed for its liquorice confectionery, especially 'Pontefract cakes' – discs of liquorice stamped with the town emblem, an owl and gate.

COOKING

The sweet roots are sold as dried 'liquorice sticks' for chewing, or boiled to extract the glossy black substance used in confectionery. Liquorice extracts are added to various sweet and baked products, ice cream, chewing gum and soft drinks. They also serve as a foaming agent in beer and as a flavouring for tobacco, cough mixtures and dark beers, such as stout and porter. Chinese liquorice is also used as a sweetener and flavouring in foods and tobacco.

HEALING

Liquorice roots contain glycyrrhizin, a substance fifty times sweeter than sucrose, that has cortisone-like effects. Extracts detoxify and protect the liver, soothe irritated tissues, control coughing, and are anti-inflammatory and expectorant. Liquorice is used in the treatment of Addison's disease, asthma, bronchial infections, peptic ulcer, and allergic complaints, and given following steroid therapy. In Chinese medicine, liquorice is added to almost all prescriptions to 'tune' other ingredients. In spite of its associations with childhood treats, liquorice as a herb is not for amateur use. It is incompatible with some herbs, reduces the effectiveness of others, and interacts with a number of commonly prescribed drugs. In fact, there can be serious side-effects from excessive intake of liquorice, and it should under no circumstances be taken during pregnancy, or by anyone with high blood pressure, kidney disease, or when taking digoxin-based medication.

NOTES FOR GARDENERS

Liquorice is not very ornamental but, being tall, can be grown as a background plant in the border. It thrives in deep, rich, sandy, slightly alkaline, moisture-retentive soil, and sun. Propagation by seed is slow: the hard seeds require soaking in hot water or scarifying to speed germination. Larger plants are produced more quickly by division of the main crown or by cuttings taken from stolons (runners) 20–50cm (8–20in) long and inserted vertically in the soil in spring. To harvest the roots without destroying the plant, excavate and remove up to a third in autumn.

Hamamelis virginiana   VIRGINIAN WITCH HAZEL

PORTRAIT

A hardy deciduous shrub, reaching 4–5m (12–15ft) tall, with upward-pointing branches and broadly oval, deeply veined, hazel-like leaves that turn yellow in autumn at the same time as the spidery, scented, yellow flowers appear. The flowers are followed by capsules that open explosively when ripe, ejecting the glossy black seeds at some distance from the plant. Virginian witch hazel occurs in moist woodland in eastern United States. The Ozark witch hazel, *H. vernalis,* which is also used medicinally, is similar but native to south-central United States and bears yellow to orange or red-flushed flowers in late winter and early spring.

HISTORY

Witch hazel is a traditional healing herb used by countless generations of native North Americans. The Mohawks made an eyewash by soaking the bark in water, and the Potawatomi infused twigs in water, adding hot stones to create a soothing steam to relieve sore muscles. In the 1840s, Theron T. Pond of Utica and the medicine man of the Oneida Indians of New York worked together to produce and market an extract they named Golden Treasure. This venture founded the witch hazel industry in Connecticut, where most production is still based to this day.

BEAUTY

Distilled witch hazel is one of the main ingredients in skin toning lotions, face masks, after-sun creams and eye creams. Undiluted witch hazel makes a good toning lotion on its own, or can be

Hamamelis virginiana L.

mixed with rose water (or with rose water and glycerin) for dry skins. It also makes a soothing wipe or compress for sore or tired eyes.

HEALING

Witch hazel is soothing, astringent and slightly aromatic. It reduces inflammation, relieves minor discomfort and itching, and controls bleeding and discharges. Bark, stems and leaves are used to produce extracts, bark being the most potent. Extracts can be used internally to treat problems such as diarrhoea, colitis, and heavy periods. Mainly they are used externally – in the form of lotions, creams or ointments – for sprains, burns, chapped skin, injuries caused by crushing or trapping, muscular pain, bruises, haemorrhoids, varicose veins, eye inflammations and sore throats – but not cuts or wounds where the skin is broken. Distilled witch hazel can be obtained from any pharmacy for home remedies and cosmetics. For internal use a tincture would be more effective.

NOTES FOR GARDENERS

Asian, hybrid, and Ozark witch hazels are popular ornamentals, flowering spectacularly on bare branches. The true medicinal witch hazel is not as eye-catching, as the flowers are rather hidden among the yellowing leaves. Grow in moist, rich, neutral to acid soil in sun or partial shade. To propagate, sow seed when ripe in containers in a cold frame and be patient; germination is usually slow and erratic over 18–30 months. You can also try softwood cuttings in summer.

Hedera helix   IVY

PORTRAIT

A hardy, evergreen climber or creeper with tough, sinuous stems clad in self-clinging roots and glossy, dark green leaves and umbels of nectar-rich, yellow-green flowers in autumn, followed by poisonous, round, black berries. In young plants the leaves have three to five lobes, becoming broadly oval as the plant matures. Flowering occurs only on adult plants and in a sunny position. Ivy grows wild in woods and hedges and on walls throughout Europe.

HISTORY

Ivy was dedicated to Bacchus (Dionysius), god of wine, who was hidden under ivy after his mother deserted him. Bound to the brow, it was supposed to prevent intoxication. In ancient Greece, wreaths of ivy symbolized fidelity and were part of the marriage ceremony. The early Christian church banned them as pagan custom.

BEAUTY

Ivy extracts are added to creams and lotions that help reduce cellulite.

HEALING

Ivy is a bitter, anti-bacterial herb with a distinctive aroma and nauseating taste. It contains emetine, an alkaloid that kills the organisms responsible for amoebic dysentery and, as the name suggests, causes vomiting. Other constituents include saponins that are effective against liver flukes, intestinal parasites and fungal infections. Ivy is a poisonous herb that in excess causes irritability, diarrhoea and vomiting, and destroys red blood cells. It is not therefore a herb for internal use by amateurs. External use is less risky, and leaf extracts may help relieve pain and constrict veins. They can be used to relieve skin eruptions, swellings, painful joints, neuralgia, scabies, impetigo, gout and sciatica. Leaves are best use fresh rather than dried.

NOTES FOR GARDENERS

Ivy is very easy to grow, being tolerant of most soil types and conditions, apart from water-logged, and coping equally well with deep shade and full sun. It is a very variable plant and there are more than 300 named cultivars, varying in habit, as well as in shape, size and colour of leaf. 'Erecta' is very distinctive, having small, tightly packed leaves and completely upright stems that form an interestingly shaped bush. Most of the green-leaved varieties are, like the species, very hardy, but variegated kinds are more sensitive and may be damaged by both strong sun and severe cold. The more tender varieties make excellent pot plants for unheated rooms and poorly lit areas where little

HEDERA HELIX

else will thrive. Propagation is child's play from semi-ripe cuttings, or by shoots or sections of stem that are already developing roots.

Hydrastis canadensis — GOLDENSEAL

PORTRAIT

A hardy perennial, 20–38cm (8–15in) high, with dense, wiry, golden yellow roots and two matt-textured leaves that have between five and nine lobes and toothed margins. Small clusters of inconspicuous green-white flowers appear in spring. They are borne on a short stalk that arises from the base of the leaf and are followed by a red, inedible fruit that 'sits' on the leaf, resembling a raspberry. Goldenseal is native to rich, moist woodland in eastern North America, and is increasingly rare in the wild.

HISTORY

Goldenseal grows in the same kinds of places as American ginseng (*Panax quinquefolius*), and traditionally 'seal' was collected by 'seng' diggers, settlers who supplemented their income by collecting medicinal herbs. As long ago as 1909, goldenseal was over-collected and fetching high prices. It is now a protected species in many areas. The name goldenseal refers to scars on the rhizome that are similar in shape to the old-fashioned wax seals used to close envelopes. Goldenseal was used for a range of different purposes by native Americans, both medicinally and as a dye plant. Its first mention – as a remedy for cancer among the Cherokee – was made by B.S. Barton in *Collections for an Essay towards a Materia Medica of the United States* in 1798, and the first detailed discussion of its uses appeared in *The Eclectic Dispensatory of the United States* by John King in 1852.

HEALING

Goldenseal is an alterative herb with many different applications, but today is primarily valued as an anti-infective that acts mainly on the mucous membranes. This makes it an excellent remedy for

eye and ear infections, gum disease, catarrh, sinusitis, inflammatory conditions of the digestive and reproductive tracts (such as peptic ulcers and pelvic inflammatory disease, respectively). It also has a tonic effect on the liver, comparable with *Berberis*, which similarly has bright yellow roots that contain liver-stimulating alkaloids. In addition, goldenseal stimulates the uterus and controls bleeding, and is used for gynaecological problems, including post-partum haemorrhage. It is not suitable for use during pregnancy. In view of the herb's scarcity in the wild, and limited supplies from certified cultivated stocks, many herbalists prefer to use *Berberis* or, for more general purposes, yerba mansa (*Anemopsis californica*), which is similar in effect.

NOTES FOR GARDENERS

Goldenseal is challenging to grow. It needs rich, moist, well-drained, acid soil, and the kind of shade produced by deciduous trees, giving maximum light as goldenseal starts into growth and providing 75 per cent shade by the time its new leaves have developed. Propagate plants by seed sown as soon as it is ripe: it loses viability on drying. Sow seed in sandy compost and subject to

Hypericum perforatum

Publish'd by D.ᵣ Woodville Feb.ʸ 1. 1790.

low temperatures in a cold frame or fridge for three months: the seedlings are fragile and slow growing. An easier method is to divide rhizomes or roots with 'eyes' (buds) when dormant. Small divisions may not sprout at all the first season, so patience is required, even for vegetative propagation.

Hypericum perforatum — ST. JOHN'S WORT

PORTRAIT
A hardy rhizomatous perennial, reaching 30cm–1m (1–3ft) high, with blunt, narrowly oval leaves and bright yellow, five-petalled, gland-dotted flowers, 2cm (¾in) across, in summer. St. John's wort grows wild in woods and hedgerows in Europe and temperate parts of Asia. It is naturalized in many other countries, notably in North America where by 1830 it had become a serious weed, and where eradication programmes are carried out to protect livestock from phototoxicity (sensitivity to sunlight) caused by eating the plant.

HISTORY
St. John's wort has been known throughout history as a vulnerary (wound healer) and was in its heyday on the battlefields of the Crusaders. It was also credited with keeping evil away, for which purpose it was hung above doors on the Eve of St. John's Day (24 June), when witches were thought to be most active. Its mystique was confirmed by the way the juice of the plant turns red on exposure to air – a phenomenon thought to symbolize the blood of St. John the Baptist.

HEALING
Though St. John's wort is best known today as an anti-depressant and sedative – 'nature's Prozac' – it is historically more important as a healing herb. Traditionally the plant was cut as it came into flower, chopped and packed into jars of vegetable oil which in due course it turned red. The oil was used as a dressing for burns, bruises, injuries, sprains, tennis elbow, sciatica and surgical scars. It is particularly effective for deep wounds, injuries caused by crushing, or any other kind of trauma or condition associated with nerve damage. As an anti-depressant, St. John's wort can be taken in the form of a tea, tablets or tincture to relieve anxiety, nervous tension, menopausal syndrome, bedwetting in children, and shingles, as well as mild clinical depression. It is not given to patients suffering from severe depression, or to patients who are already taking certain kinds of medication. High doses of St. John's wort may cause photosensitivity, especially in fair-skinned people.

NOTES FOR GARDENERS
St. John's wort is easy to grow in well-drained to dry soil, including clay, in sun or partial shade. It is an obvious candidate for the woodland garden or hedgerow, and is equally at home in a perennial wildflower meadow. Start it from seed in autumn or spring, or propagate plants by division when dormant or as new growth begins in the spring. Where conditions suit it, St. John's wort usually self-sows and forms handsome colonies.

RICINUS COMMUNIS

COLCHICUM AUTUMNALE

MANDRAGORA OFFICINARUM

Herbal

SOME OF THE DEADLIEST POISONS KNOWN are produced by plants. As far as can be determined, none is required for plant growth; it seems they are chemical weapons to make tissues unpalatable or to poison animals that eat them. Warfare between plants and animals has resulted in a staggering array of toxins, which human beings have learnt to manipulate to provide medicines. Although a normal healthy person might still react adversely to these substances, they can provide the necessary stimulus to correct an imbalance when the body is malfunctioning. It is all a question of degree. In the words of Swiss physician Paracelsus (*c*.1493–1541), 'All substances are poisons. Only the right dose differentiates a medicine from a poison.' Needless to say, herbs as toxic as those described below are almost always subject to legal restrictions regarding medicinal use, though gardeners are often free to grow them as ornamentals.

Jequirity (*Abrus precatorius*) is a tropical climbing pea. Its common name is from a Portuguese version of the South American Tupi-Guarani tribe's word for 'lucky bean' and the red, black-tipped seeds are often strung into necklaces as good luck charms. The seeds contain abrin, one of the most poisonous substances known. Chewing just one raw seed may cause serious symptoms, if not coma and death. In Ayurvedic medicine, seeds, leaves and roots are used medicinally after skilled preparation.

Castor oil (*Ricinus communis*) is a handsome shrub, often grown as an annual for a subtropical effect. The seeds contain ricin, the most toxic of all natural poisons. Again, the pretty seeds, mottled like birds' eggs, are often threaded into necklaces, though it would take only a couple to fatally poison a child. Ricin-free castor oil, extracted from the seeds, has been a popular purgative since the eighteenth century and it still has innumerable other uses in medicine, cosmetics and industrial processes.

The crocus-like flowers of meadow saffron (*Colchicum autumnale*) look harmless enough, but this plant is not called 'vegetable arsenic' without good reason. All parts are toxic, especially the bulb. It contains an alkaloid called colchicine that affects cell division, and plays an important role in plant breeding and genetic engineering. In minute doses, meadow saffron has been used since classical times – and is still prescribed today – to treat gout. Do not use the flowers in salads, or as a substitute for saffron: they might prove fatal. Glory lilies (*Gloriosa superba*) also contain colchicine.

Few herbs rival mandrake (*Mandragora officinarum*) in magic and mystery. The fact that the forked root resembles a human form was taken to indicate aphrodisiac effects and inspired much superstition. In reality, it contains narcotic alkaloids that have pain-killing effects and cause unconsciousness

Poisons

ACONITUM NAPELLUS

– properties that were utilized, not without risk, in the early days of surgery. The cabbage-like plant, with violet-green bells and yellow berries, grows easily in a dry sunny spot, though it resents being disturbed; according to legend, it shrieks if uprooted. American mandrake or May apple (*Podophyllum peltatum*) and Himalayan mandrake (*P. hexandrum*) have a different chemistry. Their toxic principle is a resin that was first used medicinally as a purgative. Today it is important as the basis of etoposide, a potent anti-tumour drug.

Monkshoods (*Aconitum* species) are popular garden ornamentals with purple-blue, helmet-shaped flowers in late summer. They should be handled with care (and always wearing gloves) as all contain the alkaloid aconitine, a deadly poison that can be absorbed through the skin. The European *A. napellus* and Chinese *A. carmichaelii* are both used medicinally for their sedative pain-killing effects. Foxgloves (*Digitalis*) are also favourite but very poisonous garden plants. They contain glycosides such as digitoxin that are the mainstay of cardiac medicines. Similar compounds are found in the roots of Christmas rose or black hellebore (*Helleborus niger*). The American green hellebore (*Veratrum viride*) is a handsome woodland species with pleated foliage and starry green flowers. Ingested, the root causes violent irritation to the mucous membranes, followed by collapse, but in minute doses was once used to lower dangerously high blood pressure.

ATROPA BELLA-DONNA

Deadly nightshade (*Atropa bella-donna*) has a macabre history in criminal poisoning and witchcraft, but is important as a source of alkaloids that have many uses in modern medicine. It is a member of the nightshade family, Solanaceae, which includes species with edible parts such as potatoes, tomatoes, and peppers but the plants themselves invariably contain toxic alkaloids. Another relative is jimsonweed or thornapple (*Datura stramonium*), which is used to relax spasms in asthma. Jimson is a corruption of Jamestown, in Virginia, USA, where in 1676 soldiers cooked and ate *Datura stramonium* leaves as a vegetable and were delirious for days.

Yew (*Taxus baccata*) is among the most poisonous of trees. It contains the alkaloid taxin, which is absorbed very rapidly, giving little chance to save the victim. In the 1960s a compound called paclitaxel (brand name Taxol) was found in Pacific yew (*T. brevifolia*); it proved effective against various cancers, especially of the breast and ovaries. As a result, Pacific yews became endangered through over-collection for the pharmaceutical industry. Then in 1996 it was discovered that the compound actually exists in a fungus that grows on the trees. As a result, anti-cancer drugs can now be produced more cheaply, and with less impact on the environment.

See also: *Hedera helix, Lobelia inflata, Viscum album.*

TAXUS BACCATA

147

Hyssopus officinalis

HYSSOP

Portrait

A hardy, semi-evergreen perennial, 45–60cm (18–24in) tall, with woody-based stems, linear leaves 2.5cm (1in) long, and dense spikes of blue, or occasionally pink or white flowers in summer. Hyssop is native to central and southern Europe, western Asia and northern Africa.

History

The word hyssop is derived from the Hebrew *ezob*, holy herb, a plant used to cleanse holy places, though the hyssop mentioned in the Bible is probably a kind of marjoram. Hippocrates (*c.*460–377BC) recommended hyssop for bronchitis and pleurisy. Later on, Dioscorides (*c.*AD40–90) prescribed a mixture of hyssop, rue, figs and honey for bronchial and respiratory complaints. It was valued as a bee plant in Cistercian monasteries.

HYSSOPUS OFFICINALIS

Cooking

Hyssop leaves have a bitter, sage-mint flavour and can be used sparingly with pulses, soups, sauces and meat dishes. The leaves can be made into tea and flowers added to salads. Essential oil of hyssop is added to liqueurs such as Chartreuse.

Healing

Hyssop contains a camphoraceous volatile oil and substances similar to those in horehound (*Marrubium vulgare*), which is a classic herb for bronchial complaints. Extracts of the flowering plant are useful for relieving bronchial congestion and coughs. They also have a tonic effect on the digestive, urinary and nervous systems, and help to lower fever. Applied externally, hyssop reduces inflammation, and is made into a bath oil for nervous exhaustion, and a medicated oil for rubbing on the chest in bronchitis. Essential oil of hyssop should be treated with caution as it can cause epileptic fits. However, mixed half and half with betony (*Stachys officinalis*) as a tea, it has been used to treat epilepsy.

NOTES FOR GARDENERS

This colourful, late-flowering, shrubby herb is a must for the herb garden. Dwarf or rock hyssop (subsp. *aristatus*) is also useful: it bears later and smaller spikes of blue flowers, reaches only 30cm (12in) and has a very neat habit for the edges of paths, containers or other confined spaces. All enjoy well-drained to dry, neutral to alkaline soil in sun, and are easily propagated by softwood cuttings in summer, or by seed in spring or autumn (varieties may not come true from seed).

Inula helenium   ELECAMPANE

PORTRAIT

A giant hardy perennial, up to 3m (10ft) tall, with thick aromatic rhizomes, stout upright stems and pointed, oval leaves, reaching 80cm (32in) long. Yellow daisy-like flowers, about 7cm (3in)

INULA HELENIUM

across, with narrow, shaggy ray petals, appear in summer. Elecampane occurs on banks and along hedgerows and ditches in southern Europe and western Asia, and is introduced elsewhere in Europe, and in North America and Japan.

HISTORY

Elecampane has a long history of use. In Ancient Rome, Pliny regarded it as an antidote to poisons, as did his near contemporary in Ancient Greece, Dioscorides, who used it to treat snake bite. A century later, Galen recommended it for sciatica. In the Middle Ages it was known as hors-helne (later horse-heal) and given as a tonic for horses, and also as scabwort because it was used to treat scab in sheep. In the late sixteenth and early seventeenth centuries, both Gerard and Culpeper valued it for chest complaints (as do modern herbalists). The roots were often candied as medicinal cough lozenges, or made into a syrup or cordial. Japanese elecampane (*I. britannica* var. *chinensis* syn. *I. japonica*) was first recorded in Chinese medicine almost 2,000 years ago.

AROMATIC USES

The camphor-scented essential oil is used in perfumery.

COOKING

The roots were once popular as a flavouring for puddings and sauces for fish, and have uses in brewing and distilling, notably in vermouth and absinthe.

HEALING

Elecampane is an expectorant and anti-inflammatory herb that relaxes spasms and increases perspiration, thus lowering fever. It acts as an alterative, improving the excretion of toxins, and stimulating the immune and digestive systems. Research shows that it is effective against bacterial and fungal infections, and contains a substance that expels intestinal parasites. Herbalists today use it mainly for respiratory congestion, coughs, chronic bronchitis and bronchial asthma. The flower heads of Japanese elecampane are used in Chinese medicine for similar purposes, and for hiccoughs.

NOTES FOR GARDENERS

This commanding plant needs plenty of space at the back of a border or the edge of woodland, with at least 1m (3ft) between it and its neighbours. Though tolerant of most conditions and positively enjoying clay, it will reach maximum proportions in rich, moist, acid soil, in sun or partial shade. If too dry, the foliage may be spoilt by powdery mildew – a sure indication that a plant needs to drink deep and often. Propagate elecampane by seed or division in autumn or spring. Established plants usually produce a few self-sown seedlings but rarely make a nuisance of themselves. Harvest the roots at the onset of dormancy: if you do not want to sacrifice the plant, excavate just sufficient for your needs. Otherwise, grow several plants closer together and harvest them, roots and all, in autumn of their second year.

Juniperus communis   JUNIPER

PORTRAIT

A very hardy, very variable, evergreen coniferous shrub, ranging from prostrate varieties to specimens 4m (12ft) tall, with red-brown bark and grey-green, linear, sharply pointed leaves, 1–2cm (¼-½in) long. Insignificant male and female flowers are borne on separate plants, followed on female plants by rounded, aromatic 'berries' (really cones) that ripen black with a grey bloom in the third year. Juniper is found on both acid and calcareous soils, usually in coastal or upland regions, throughout the northern hemisphere.

HISTORY

Juniper berries give gin its distinctive flavour. The manufacture of gin began in the sixteenth century when Francisco Sylvius, a physician at the University of Leiden in Holland, distilled crushed juniper berries with pure spirit alcohol for medicinal purposes. It was first known as *genever*, the Dutch word for juniper. This was shortened to gin when it was introduced to Britain in the seventeenth century, during the Thirty Years' War, by English mercenaries who found it gave them

'Dutch courage'. Gin grew in popularity when William of Orange (1650–1702) banned imports of French brandy, reaching its height in the mid-eighteenth century, as illustrated in Hogarth's engraving of Gin Lane and the consequences of 'mother's ruin'. In 1736 the imposition of duty caused riots. The combination of gin and tonic arose in India when colonial officers added it to quinine – the intensely bitter anti-malarial – to make their daily dose more palatable.

AROMATIC USES

Juniper oil, distilled from the berries, is used in spicy fragrances.

COOKING

Juniper berries are added to sauerkraut, pickles, game, pâtés, ham, and pork. They reduce the odour of cabbage and turnips if added while cooking. Westphalian ham is smoked using juniper twigs and berries. In addition to flavouring gin, juniper berries and oil are used in *genevrette*, a French barley beer, and in *ginepro*, a liqueur.

JUNIPERUS COMMUNIS

HEALING

Juniper is a potent diuretic and urinary antiseptic that reduces inflammation and benefits the digestion. Though effective for urinary tract infections, it is irritant and best taken with soothing herbs such as marsh mallow (*Althaea officinalis*) or cornsilk (*Zea mays*). It works well with parsley piert (*Aphanes arvensis*) for cystitis. Juniper is also helpful in clearing toxins and reducing swelling in rheumatism, arthritis and gout, and the diluted essential oil can be applied externally to relieve muscular and joint pain, and neuralgia. It is not a herb that should be used by pregnant women or those with kidney disease.

NOTES FOR GARDENERS

Juniper is a very adaptable plant. It will grow in almost any soil, acid or alkaline, wet or dry, hot or cold, and in exposed conditions. A sunny, open position is best but dappled shade is acceptable. There are numerous ornamental junipers in the horticultural trade but most of these are propagated from male plants and will not bear fruit. Tracking down common junipers that are clearly labelled male or female is difficult, and the only reliable sources are herb nurseries and native plant or tree specialists. You can propagate juniper from seeds removed from berries as soon as ripe, or from ripewood cuttings in early autumn. Seeds may take up to five years to germinate. Harvesting juniper berries is no easy task and may be the origin of the expression 'beating about the bush', as there is no better way than laying a sheet on the ground to catch the berries and hitting the branches with a stick.

Lactuca serriola   PRICKLY LETTUCE

PORTRAIT
A foetid, hardy biennial, 1–1.5m (3–5ft) tall, with prickly stems and jagged, glaucous, prickle-edged leaves up to 30cm (12in) long. Yellow flowers, resembling miniature dandelions, appear in summer. Originally from Europe, prickly lettuce is a cosmopolitan weed, often forming large stands by the side of roads and on waste ground.

HISTORY
The milky sap or latex of wild lettuce species contains mildly narcotic compounds that are known as 'lactucarium' when dried. These compounds are most abundant in flowering plants – young, first-year plants contain very little. Lactucarium is a natural sedative and first entered medical practice in the eighteenth century to adulterate opium, having similar, but non-addictive effects. The other main sources of lactucarium are wild lettuce (*L. virosa*) and American wild lettuce (*L. canadensis*). Centuries of breeding to improve eating qualities have greatly reduced the amounts in garden lettuce (*L. sativa*).

COOKING
Young leaves of first-year plants can be eaten raw in salads or cooked briefly in stir-fries or as a vegetable. Lettuce seed oil is popular in Egypt.

HEALING
Lettuce extract or latex is a common ingredient of herbal sedatives and tranquillizers. It is often combined with other sedative herbs, such as hops (*Humulus lupulus*), passionflower (*Passiflora incarnata*), valerian (*Valeriana officinalis*), and skullcap (*Scutellaria lateriflora*). Herbal sedatives are a natural remedy for insomnia, nervous tension, anxiety and hyperactivity. Lettuce extracts are also expectorant and soothe irritated tissues, making a good remedy for dry coughs that disturb sleep. Although lettuce extracts in sedatives cause drowsiness, in excess they may cause restlessness.

NOTES FOR GARDENERS
Most gardeners would shun such a weed, but in its defence it is smarter in appearance than a sow thistle, and has a certain attraction in the way its leaves line up in the same plane, orientated toward the sun. Another of its names is compass plant, referring to this interesting phenomenon. If you are tempted to grow it, collect some ripe seeds from wayside plants and sow directly where you want them to flower. As you might guess from its roadside haunts, prickly lettuce enjoys dry, preferably well-drained, alkaline soil in sun. Otherwise it is undemanding and will grow like a weed.

Lactuca Scariola

Laurus nobilis

BAY

PORTRAIT
A dense, frost-hardy to hardy, evergreen, large shrub or small tree, 3–15m (10–50ft) tall, with leathery, pointed, oval leaves, and clusters of cream flowers, about 1cm (½in) across, in spring, followed by dark purple berries. Bay trees grow wild in the Mediterranean region.

HISTORY
Bay, bay laurel or sweet bay, call it what you will, has always been associated with success. In ancient Rome, victors and leaders wore a crown of bay leaves, and garlands of bay were a feature of the festival of Saturnalia in December. In ancient Greece, bay leaves were chewed by priestesses at Delphi before reading oracles. Historically, bay is a great protector too. Keeping a bay leaf in your mouth was meant to guard against misfortune, and wearing a garland of bay on

LAURUS NOBILIS

your head during a thunder storm was one way to avoid being struck by lightning. The genus *Laurus* is derived from the Latin *laus*, praise, from which we also get the title Poet Laureate. At one time, newly qualified doctors were crowned with bay, a gesture known as *bacca laureus* – laurel berry – which gave us the term baccalaureate (university degree) and bachelor (as in Bachelor of Arts, B.A.).

AROMATIC USES
The essential oil is sometimes used in perfumery.

COOKING
Bay leaves are a key ingredient of *bouquet garni*, and are much used as a flavouring for soups, stews, stock, stuffings, sauces, meat and fish dishes, and desserts. The bark was once used as a spice, and the berries are still used to make the Italian liqueur *fioravanti*. Bay leaves are used in packing figs and liquorice to deter weevils.

BEAUTY

Bay oil is added to anti-dandruff products.

HEALING

Like many culinary herbs, bay improves digestion, especially of rich or relatively indigestible food. Though seldom used medicinally, a tea made from the leaves would improve appetite and relieve wind and indigestion. The essential oil can be diluted with a carrier oil as a rub for painful muscles and joints, sprains, and bruises. It should not be taken internally.

NOTES FOR GARDENERS

In areas with cold winters, the hardiness of bay largely depends on position. Choose somewhere sheltered from wintry blasts and well away from frost pockets. Otherwise, the main requirements are sun and well-drained soil. Bay trees tolerate drought but need ample moisture when in full growth. If you fancy something different, there are varieties with yellow leaves ('Aureus') and narrow, willow-like leaves ('Angustifolia'), though for clipping and topiary, the classic dark green bay tree is best. Trim trained bays in summer and remove suckers as they appear. Propagate plants by seed sown in autumn or by semi-ripe cuttings in summer. Either way is slow, so look out for pots of bay in markets and garden centres that consist of a clump of seedlings – usually about 20 in a pot, ranging from 15–20cm (6–8in) tall – which represent a considerable saving in time and money. Detaching suckers with a bit of root is also a way of speeding things up.

Lavandula angustifolia LAVENDER

PORTRAIT

A compact hardy shrub, up to 1m (3ft) tall and 1.2m (4ft) wide, with grey-green, linear leaves, about 5cm (2in) long, and spikes of fragrant, pale to deep purple flowers on long, unbranched stalks in summer. Lavender grows wild in Mediterranean regions.

HISTORY

For more than 2,000 years lavender has been the most popular perfume for toilet water, soap and bath essences. The words lavender, *Lavandula* and launder are all from the Latin *lavare*, meaning 'to wash'. Traditionally laundry was rinsed in lavender-scented water, and in Elizabethan times a washerwoman was known as a 'lavender'. The finest perfume oils come from forms of *L. angustifolia*. Crossing *L. angustifolia* with spike lavender (*L. latifolia*) gives lavandin (*L. x intermedia*), whose flowers have a more camphoraceous scent.

COOKING

Though not obviously a culinary herb, lavender has some interesting uses. Individual florets can be crystallised; less fiddly, they can be added to scones, biscuits, homemade conserves, vinegars and mustards. You can make an interesting marinade for pork using lavender, which after all is an ingredient of *herbes de Provence*. Lavender ice cream is a classic, and the flavour goes well with apples too. The leaves can be used as well as the flowers.

BEAUTY

Lavender adds a vital note to *fougère*-type perfumes and colognes, and is the bath herb par excellence, stimulating the skin and relieving stress. Any good-quality lavender product will do the trick, or make your own bath oil by adding essential oil of lavender to almond or avocado oil. Even more simply, pick stems of lavender and place in a muslin bag under the hot tap.

HEALING

Medicinally, lavender has tonic, sedative effects, stimulating the circulation and relaxing spasms. Applied to the skin, it relieves pain and is antiseptic and healing. Lavender oil should be in every first-aid kit for on-the-spot relief of minor burns and insect bites. Diluted with almond oil, it can be applied to larger areas of sunburn, or for massaging tense muscles. Internally or externally, lavender eases nervous tension and stress-related headaches, insomnia, digestive problems and emotional disturbance. You will sleep easy on a lavender pillow; or try relaxing with a cup of lavender tea, or regaining your composure by taking drops of lavender oil in a teaspoon of honey.

LAVANDULA ANGUSTIFOLIA

NOTES FOR GARDENERS

Lavender needs well-drained soil in full sun, but is undemanding. It is best when young, becoming sparse and twiggy with age. Take cuttings in summer from non-flowering shoots to replace ageing specimens. Pruning should be done after flowering to encourage strong new growth for flowering the following summer. Alternatively, give a plants a 'haircut' in spring and a light trim after deadheading. Lavender is easy from seed but plants will vary, so propagate from cuttings of a named variety to plant a uniform hedge. There are numerous kinds to choose from, varying in habit and flower colour. All make delightful garden plants.

VALERIANA OFFICINALIS

Herbal

RELAXATION SHOULD BE PART OF A NORMAL, active, energetic life – not just reserved for the odd day off or for holidays. It can be likened to recharging batteries – many of us remain 'switched on' almost continuously, which can lead to anxiety and stress-related health problems. Ironically, when we reach this state, it can be very difficult to relax. Stress is not harmful in itself – without challenge and episodes of the unexpected, we become bored and fed up. Likewise, the feeling of tension or excitement is a healthy response to stress, but when stresses exceed our ability to respond positively, tension becomes a chronic energy-sapping state. If we reach this state, we need help. Herbs cannot change your life, resolve deep-seated disturbances or cure physical problems caused by lack of exercise, inadequate nutrition and poor posture, but they can help relax mind and body, and uplift the spirit, which may be all that is needed for you to make the necessary changes. Some people find that Flower Remedies – very diluted flower essences that capture the energy of the plant – work well, while others prefer to vaporize relaxant essential oils, such as lavender, jasmine, rose, myrtle or orange, while meditating or listening to music.

Relaxant herbs are available as over-the-counter remedies. These can work well for brief periods of undue stress, but for chronic tension associated with deteriorating health, there is no substitute for seeing a herbalist or aromatherapist.

The word 'tranquillizer' was coined in 1953 to describe the effect of Indian snakeroot or rauwolfia (*Rauvolfia serpentina*). The roots of this small tropical shrub contain alkaloids that calm the nervous system, slow heart rate and lower blood pressure. Though a recent introduction to Western medicine, it was first mentioned in Indian medical texts dating to around 600BC as a remedy for insanity, hysteria and restlessness. It was also taken as a relaxant tea when under stress – notably by Mahatma Gandhi.

A homely bowl of porridge a day can help you relax. Oats (*Avena sativa*) are a simple, cheap, readily available herbal relaxant that can help put you back on your feet after illness or trauma, or at times of low vitality. Herbalists use the whole plant, grains and stems or 'straw', often in the form of a tincture or infusion, but rolled oats or oat flakes (preferably oganic) are the next best thing. The oat plant contains much more than starch, proteins minerals and vitamins: there are alkaloids, flavonoids and sterols as well, which support the nervous system and raise energy levels.

The relaxant effect of beer is not just a consequence of the alcohol. Hops (*Humulus lupulus*), the main flavouring in ales, lagers and stouts, are a potent sedative and soporific. In hop fields on warm, still days, when volatile oil

LEONURUS CARDIACA

Relaxants

from the hops lingers on the air, workers can become drowsy. Female hop catkins contain golden specks of an oleo-resin, rich in aromatic substances that relax spasms, reduce irritability and encourage sleep. There is no need to drink beer to benefit: take them as a tincture, infusion or capsules, or in remedies combined with other sedative herbs. But avoid hops if you are depressed; they could make you feel worse.

Hops are often combined with valerian (*Valeriana officinalis*), a non-addictive tranquillizer that has been extensively researched for its sedative effects. Trials have show that in combination with St. John's wort (see p.145), valerian is even more effective than diazepam in relieving anxiety. The flavour and smell of valerian root – though irresistible to most cats – are not to everyone's taste, but can be fairly well disguised in a number of relaxing bedtime herb teas. Stronger valerian-based remedies positively induce sleep and should not be taken in conjunction with sleeping pills or during the day when you need to stay alert.

Motherwort (*Leonurus cardiaca*) is another effective relaxant, often used in combination in anti-stress remedies. While calming the nerves, it has a tonic effect on the heart, and is often prescribed for anxiety-related palpitations. It also stimulates the uterus and, as the name suggests, has a particular affinity with women's problems.

Vervain (*Verbena officinalis*) was once regarded as a cure-all, and for good reason. Its complex chemistry has both tonic and relaxant effects that alleviate a range of conditions. Mainly though, vervain relieves anxiety and tension, especially when there is an element of exhaustion, and is a good anti-depressant following viral infections and feverish illnesses.

Kava kava (*Piper methysticum*) is a Polynesian herb. Its roots are traditionally fermented to make a ritual drink that induces euphoria and heightened states of awareness. Clinical testing in the 1990s showed that kava kava relieves anxiety as effectively as benzodiazepene, but does not cause dependency, drowsiness or other side effects in recommended doses. Kava kava also relaxes muscles and relieves pain. Jamaican dogwood (*Piscidia erythrina*) is a tropical West Indian tree. Extracts of the root bark were traditionally used to relieve insomnia caused either by nervous tension or painful conditions, such as neuralgia. Today it is often combined with valerian, hops and other relaxant herbs in sedative remedies.

See also: *Chamaemelum nobile* and *Matricaria recutita*, *Hypericum perforatum*, *Lactuca* species, *Lavandula officinalis*, *Melissa officinalis*, *Myrtus communis*, *Papaver* species, *Passiflora incarnata*, *Primula veris*, *P. vulgaris*, *Salvia sclarea*, *Scutellaria* species, *Tilia* species, *Viscum album*.

Verbena officinalis

Avena sativa

Papaver rhoeas

Levisticum officinale

LOVAGE

PORTRAIT

A robust hardy perennial, up to 2m (6ft) tall, with smooth, compound, divided leaves that smell strongly of celery. Tiny yellow-green flowers are produced in umbels in summer, followed by elliptic, winged seeds. Lovage is native to eastern Mediterranean regions.

HISTORY

In medieval times lovage was associated with love potions and aphrodisiacs. More mundanely, however, the word lovage is derived from *luvesche*, which started off as *levisticum* or *ligusticum*, meaning Ligurian (from the Liguria area of Italy, where lovage grows in abundance). Coincidentally, the word *luvesche* sounds very like *loveache*, *'ache'* being an old word for parsley, which gives us another of its common names today, love parsley.

LEVISTICUM OFFICINALE

COOKING

The new shoots are blanched and eaten like celery, and the young stems can be candied like angelica. The seeds make a tasty addition to breads, savoury biscuits and soft cheese, but it is the leaves that are most useful of all. With a flavour reminiscent of celery and yeast extract, they are an excellent addition to soups, casseroles and almost anything savoury. Young leaves also make delicious fritters.

HEALING

Lovage roots have effects similar to those of Chinese angelica (*Angelica polymorpha* var. *sinensis*) but none of the kudos. Nevertheless, when there were shortages of Chinese angelica in China during the 1960s, it was used instead, reinforcing its effectiveness for treating painful menstruation and slow labour. Traditionally in western herbal medicine it is more likely to be used for poor appetite, indigestion, cystitis or kidney stones, or added to prescriptions for problems caused by sluggish, congested systems.

NOTES FOR GARDENERS

Lovage tolerates most soils and conditions but does best in moist, rich, well-drained soil in sun or part-shade. It is easily grown from seed, sown when ripe, though it will probably not germinate until the following spring. Plants can also be divided in early spring. The worst problem with lovage – apart from its size if planted in the wrong place – is likely to be an attack by leaf miners which tunnel into the leaves and make them unsightly and, more importantly, unusable. The only solution that does not involve toxic chemicals is to pick the offending leaves and destroy them at the first sign of infestation.

Liatris spicata

GAYFEATHER
BLAZING STAR. BUTTON SNAKEROOT

PORTRAIT

A hardy, stiffly upright, clump-forming perennial, reaching 1.5m (5ft) tall, with linear leaves up to 40cm (16in) long, and dense spikes of thread-like, purple-pink flowers that, unusually, open from the top downwards over many weeks in summer. *Liatris spicata* grows wild in boggy ground in pine barrens, woodland and grassland in the eastern United States. Other species, such as *L. punctata, L. scariosa,* and *L. pycnostachya,* which are also used medicinally, prefer drier sites.

HISTORY

Gayfeathers are traditional medicinal herbs among many native North American tribes, from whom settlers learnt some of their uses. An early report was made by Edwin James, botanist on the Stephen Long expedition, who in 1819 recorded that the gayfeather or 'pine of the prairies' was used to cure gonorrhoea. The first description of its uses in American medical literature was by Finley Ellingwood in *A Systematic Treatise on Materia Medica and Therapeutics* (1902), which stated that it was an effective diuretic 'but we have more direct and efficient remedies'.

HEALING

Liatris spicata is indeed a good diuretic, used to treat kidney disease. Its astringent properties are also useful in gargles for sore throat, and in New Mexico the roots are burned as incense to inhale for throat infections and headaches.

NOTES FOR GARDENERS

Gayfeathers get ten out of ten as garden plants and cut flowers, having a long flowering period and tidy foliage. *Liatris spicata* makes a good companion for hostas, astilbes, and other moisture-loving perennials, giving a strongly vertical accent and a vivid touch of colour from high summer to autumn. Propagate plants by seed sown when ripe, or by division in spring. In addition to the usual form, there are dwarf and white-flowered varieties that are well worth growing too.

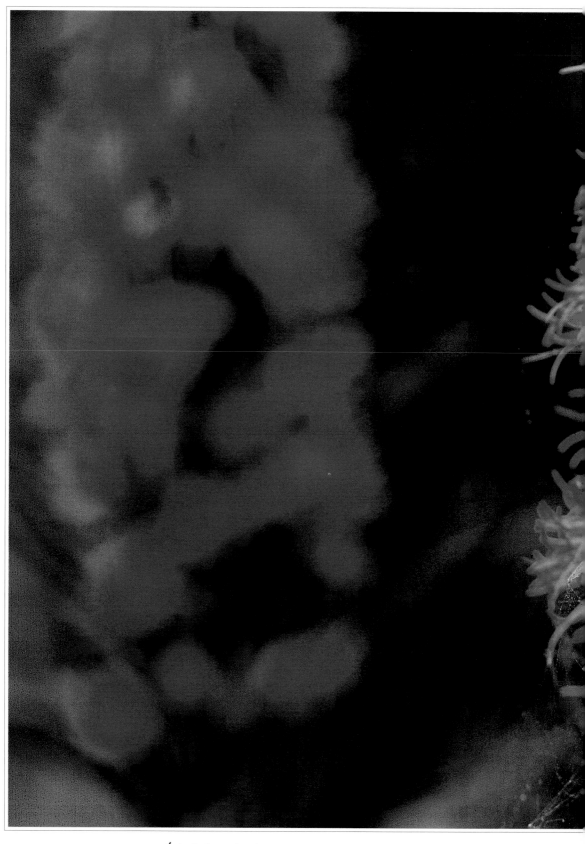

Liatris spicata

Linum usitatissimum

FLAX
LINSEED

PORTRAIT

A slender hardy annual, 80cm–1.2m (2½–4ft) tall, with pointed, linear leaves, about 2.5cm (1in) long, and sky-blue, five-petalled flowers in summer, followed by spherical capsules containing shiny, oval, flattened seeds. Flax has been cultivated for so long that its origins are uncertain. Though classified as a species, *L. usitatissimum* was probably derived from *L. bienne* during its very long history in cultivation.

HISTORY

Flax has been grown since 5000BC for its stems, which yield linen fibre, and for its seeds, which contain 30–40 per cent linseed oil. The sails of ancient Greek ships were made from linen, and the words linen, linseed and line are all derived from the Latin *linum* and Old English *lin*, meaning flax.

LINUM USITATISSIMUM

In ancient Egypt, linseed oil was important for cooking and burning in lamps, but today its main use is as a fast-drying oil in paints. Over the centuries, two strains of flax have been developed: a tall one with few branches and flowers, that yields long fibres; and a shorter one with numerous flowers and seeds capsules for oil production.

COOKING

The seeds can be added to breads. The oil is still used in Egypt for cooking as it is cheaper than olive oil.

HEALING

The crushed seeds act as a non-irritant bulk laxative that is especially useful for sufferers of inflammatory bowel conditions, such as diverticulitis. One tablespoon a day, mixed with muesli or other cereal, and ample liquid, is the recommended quantity. They also have expectorant and sedative effects on the respiratory system and can be used in cough remedies. Flax seed oil consists mainly of linoleic and linolenic acids – essential fatty acids (EFAs) that are important for the functioning of hormonal systems. Alpha-linolenic acid is converted in the body to omega-3 fatty acids. It is needed in large quantities, but is highly unstable and easily lost from foods during processing and storage. The oil is marketed in capsules as a dietary supplement to protect against skin, circulatory and joint problems. Eczema, PMT, arthritis and arteriosclerosis are some of the conditions that may benefit from EFA supplements. Linseed oil is a lower grade product, suitable only for industrial purposes.

NOTES FOR GARDENERS

Several blue-flowered species of *Linum* are grown as garden plants but *L. usitatissimum* is not one of them. Your best chance of finding seeds is not in a seed catalogue, but in a health food store. Sow them in spring in well-drained to dry, sandy soil where you want plants to flower; seedlings do not transplant successfully. If you succeed in producing your own crop of seeds, make sure they are fully ripe before harvesting, as immature seeds contain toxic substances.

LOBELIA INFLATA

Lobelia inflata

INDIAN TOBACCO

PORTRAIT

A spreading, hardy annual, reaching 30–60cm (1–2ft) or more in cultivation, with downy, oval, toothed leaves, 5–8 cm (2–3in) long. Pale blue, often pink-tinged, two-lipped flowers are produced in summer, followed by inflated, two-valved capsules, containing very tiny seeds. Indian tobacco grows wild in open woods and fields, and near water in eastern and central North America.

HISTORY

Indian tobacco was a traditional remedy among native Americans before being adopted by the herbalist Samuel Thomson (1769–1843) as his 'No 1' herb. He regarded it as central to his system of Physiomedicalism, which encouraged therapeutic sweating and vomiting to restore health. In 1809 he was unsuccessfully prosecuted for prescribing an allegedly fatal dose of lobelia.

The trial aroused a great deal of controversy over the practice of medicine, which at that time needed no licence, and gained a great deal of publicity for both Thomson and this toxic but highly efficacious herb.

HEALING

Also known as asthma weed and puke weed, lobelia stimulates the respiratory system, relaxing the bronchial airways, and expelling phlegm. In larger doses it causes nausea and vomiting, and may be fatal in excess. Traditionally it was smoked to relieve asthma, hence one of its common names. Today, it is sometimes added to anti-smoking remedies, having similar effects to nicotine but being non-addictive. Herbalists prescribe it in the form of an infusion for bronchitis, or as a tincture or tablets, often combined with other herbs, to relieve asthma. It can also be applied externally to relax bronchial muscles or muscles elsewhere in the body that are in spasm, as commonly happens in back problems. Lobelia is not a herb for self-medication and is especially dangerous as a fresh plant. Various other lobelias contain similar alkaloids that stimulate respiration and cause vomiting. These include popular ornamentals, such as *L. tupa* (devil's tobacco), a Chilean narcotic used to relieve toothache, and *L. siphilitica* (blue cardinal flower), a remedy for venereal diseases.

NOTES FOR GARDENERS

Though by no means ornamental, Indian tobacco is interesting to grow as a curiosity and, like many rather unassuming plants, repays close examination. It likes rich, moist, slightly acid soil in sun or partial shade, and is easily grown from seed sown in autumn or spring, either where plants are to flower, or in trays of seed compost. The seed is very fine and must be sown on the surface as it needs light to germinate. Avoid overhead watering, which may wash the seed into the compost. Keep it just moist until seedlings are large enough to prick out; they are sensitive to both dry and wet conditions when small. The only other requirement is to remember that it's a poisonous plant and to site it accordingly.

Melaleuca alternifolia — TEA TREE

PORTRAIT

A half hardy shrub or small tree, reaching 3–5m (10–15ft) tall, with papery bark and aromatic, pointed, linear leaves, up to 3.5cm (1½in) long. White fluffy flowers are borne in a dense, bottlebrush spike about 5cm (2in) long, in spring, followed by woody capsules. Tea tree is an Australian paperbark that grows wild in coastal swamps and along streams in New South Wales and Queensland.

HISTORY

Long used by Bundjalong Aborigines as a remedy for coughs, colds and skin infections, the tea tree was so-named because the crew of Captain Cook's *Endeavour* picked its aromatic leaves to make tea when they landed in Australia in 1770. Tea tree oil was used by Australian forces in World War II for dressing wounds, following clinical trials in the 1920s that proved its effectiveness as an antiseptic. It fell into disuse as synthetic drugs were developed, re-emerging towards the end of the twentieth century when natural products began their meteoric rise in popularity. Now it is recognized as one of the most important and widely used natural antiseptics.

BEAUTY

Tea tree extracts are added to hair products, deodorants, soaps, face washes and skin creams where back-up treatment for scalp or skin problems is required, or where anti-bacterial hygiene is a priority.

HEALING

Tea tree oil should be in every medicine cabinet and first aid kit for on-the-spot treatment of minor injuries, infected wounds, bites and stings. Longer term, it is an effective anti-fungal, anti-viral and anti-bacterial for conditions such as athlete's foot, ringworm, cold sores, boils, verrucae, warts, thrush and acne. Unlike most essential oils, tea tree can be applied directly to small, relatively insensitive areas, but for other uses should be diluted with vegetable oil. It makes a good gargle or mouthwash for oral problems and sore throats, and can also be taken internally, in the form of a tea made from the leaves, to strengthen the immune system in chronic infections, such as glandular fever and cystitis. In hospitals it is used against 'superbugs' – MRSA (methycillin-resistant *Staphylococcus aureus*).

MELALEUCA ALTERNIFOLIA

NOTES FOR GARDENERS

Tea tree thrives in moist to wet, neutral to acid soil in sun. In cool areas it can be grown in a pot, with protection from frost in winter, and exposure to sun and wind outdoors in the summer. It makes an elegant foliage plant, but needs long, hot summers to encourage flowering and fruiting. The main advantage of growing your own is access to the leaves for tea. Pinch out containerized plants to maintain a neat, bushy shape, and use the trimmings for tea. Producing your own essential oil is a much more difficult undertaking. Propagation is by seed sown in spring at 13–24°C (55–75°F), or by semi-ripe cuttings in summer.

Melissa officinalis

LEMON BALM
MELISSA

PORTRAIT
A hardy, lemon-scented perennial, reaching about 80cm (32in) tall, with square stems and oval, neatly toothed leaves, 3–7cm (1½–3in) long. Small, pale yellow flowers that age pinkish-white, appear in summer. Lemon balm is widely distributed in southern Europe, western Asia and North Africa.

HISTORY
Lemon balm has been cultivated for more than 2,000 years. Its role in encouraging good spirits and longevity were promoted by Arab physicians in the tenth and eleventh centuries, and Paracelsus, the sixteenth-century Swiss physician and alchemist, called it 'the Elixir of Life'. *Melissa* is the Greek word for a honey bee, referring to lemon balm's long history as a bee plant, both as a source of nectar and as a herb traditionally rubbed on hives to encourage bees to return.

MELISSA OFFICINALIS

COOKING
Fresh leaves give a delicious lemon flavour to salads, soups, sauces, vinegars, stuffings for poultry and game, and fish dishes. They can also be added to wine cups and are an ingredient of liqueurs such as Benedictine and Chartreuse.

HOME
Dried leaves are good in pot-pourris and herb pillows.

HEALING
No herb garden should be without this useful herb. Though primarily a sedative and anti-depressant, relieving stress-related headaches and digestive problems, and calming anxiety, panic attacks, hyperactivity and irritability, it is mild enough to give to over-excited children, and sufficiently pleasant-tasting to drink regularly as tea. On a more serious note, clinical trials have shown that in therapeutic doses, it inhibits thyroid activity and can be used to treat hyperthyroidism, in

MELISSOPHYLLVM
ADVLTERINVM.

Wantzenkraut.

t 4

conjunction with other herbs and conventional drugs. Applied externally in the form of a cream, lemon balm has proved successful against cold sores if used at the first sign of symptoms. The essential oil has insect-repellent effects and is used in aromatherapy to relax and rejuvenate. It can also be used, diluted in a carrier oil, as a massage for painful areas caused by shingles. The fresh plant has its uses too – a crushed leaf brings relief from insect bites and stings.

NOTES FOR GARDENERS

Ordinary lemon balm is not a very exciting plant visually. Much better as a garden plant, and with exactly the same uses, is the variegated form, 'Aurea'. There is also a dwarf form, 'Compacta', which is useful for edging and containers, and a yellow-leaved variety, 'All Gold'. The latter is lovely in spring but needs dappled shade to protect the foliage from sun-scorch. Grow them all in moisture-retentive soil, and cut back after flowering for a new flush of leaves. Propagate by division in autumn or spring; the species can also be propagated by seed sown in spring.

Mentha x piperita PEPPERMINT

PORTRAIT

A robust, invasive hardy perennial, about 90cm (3ft) tall, with dark green, purple-tinged, oval, toothed leaves 4–8cm (1½–3in) long. Whorls of tiny, two-lipped, lilac-pink flowers are borne in summer. Peppermint (*Mentha* x *piperita*) is European in distribution. It is a hybrid between water mint (*M. aquatica*) and spearmint (*M. spicata*), occurring where the two species overlap in the wild. There are two varieties: black peppermint (*M.* x *piperita* var. *piperita*), which includes Mitcham kinds; and white peppermint (var. *officinalis*), which has a more mellow flavour.

HISTORY

Remains of peppermint were found in a bouquet in an ancient Egyptian tomb dating from the Late Period (1035–332BC). According to Pliny, peppermint was popular both for adornment and flavouring in classical times, after which its only mention for many centuries was in a thirteenth-century Icelandic pharmacopoeia. It rose to prominence from the seventeenth century onward, being highly rated as a digestive remedy by Culpeper. Commercial cultivation began in England in around 1750, but today the United States is now the largest producer. Peppermint oil is of major importance in the pharmaceutical and food industries.

COOKING

Cool, refreshing peppermint is a favourite flavour for chewing gum, confectionery, ice cream and liqueurs, such as *crème de menthe*. It is used only in sweet foods as the anaesthetic effect overwhelms subtle flavours. Peppermint tea is one of the most popular of all herb teas, while after-dinner mints combine enjoyment of the flavour with the practical benefit of aiding digestion.

HEALING

Peppermint improves digestion and calms the digestive system, reducing wind, griping pains, colic and nausea. It is a key ingredient of many remedies for indigestion and irritable bowel syndrome.

The aroma of peppermint has decongestant effects and extracts are widely used in inhalants and chest rubs for colds and catarrh. The main constituent of the essential oil is menthol, a potent antiseptic that has a cooling effect on skin and mucous membranes, due to its mild anaesthetic effect. Both peppermint oil and menthol are used in oral hygiene products. The cooling, numbing effect is also utilized in lotions for itchy skin and scalp. Corn mint (*M. arvensis*), known as *bo he* in Chinese medicine, is used for similar purposes. Japanese corn mint (*M. arvensis* var. *piperascens*) has a strong peppermint aroma and is a commercial source of oil, which is used as a substitute for, or adulterant of true peppermint oil. Horsemint (*M. longifolia*) is another source of peppermint oil. *Mentha* x *piperita* f. *citrata*, variously known as eau-de-Cologne mint, lemon mint or bergamot mint, has a lavender-like aroma and its uses are more akin to lavender than peppermint; it is a source of lavender-like oil for perfumery and household fragrances. The typical aroma of lavender is associated with certain components (linalool and linalyl acetate) and some cultivars of f. *citrata*, such as 'Lavender' and 'Lanvanduliodora', have a particularly high content.

MENTHA X PIPERITA

NOTES FOR GARDENERS

The advantage of growing peppermint is having fresh leaves for tea, which are infinitely better than the dried herb or tea bags. The disadvantage is that, like all mints, it is a space invader. Either grow it in a large container of rich soil and replant each spring in fresh compost, discarding surplus runners in the process, or plant in moist soil where it has stiff competition from large-leaved perennials, such as hostas or Chinese rhubarb (*Rheum palmatum*), that form a dense canopy to curb its exuberance.

Mentha pulegium   PENNYROYAL

PORTRAIT

A hardy perennial with upright to sprawling stems, clad in bright green, highly aromatic, rounded leaves up to 3cm (1½in) long. Whorls of tiny, two-lipped, lilac flowers appear in summer. Pennyroyal is widely distributed from Europe to western Asia but has rather specialized ecological requirements, growing in damp places that dry out in summer. It is becoming scarce in many areas. Hart's pennyroyal (*M. cervina*) has narrow leaves and a more restricted distribution in south-western Europe. American pennyroyal (*Hedeoma pulegioides*) is an annual, growing in eastern fields and woodlands. Its western equivalent is mountain pennyroyal (*Monardella odoratissima*). There is an Australian pennyroyal, too – *M. satureioides* – which grows in all states but Tasmania and has white flowers in spring.

HISTORY

From classical times until at least the Middle Ages, European pennyroyal was well-known – if not notorious – as an anti-fertility herb and one that in sufficient quantity would cause abortion. It had other uses though. Pliny, writing in the first century AD, noted that it deterred fleas, which gave it the name *pulegium*, from the Latin *pulex*, a flea. By the seventeenth century, it was put to quite a different use – to sweeten drinking water that was stored for weeks on long sea voyages. American pennyroyal was used by native American tribes to ease headaches and stomach cramps.

MENTHA PULEGIUM

COOKING

Though little used in cooking, pennyroyal is popular in some parts of Europe. It is added to black pudding in northern England, to sausages in Spain, and to artichokes in Italy to make *carciofi alla Romana*.

HEALING

All the pennyroyals mentioned contain pulegone, a major component of the volatile oil that gives them their characteristic aroma. Pulegone stimulates the uterus and in excess is exceedingly toxic, causing liver, kidney and lung damage. As little as half a teaspoon of pennyroyal oil induces convulsions and coma. Infusions of the herb are, in sensible amounts, good for indigestion, colic, feverish colds, catarrh and asthma, and difficult, painful menstruation. The same infusion, cooled, can also be used topically for itching and inflamed skin conditions, such as eczema. The oil is best left well alone, and pregnant women should not take the tea either. Pennyroyal oil is an ingredient in insect repellents.

NOTES FOR GARDENERS

European pennyroyal enjoys rich, moist, well-drained, sandy soil in sun or part-shade. It can be planted as a lawn or in shady areas of gravel, paving and borders. There are one or two different forms in cultivation – a creeping one, sometimes called 'Cunningham Mint', and one with a more upright habit. European pennyroyal may be cut back by severe winter weather, but usually re-emerges in spring. Propagate it by seed or by rooted runners in spring. American pennyroyal must be grown from seed every year. Mountain pennyroyal is both prettier and perennial, and easily grown from seed or divisions.

Mentha spicata   SPEARMINT

PORTRAIT

A fast-spreading, sweet-smelling, hardy perennial, up to 1m (3ft) tall, with bright green, wrinkled, regularly toothed, oval leaves 5–9cm (2–3½in) long. Tiny lilac, pink or white flowers

MENTHA SPICATA

MENTHA SUAVEOLENS

are produced in tapering spikes in summer. Spearmint (*Mentha spicata*) is native to western and central Europe but widely naturalized elsewhere. Red mint (*M. x smithiana*), and American applemint (*M. x gentilis*) – also confusingly called red mint – have a spearmint aroma too, as does Bowles 'mint (*M. x villosa* var. *alopecuroides*). Applemint (*M. suaveolens*), pineapple mint (*M. suaveolens* 'Variegata') and ginger mint (*M. x gracilis* 'Variegata') have a fruity spearmint aroma, while doublemint (*M. x gracilis* 'Madalene Hill') combines both spearmint and peppermint flavours.

HISTORY

Spearmint was used to scent bath water and for oral hygiene by the ancient Greeks. This favourite aromatic was probably introduced to northern Europe by the Romans. It was grown as a garden plant in Chaucer's time (1300s) and the leaves were rubbed on the teeth and gums as a cleanser. Culinary uses have a long history too. In *A New Herball* (written between 1551 and 1568), William Turner notes that it 'hath a singulare pleasantnes in sauces'.

COOKING

Spearmint, and other mints with a spearmint-like aroma, have high concentrations of carvone – the predominant oil in caraway – and less menthol and pulegone than peppermint and pennyroyal respectively. The flavour of spearmint is therefore much easier to marry with other flavours in foods and drinks. The fresh leaves are used for flavouring and garnishing iced drinks, such as Pimm's and – with Bourbon whisky – mint julep. Fresh or dried, spearmint is an excellent ingredient for herb teas: not so much on its own, but with other herbs. Finely chopped fresh spearmint is an ingredient of *tzatziki* in eastern Europe, *tabbouleh* in the Middle East and mint sauce to serve with lamb in Great Britain. Sprigs of mint, added to the cooking water, give a subtle spearmint flavour to potatoes and peas. Whole sprigs of *M. x gentilis* are served with Vietnamese dishes.

HEALING

Spearmint is a good remedy for indigestion, wind and hiccoughs. It is less pungent and more relaxing than peppermint, and favoured by herbalists for cooling and soothing feverish children. Spearmint oil is an important ingredient of oral hygiene products and chewing gum.

NOTES FOR GARDENERS

As spearmint is the top culinary mint, flavour is all-important. Among the finest varieties are 'Moroccan', Tashkent', and 'Kentucky Colonel', which are often grown commercially as fresh-cut or potted herbs for supermarkets. Vietnamese red mint is good too. Bowles' mint has many admirers for flavour, but woolly leaves are not perhaps the best for salads or garnishing. The cultivation of spearmint and spearmint-like mints carries exactly the same warnings and recommendations as for peppermint. Spearmint is just as invasive and no great beauty, but pineapple mint and ginger mint can be controlled among other vigorous plants in the border, and make attractive foliage plants.

Menyanthes trifoliata BOGBEAN

PORTRAIT

A hardy aquatic perennial with thick, creeping rhizomes up to 1.2m (4ft) long, and long-stalked leaves, divided into three oval leaflets 6–10cm (2½–4in) long. White, star-shaped, fringed flowers, 2.5cm (1in) across, and pink in bud, are borne on tall spikes in summer. The plant's total height is 20–30cm (8–12in). Bogbean grows wild in shallow water and wetter areas of bogs in Europe, northern Asia, north-western India, and North America. It is a protected species in some areas.

HISTORY

Bogbean has long been used in folk medicine for arthritis and rheumatism, and to treat scabies, malaria and intermittent fevers. The starchy rhizomes are a famine food in northern regions.

COOKING
The bitter leaves can be made into tea and used as a substitute for hops in brewing beer.

HEALING
Bogbean is related to gentians and is similarly very bitter. It has diuretic and laxative effects and is mainly used to stimulate the digestion and improve appetite in anorexia, chronic infections, rheumatoid arthritis and ME (myalgic encephalomyelitis or chronic fatigue syndrome). In excess it causes vomiting and irritates the digestive tract. It should not be taken by anyone with irritable bowel syndrome or an inflammatory condition of the digestive tract, such as colitis.

NOTES FOR GARDENERS
Bogbean is a beautiful plant for the water garden, with distinctive foliage and detailed flowers. It can be planted directly in the mud at the edge of a pond, or in aquatic planting baskets in water no deeper than 23cm (9in). It needs full sun to encourage flowering, so plant in an open site. Propagation is by seed sown when ripe into pots of compost stood in water, or by division of young rhizomes in summer.

MENYANTHES TRIFOLIATA

Monarda species

BERGAMOT
HORSEMINT, BEE BALM

PORTRAIT
Monarda didyma is a clump-forming, sweetly fragrant, hardy perennial, reaching 1–1.2m (3–4ft), with square stems and oval, toothed leaves 8–10cm (3–4in) long. Bright red, claw-shaped flowers, with red-green bracts, are borne in two whorls in summer. Bergamot grows wild in moist woods and along streams in eastern North America. Lemon bergamot (*M. citriodora*) is a short-lived prairie plant with pale lavender flowers. Wild bergamot or beebalm (*M. fistulosa*) is about the same size as *M. didyma* but has pink, lavender or white flowers and grows in drier places. The variety *menthaefolia* (*oregano de la sierra*), which grows in south-western North America, has an oregano-like aroma. Horsemint (*M. punctata*), a species of the eastern coastal plains, has a thyme-like aroma, yellow flowers and pale pink bracts.

HISTORY

Native American tribes have long used *M. didyma* and *M. fistulosa* for tea and flavouring. They used them medicinally too, mainly for digestive problems, headaches, colds and flu. The leaves of *M. citriodora* were used by the Hopis for flavouring hare and other game. Oswego tea, a common name for *M. didyma*, is so-called because the Oswego Indians made tea from it. It was adopted by settlers as the daily brew following the Boston Tea Party in 1773, when colonists boarded ships in Boston harbour and threw crates of tea into the water in protest at the tax imposed on the commodity by the British.

COOKING

Confusingly, bergamot is not the flavouring in Earl Grey tea: it comes from oil of bergamot, extracted from the bergamot orange (*Citrus bergamia*, see p.83). Bergamot was presumably named after the bergamot orange (which in turn was named after Bergamo in Italy), because of its similar aroma. All monardas can be used for making tea, though *M. didyma* probably has the edge for flavour. The leaves, which really are like Earl Grey tea in aroma, give a subtle flavour to fruit salads

MONARDA DIDYMA

and iced drinks, and the red florets are edible too. The aroma of *M. fistulosa* is more robust and better suited to meat and vegetable dishes. *Monarda fistulosa* var. *menthaefolia* is the traditional flavouring for wild game in areas where it grows wild.

HEALING

Monarda punctata is the most important medicinally, being used to treat indigestion, colic, nausea and vomiting, diarrhoea, fevers, colds and flu. It also stimulates the uterus and may bring on menstruation. Externally, oil of horsemint is used in liniments for neuralgia and rheumatism. The oil is about 60 per cent thymol and is a commercial source of this compound, which is widely used in mouthwashes and antiseptics. *Monarda fistulosa* is also used for gastric and bronchial complaints, and to lower fevers.

NOTES FOR GARDENERS

Most of the bergamots in cultivation are selected from *M. didyma* or are crosses between *M. didyma* and *M. fistulosa*. Any bergamot with *M. didyma* in its blood needs moist, rich, slightly acid soil in partial

NOTES FOR GARDENERS

This is a rewarding herb to grow, with elegant foliage and a unique aroma. Botanically, it is related to citruses — so closely that it can serve as a rootstock for grafting lemon trees. Curry leaf bushes need moist, humus-rich, well-drained soil in sun or part-shade, and an average minimum temperature of 15–18°C (59–64°F). Propagate them by seed sown in warmth in spring, or by semi-ripe cuttings in summer. Plants grown under cover in cool areas are rather prone to scale insects, aphids and red spider mites.

Myristica fragrans   NUTMEG

PORTRAIT

A tender, evergreen tree, 10–20m (30–65ft) tall, with glossy, pointed, oblong leaves about 12cm (5in) long. Pale yellow flowers, 1cm (½in) across, are produced in clusters, followed by fleshy, dull yellow fruits, 6–9cm (2½–3½in) long, which split in half when ripe, revealing a lustrous, dark brown nut enclosed in a lacy, scarlet aril (mace) that turns yellow when dry. Inside the nut is a seed — the nutmeg. The nutmeg tree is native to the Molucca Islands, formerly known as the Spice Islands, and is extensively cultivated in Indonesia, Sri Lanka and Grenada (West Indies).

HISTORY

Nutmegs have been traded for thousands of years. They were first mentioned in a Chinese herbal in about AD600 and may have reached Europe via Arab traders in the same era. Large-scale cultivation of nutmegs followed Portuguese settlement of the Moluccas in the early sixteenth century, and throughout the following century when the islands were taken by the Dutch. Initially, nutmeg was promoted as a tonic. The first report of its hallucinogenic effects was in 1576 when a pregnant English woman consumed about a dozen nuts and became 'deliriously inebriated'. The essential oil extracted from the leaves has herbicidal properties and is used today medicinally and in aromatherapy. A fatty oil, known as 'nutmeg butter', is steam-extracted from crushed kernels and used in the pharmaceutical industry and in the manufacture of perfumes, soaps and candles.

COOKING

Nutmeg and mace are very similar in aroma and uses, and go equally well with sweet and savoury dishes. Mace is slightly less pungent and, being paler in colour, is often preferred for foods with subtle flavours and colours, such as sauces, clear soups, soufflés and fish dishes. It is difficult to grind finely at home, so ground mace is very convenient, while nutmegs can be grated in a jiffy. Nutmeg has a particular affinity with custards, milk puddings, cakes, spinach and mushrooms. It is traditionally used to flavour pasta sauces and fillings, eggnog and béchamel sauce. Both nutmeg and mace are ingredients of the Middle Eastern spice mixture, *ras el hanout*. The flesh of the fruits is edible: it has a delicate nutmeg flavour and may be pickled, candied or made into rose-coloured jams, jellies and syrups.

HEALING

In both western, Chinese, and Ayurvedic medicine, nutmeg is used mainly as a digestive remedy, relieving wind, bloating, diarrhoea and vomiting. The fixed oil from the seeds, which is quite

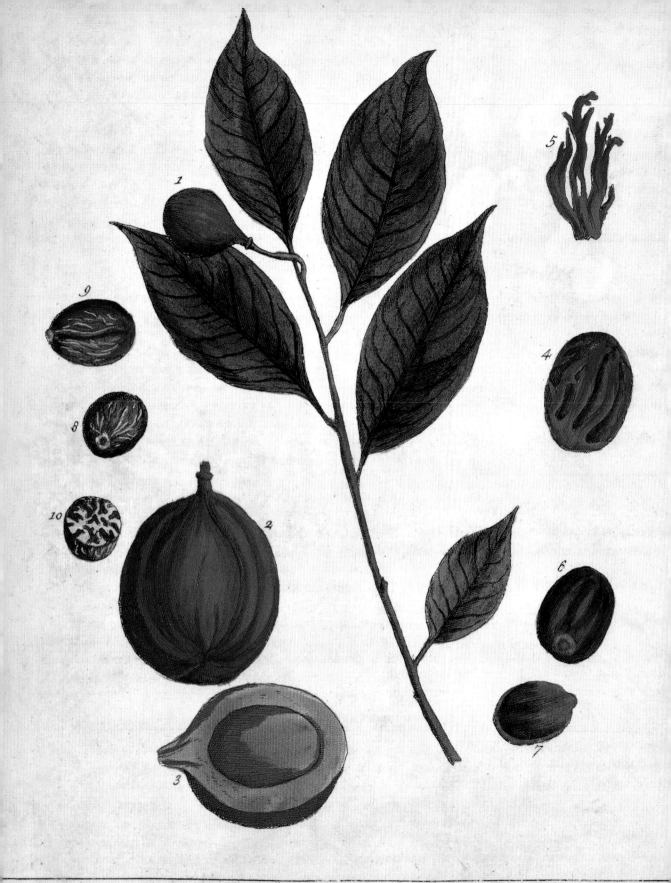

The Nutmeg.

1. unripe Fruit.
2. ripe Fruit.
3. Fruit open.
4. Shell with its Mace
5. Mace.

6. Shell.
7. Shell open.
8. Female Nutmeg.
9. Male Nutmeg.
10. Nutmeg open.

Nux Moschata.

Eliz. Blackwell delin. sculp et Pinx.

different in composition from the essential oil, is used externally for toothache, rheumatic and abdominal pains (including labour pains), eczema and ringworm. In India, nutmeg is regarded as an aphrodisiac, and according to the *Medical Book of Malay Medicine*, it can be used to treat madness. Excess is extremely toxic, causing hallucinations, convulsions, stupor and possibly death.

NOTES FOR GARDENERS

Unless you live in the tropics, there is little prospect of growing nutmeg trees They need humus-rich, well-drained, sandy soil, and tropical quotas of light, heat and humidity. Nutmegs must be sown within 24 hours of ripening as they have an extremely short period of viability. There is no hope of success with a nutmeg from a supermarket. Seeds take four to five weeks to germinate, and young plants don't flower for up to eight years. Only then can you tell which are males and females. Commercially, propagation is often done by air-layering. The alternative to growing nutmegs is to visit Grenada in the Caribbean, see them growing in the mountains, and enjoy the sight and smell of the nutmeg factory and its products.

MYRTUS COMMUNIS

Myrtus communis　　　　　　　　　　　　MYRTLE

PORTRAIT

An upright, evergreen, frost-hardy shrub, 3–5m (10–15ft) tall, with lustrous, dark green, oval leaves up to 5cm (2in) long. White, five-petalled flowers, 3cm (1½in) across, with golden stamens, appear in summer, followed by purple-black berries 1cm (½in) long. Myrtle is native to Mediterranean regions.

HISTORY

In classical times, myrtle was sacred to Aphrodite, goddess of love (Venus in Roman mythology), and is carried in wedding bouquets to this day. Traditionally, a sprig from the bride's bouquet was struck as a cutting to provide myrtle for her future daughter's wedding. Myrtle flowers were the main ingredient of *eau d'anges*, a skin-care lotion supposedly used by Venus herself.

Cooking

The leaves are a popular flavouring for pork, lamb, poultry and small birds in the Mediterranean, especially on Corsica, Sardinia and Crete. In Corsica, myrtle liqueur (*myrthe*) is made, while in the Middle East the berries (known as *mursins*) are used as a spice. Aromatic myrtle wood makes good charcoal and is used for smoking foods.

Beauty

Essential oil of myrtle is used in soaps and skin-care products.

Healing

Myrtle leaves are sometimes used as a substitute for buchu (*Agathosma crenulata*) in treating urinary infections. In Unani medicine – an ancient system practised in parts of India – they are used for chronic womb infections. More generally, they are helpful for bronchial infections and are mild enough for children. Externally, their antiseptic, astringent properties help in healing minor injuries, gum infections and haemorrhoids.

Notes for Gardeners

Myrtle is an ideal evergreen shrub, with small, neat, delightfully aromatic foliage and beautiful flowers. It is not terribly hardy, especially when young, so in areas with cold winters it may need the protection of a wall. Alternatively, grow it in a container that can be moved under cover in winter. The variegated form makes a very pretty pot plant. There is a double-flowered form too, with longer-lasting flowers. Myrtles are quite easy to propagate from semi-ripe cuttings in summer, with bottom heat. The species can also be propagated by seed sown when ripe. All myrtles need well-drained, neutral to alkaline soil in full sun, though in Mediterranean regions they often grow in the shade of olive trees.

Nepeta cataria

CATNIP
Catmint

Portrait

A strongly scented, hardy perennial, 30–90cm (1–3ft) tall, with upright, branched stems and grey-green, oval, toothed leaves 3–7cm (1½–3in) long. Very small white, purple-spotted, two-lipped flowers are borne in whorled spikes in summer. Catnip grows wild on dry banks, waste ground and roadsides in many parts of Europe and Asia.

History

The uses of catnip in classical times were described by Pliny, and mentioned in herbals throughout the ages. In medieval times it was grown as a culinary herb for rubbing on meat before cooking. Catnip is well-known for its effect on cats, though some cats lack the gene that causes the response. The constituent responsible is variously given as nepetalactone, or as actinidine, an iridoid glycoside that primarily occurs in *Actinidia polygama*, a Chinese shrub that is traditionally used in Asia to calm captive 'big cats'. Interestingly, both catnip and *A. polygama* are known to produce a feeling of well-being and mild hallucinations in humans too. A similar glycoside is found in the roots of valerian (*Valeriana officinalis*, see p.158).

COOKING

Mint-flavoured leaves and shoot tips can be added to salads, used for tea, or as a flavouring for sauces, soups, and meat dishes. Lemon catnip ('Citriodora') has a different aroma but similar uses.

HOME

Dried catnip is used to stuff toys for cats.

HEALING

Catnip is a cooling, sedative herb that relaxes spasms and lowers fevers. It is a good remedy for feverish colds and flu, and the antispasmodic effect soothes the digestive system too.

NOTES FOR GARDENERS

There is a saying that 'if you sow it cats won't know it, if you set it cats will get it'. Which ever way you choose, catnip is extremely easy to grow, either from seed or division in autumn or spring. It

NEPETA CATARIA

usually self-sows enthusiastically too. Catnip is not fussy about conditions, though is most aromatic when grown in poor, dry, neutral to acid soil in sun. There are certainly more ornamental catmints than *N. cataria*, but if you want plants for any of the purposes given above, then this is the one to grow. However pretty, none of the others has quite the same effects, either on humans or felines.

Ocimum basilicum   SWEET BASIL

PORTRAIT

An erect, branched, very variable annual or short-lived tender perennial, 20–60cm (8–24in) tall, with bright green, oval leaves about 5cm (2in) long, which occasionally are purple-tinged. Whorls of tubular, two-lipped, white to pinkish-purple flowers are produced in lax spikes in summer. Sweet basil is native to tropical Asia, where it grows along roadsides and in fields. Other basils common in cultivation include: bush or Greek basil (*O. minimum*), a dwarf, small-leafed species which is hardier than sweet basil; holy basil (*O. tenuiflorum*), a softly hairy plant, highly revered in the East, with a clove-like aroma; tree or East Indian basil (*O. gratissimum*), a shrubby species with medicinal and insect-repellent properties; and camphor basil (*O. kilimandscharicum*), a pungently scented African shrub with downy leaves, used to lower fever and repel mosquitoes.

HISTORY

The words 'basil' and *basilicum* are derived from the Greek *basilikon,* meaning 'royal'. Basil was known to the ancient Egyptians and popular in classical times, but in the course of history acquired a dubious reputation through association with the word *basiliscus* or basilisk – a mythical reptile whose gaze or breath caused instant death. In time, this confusion transmogrified into stories that basil 'ingendreth worms' or caused scorpions to breed in the brain. Both sweet basil and bush basil were grown in Britain prior to 1550, but were probably little used until the seventeenth century when superstitions such as these were disregarded. Certainly basil was used medicinally by the time Parkinson's herbals were published in 1629 and 1640, and in the early eighteenth century some 50 varieties were recorded. Today, essential oils, differing in aroma depending on the variety of basil, are used in perfumery and to make insect repellents.

COOKING

Basil is the tomato herb *par excellence*, offsetting the acidity of tomato-based salads, soups and sauces. It also goes well with peppers, aubergines, courgettes (zucchini) and beans of all kinds. *Pesto* sauce is made by pounding basil leaves with garlic, pine nuts, Parmesan cheese and olive oil, as a dressing for pasta. The variety 'Horapha' (also known as 'Anise' and 'Glycyrrhiza') is used in Thai and Vietnamese cuisine, often eaten raw with spring rolls. The lemon-scented 'Meng Luk' or *manglak* (*O. x citriodorum* – a hybrid between *O. basilicum* and *O. americanum*) is also much used in south-east Asia.

HEALING

Basil is a warming, relaxing herb that lowers, fever, eases spasms and improves digestion. It makes a good home remedy for nervous indigestion, wind, nausea, tension headaches and sleeplessness when over-excited or anxious. Anti-bacterial properties may help prevent or treat gastro-enteritis. Applied externally, a crushed basil leaf relieves insect bites and stings. Bush basil has similar effects but is milder. Basil oil may help restore a sense of smell lost through catarrh.

NOTES FOR GARDENERS

Being tropical, basil needs ample warmth and light above all, and well-drained, reasonably fertile but not over-rich soil. It dislikes dry conditions, especially when young. Cool, humid, overcast weather is anathema, causing plants to succumb to botrytis (grey mould). For success, raise seedlings at a minimum temperature of 10°C (50°F). Basil does well in pots: bush basil makes neat, compact plants, and purple- and lettuce-leafed varieties are ornamental in mixed plantings.

diet. Similar oil is also obtained from *O. glazioviana*, *O. lamarckiana*, and *O. parviflora*. When EFAs are lacking, a host of different symptoms and conditions may arise, which is why evening primrose oil can remedy many different complaints, from eczema, rheumatoid arthritis, ME (myalgic encephalomyelitis or chronic fatigue syndrome), and hyperactivity in children to premenstrual and menopausal syndromes, alcohol-related liver damage and deteriorating nerve function in diabetes. Externally, evening primrose oil is of considerable benefit to dry skin. It is often combined with vitamin E to prevent oxidation.

NOTES FOR GARDENERS
This willowherb relative is a colourful, long-flowering addition to borders and meadows, where it will self-sow for evermore. It opens its luminous flowers as many other plants close theirs for the night. Tolerant of dry, hostile conditions, such as sand dunes and railway embankments, it will grow almost anywhere but in heavy wet soil. Sow seeds in summer or autumn for flowering in a year's time. Do this for two years and you should never be without evening primroses.

OLEA EUROPAEA

Olea europaea   OLIVE

PORTRAIT
A rugged, evergreen, tree, 7–10m (22–30ft) tall, with grey, fissured bark and grey-green, silver-backed, leathery, oval leaves up to 8cm (3in) long. Numerous very small, creamy white, fragrant flowers appear in summer, followed by green fruits about 4cm (1½in) long, that turn black when ripe. Olives probably originated in south-west Asia and are characteristic of Mediterranean regions.

HISTORY
Olive trees have been grown since prehistoric times for their fruits and oil. Extensive cultivation of olives is mentioned in ancient Egyptian texts dating back to around 2500BC, though the climate in most of Egypt today is too dry for olives. The olive has been a symbol of peace worldwide for many

Olea europæa

centuries, beginning with the biblical account of the dove returning to Noah's Ark with an olive branch to show that the flood waters had abated.

COOKING
Olives are not very palatable raw, and are almost always cured or pickled in brine, salt or oil for consumption. They are an important ingredient of *hors d'oeuvres*, salads, spreads (such as *tapenade*), pasta sauces, pizza toppings, and breads. Olive oil gives a characteristic flavour to salad dressings, sauces, mayonnaise, sauces and many Mediterranean-style dishes. In southern Europe, it is often eaten with bread, instead of butter or margarine. Cold-pressed, extra-virgin olive oil often comes from unpalatable varieties. It has a much lower acidity and therefore a better flavour than oils that are extracted using heat or solvents.

HEALING
Olive leaves are infused as a tea to lower blood pressure, improve the circulation, relieve nervous tension and soothe feverish illnesses. They have antiseptic and astringent properties too, which make them useful as a lotion for cuts and grazes. The mono-unsaturated oil has soothing and softening properties, benefiting the digestive and circulatory systems, and the skin. Regular consumption of olive oil is thought to reduce the risk of circulatory disease. It reduces gastric secretions, improving digestive problems due to hyperacidity.

NOTES FOR GARDENERS
Olive trees need sharply drained soil and full sun. They are hardier when older, so gardeners in cool areas should buy the largest specimen possible if planting outdoors, and provide a sheltered position, perhaps against a sunny wall. It is also worth tracking down the hardiest variety, 'Aglandau', which is also self-fertile. Specialist suppliers will stock other self-fertile varieties and advise on their characteristics. Olives make good container plants, and there is nothing better than a large specimen in a decorative terracotta pot to create a Mediterranean atmosphere for the patio or courtyard. Propagate plants by sowing seeds in spring at 13–15°C (55–59°F), or by semi-ripe cuttings in summer.

Origanum species

MARJORAM
OREGANO

PORTRAIT
Wild marjoram (*O. vulgare*) is a variable, woody-based, hardy perennial, 30–75cm (12–30in) in height and spread, with reddish stems and oval leaves up to 4cm (1½in) long. Dense clusters of mauve-pink to white flowers with purple-flushed bracts are borne over a long period in summer. It occurs widely in Europe and central Asia, and is naturalized in eastern North America. Pungency varies considerably according to clone, habitat and climate. Sweet marjoram (*O. majorana*) is less hardy and has a more thyme-like aroma. Italian oregano or hardy marjoram (*O. x majoricum*) is similar but hardier. Pot marjoram or Greek oregano (*O. onites*) has an inferior flavour. Syrian oregano (*O. syriacum*) is a Middle Eastern species, also known as Bible hyssop. Dittany of Crete (*O. dictamnus*) grows wild only in Crete and is the trickiest species in cultivation. The

common name 'oregano' is used for many different plants, some of which are not origanums at all. Commercially dried oregano is produced mainly from Greek or Turkish marjoram (*O. vulgare* subsp. *hirtum*), Mexican oregano (*Lippia graveolens*) and others, and much oregano oil is extracted from *Thymus capitatus* (Spanish oregano).

HISTORY

The words oregano and *Origanum* are probably derived from the Greek *oros*, mountain, and *ganos*, brightness, which may be loosely translated as 'joy of the mountains'. Marjorams have always been popular in their native lands, and were extensively cultivated in monastic gardens and used as a strewing herb in the days of earthen-floored houses. Medicinal uses have been recorded since classical times. The Roman recipe book *Apicius* lists oregano as an ingredient of barley broth, a nourishing mixture of grains, pulses, cabbage, chard and leeks, which owed much to the addition of herbs for its flavour and digestibility. Both pot marjoram and Cretan dittany were grown in England before the end of the sixteenth century.

ORIGANUM VULGARE

COOKING

Marjorams or oreganos are good with strong flavours, such as chilli, garlic, onions, tomatoes and red wine, and are much used in Greek, Italian, and Mexican cooking. For maximum pungency, the herb is more often used dried than fresh. Many regard sweet marjoram as the best flavoured of all, but other species have cultivars that are outstanding too – *O. onites* 'Kaliteri', for example. Syrian oregano is ground with the tart red fruits of sumac (*Rhus coriaria*) and other ingredients to make the spice mixture *za'tar*, which in the Middle East is often mixed with oil to form a spread for bread. Marjorams of all kinds can also be used for tea.

HEALING

Wild marjoram is a warming, antiseptic herb that acts mainly on the digestive and respiratory systems. It can be taken internally, in the form of an infusion or tincture, to relieve coughs, colds, flu, tonsillitis, bronchitis, digestive problems and minor feverish illnesses. Externally, marjoram helps relieve bronchial congestion and stiff or aching muscles and joints. It stimulates the uterus, so should not be used medicinally during pregnancy. Sweet marjoram is similar in effects, with a more pronounced anti-spasmodic and sedative action.

NOTES FOR GARDENERS

Marjorams need well-drained to dry, alkaline soil in sun. Frost hardy species, such as *O. dictamnus*, *O. majoricum* and *O. onites*, usually prove hardier if planted in gritty soil in a 'rain shadow' area, such as at the base of a wall. There are variegated, golden and compact forms of *O. vulgare* that excel as garden ornamentals and, like all marjorams, attract bees and butterflies in profusion. Propagate marjorams by seed sown at 10–13°F (50–55°F) in autumn or spring, by division in spring, or by basal cuttings in late spring.

Paeonia species   PEONY

PORTRAIT

Paeonia lactiflora is a hardy perennial, 50–70cm (20–28in) tall, with fleshy roots, red-marked stems, and dark green leaves, divided into nine entire or lobed leaflets. Fragrant, single, white to pale pink flowers, 7–10cm (3–4in) across, appear in late spring and early summer. Chinese peonies grow wild in eastern Siberia, Mongolia, Tibet and northern and western China. The common peony (*P. officinalis*) is a smaller plant, native to Europe, with crimson flowers. Tree peonies (*P. suffruticosa*) occur in China, Tibet and Bhutan and are shrubs that reach 2m (6ft) tall.

HISTORY

Oriental peonies have an ancient history of cultivation and use. The Chinese peony has been grown in the East since at least 900BC, and its use in medicine began before AD500. Known as 'king of flowers' in China, the tree peony was the emperors' favourite for a thousand years and was associated with riches and honour, as well as being symbolic of spring. The medicinal uses of tree peonies were first described in the twelfth century. In European herbal medicine, the common peony was popular, especially as a remedy or charm to protect against epilepsy, up until the sixteenth century – but it is seldom used today. Herbalists recognized male and female kinds, depending on the appearance of the plant – females had more divided foliage, smaller, darker, more scented flowers, and black seeds – and prescribed them accordingly for men or women.

COOKING

Seeds of the common peony were once used as a spice to flavour beer or food, or chopped as decoration. Both common and tree peony petals are edible when cooked.

HEALING

Chinese herbalists consider that cultivated and wild-collected specimens of *P. lactiflora*, regardless of flower or root colour, yield two different drugs: *bai shao* (white peony) and *chi shao* (red peony) respectively. White peony is a tonic for liver and circulation, used mainly for high blood pressure, menstrual problems, night sweats, abdominal pains, and liver-related problems, while red peony is a cooling remedy that controls bleeding and relieves 'hot' conditions, such as

Pivoine de la Chine

Pæonia

Victor

eczema, inflamed eyes and sores. Red peony is one of the Chinese herbs used with great success to treat eczema at the Great Ormond Street Children's Hospital in London. Tree peony is a cooling, pain-killing, anti-bacterial herb that is used to control bleeding and to treat gastro-intestinal infections.

NOTES FOR GARDENERS

Peonies are exceptionally long-lived and can often be found thriving in completely overgrown gardens. However, they are not necessarily the easiest of plants to grow to perfection. For a start, they need moist, well-drained, humus-rich soil in sun or part shade, avoiding positions where early morning sun might damage new growth, buds or flowers after frost. Next, they dislike being moved and may not flower well if disturbed, too dry, or planted too deeply or too shallowly. There are numerous named varieties of all the species mentioned, but *P. lactiflora* has the most. Cultivars may not, of course, come true from seed, but the species can be propagated by seed sown in autumn. Seed may take two to three years to germinate though. Herbaceous peonies, such as *P. lactiflora* and

PAEONIA OFFICINALIS 'ROSEA PLENA'

P. officinalis and their varieties, can be divided autumn or early spring, or propagated by root cuttings in winter. To propagate tree peonies, take semi-ripe cuttings in summer.

Panax quinquefolius — AMERICAN GINSENG

PORTRAIT

A hardy perennial, about 38cm (15in) tall, with a cigar-shaped, often branched, aromatic rootstock, and leaves divided into five (occasionally three or seven) toothed, oblong, pointed leaflets, the largest reaching 15cm (6in) long. Tiny greenish-white flowers appear in a cluster above the whorl of leaves in early summer, followed by a knob of a bright red fruits. American ginseng is native to eastern North American woodlands. Its equivalent in Asia in *P. ginseng*, which grows wild in north-eastern China and is extensively cultivated, notably in Korea.

HISTORY

The use of ginseng in China goes back some 5,000 years and by the twelfth century there were already shortages due to over-collection. The first descriptions of *P. ginseng* in the wild were published in 1714 by Father Jartoux, a Jesuit missionary. He observed that forested mountains on the Korean border were so like those in Canada that a similar species must surely grow there – an observation that prompted Father Lafitau, a Jesuit priest in Canada, to search for the new species, which he found in 1716. (Millions of years ago, North America was connected to Asia, which explains why the two continents, though now distantly separated, still have some closely related species.) His discovery initiated the thriving export trade of American ginseng to China that continues to this day. In turn, American ginseng has become increasingly scarce in the wild, leading to legislation restricting its collection, and new initiatives to cultivate this valuable herb, both in North America and Europe.

COOKING

Ginseng roots and extracts are an ingredient of tonic soups, teas, soft drinks, chewing gum and liqueurs. In Asia the roots are often eaten raw, deep-fried or candied as snacks or toppings, or as ingredients for salads and stuffings.

HEALING

American ginseng is a tonic herb that increases resistance to infection and stress, improves stamina and concentration, lowers blood sugar and cholesterol levels, and strengthens the nervous system. It is usually taken for short periods as a tonic during winter or a period of undue stress, and is often very beneficial for debility in old age or during convalescence. Though similar in effects to *P. ginseng*, American ginseng is considered better for younger people, whereas *P. ginseng* is more often prescribed by Chinese herbalists to those over 40 years of age. Ginseng is unsuitable for pregnant women or anyone with a high intake of caffeine. Side effects, such as headaches, restlessness and raised blood pressure, may also occur when ginseng is taken in excess or in conjunction with alcohol, turnips or spicy foods. Externally, in ointment, ginseng helps to heal minor injuries and skin problems.

NOTES FOR GARDENERS

Ginseng needs woodland conditions – dappled shade, cool, humus-rich, acid soil and moderate warmth, moisture and humidity throughout the growing season. Natural deciduous woodland offers the best chance of success. Short of that, construct raised beds of rich, well-drained soil, with supports for a shade screen in summer. Propagation by seed is challenging. Seed must not be allowed to dry out and should be stratified before planting. Even then, it takes between six and twenty months to germinate. Young plants are also available from specialist nurseries. Outside its natural habitat, ginseng is difficult to grow with any degree of success for any length of time – particularly in pots. Given good growing conditions, roots are ready for harvesting after five or six years.

Panax quinquefolium. L.

Papaver species POPPY

PORTRAIT

Papaver rhoeas, the corn poppy, is a hardy annual, 20–90cm (8–36in) tall, with upright, soft-bristled stems and oblong, deeply divided, hairy leaves. Long-stalked, bright red (occasionally pink to white) flowers, 5–10cm (2–4cm) across, usually marked with a dark blotch at the base of each petal, appear in summer, followed by almost round capsules, containing brown seeds. Corn poppies (also known as field poppies or Flanders poppies) are weeds of disturbed ground in Europe, Asia and North Africa, and naturalized elsewhere. Opium poppies (*Papaver somniferum*) are native to western and central Mediterranean regions, and now grow in many other areas worldwide. They are larger plants, with jagged, blue-green foliage, white or lilac (occasionally pink, red, or maroon) flowers, glaucous capsules, and grey or white seeds. In Mexico, the place of opium poppies and corn poppies is taken with *chicalote* or prickly poppies (*Argemone mexicana*), which have similar properties.

PAPAVER SOMNIFERUM

HISTORY

Corn poppies were popular in ancient Egypt, and often depicted as ornamentals on wall paintings and reliefs. Seeds were found mixed with barley in Egyptian remains pre-dating 2500BC. Opium poppies were known then too; analysis of the contents of a pot found in a tomb showed not only that it was opium, but also that the drug was still potent after 1,000 years. The ancient Greeks and Romans used poppy seeds in food and, throughout the ages, poppy extracts have been taken to ease suffering and pain. Corn poppies have symbolized blood and new life since ancient Egyptian times. Artificial poppies are worn in Britain on Armistice Day (11 November) every year to commemorate those who died in battle – a tradition initiated by the poem 'In Flanders Fields', by Col. John McRae, describing the battlefields of World War I covered with poppies after being disturbed by the digging of thousands of graves.

Shirley poppies, which come in a wide range of colours but all bearing pale centres, were raised by the Reverend William Wilks of Shirley in Surrey, England, from a plant with white-rimmed flowers that he spotted in a wild corner of his garden in 1879 or 1880. White Shirley poppies

Pavot   *Papaver*

Papaver rhoeas

are worn on Armistice Day by pacifists, by way of honouring the dead but rejecting violence and war.

COOKING

Poppy seeds are non-narcotic and safe for using in breads, cakes and other baked foods. Oil pressed from the seeds is excellent for salad dressings and cooking. The red petals are used to colour wine and cordials.

HEALING

Corn poppies contain some different alkaloids from opium poppies and are much milder. The flowers – which are usually made into a syrup – have pain killing, spasm-relaxing and expectorant effects that help relieve paroxysmal coughs, nervous digestive problems, insomnia and restlessness, especially in children and the elderly.

NOTES FOR GARDENERS

As corn poppies do not contain opium, gardeners are free to grow them (in some countries it is illegal to cultivate the opium poppy in any shape or form). All they need is well-drained soil in sun. They do not transplant successfully, so sow seeds directly where they are to flower. Hoe or rake the soil first as poppies require disturbed soil and light for germination. As well as the Shirley strain, there are more recent selections, such as 'Mother of Pearl' with unusual pastel shades, including dusky lilacs and greys, and 'Cedric Morris', a taller strain with delicately speckled, pale pink to white flowers. Opium poppies have some glorious cultivars too, including fully double, peony-flowered kinds in every shade from white to dark maroon, and fringed, vividly coloured singles such as 'Danebrog', which is scarlet with a white centre. To enjoy poppies as cut flowers, seal the ends of the stalks over a flame so that they last longer in water.

Passiflora incarnata

PASSIONFLOWER
MAYPOP

PORTRAIT

A hardy perennial climber with tuberous roots, stems reaching 8m (25ft) in length, and dark green leaves, divided into three- to five-toothed lobes up to 15cm (6in) long. Fragrant pale lavender flowers appear in summer, followed by small egg-shaped yellow fruits or 'maypops', 5cm (2in) long. *Passiflora incarnata* grows wild on waste ground and along fields and roads in the eastern United States, mostly in southern parts.

HISTORY

Passionflower roots were crushed and added to drinking water as a tonic by the Houma tribe of Louisiana, and the fruits were eaten by various other tribes. The plant was described by a visiting European doctor in 1783 as a cure for epilepsy. It was used as a remedy for insomnia in the nineteenth century and included in the *US National Formulary* from 1916 to 1936. Today it is far more popular as a herbal remedy in Europe than in the United States.

COOKING

Young leaves are eaten raw or cooked as a vegetable. The flowers are edible too, and can be made into a syrup. More often used are the fruits – eaten raw, or made into jams, jellies, or drinks. Their appearance when ripe gives the plant another common name, apricot vine.

HEALING

Passiflora incarnata is a bitter, cooling, non-addictive, sedative herb that relaxes spasms and lowers blood pressure. The fresh or dried whole plant (minus the roots) is used to make tinctures, infusions and tablets to calm anxiety, nervous tension, irritability, insomnia and hyperactivity. It may also help in the treatment of high blood pressure, shingles, palpitations, irritable bowel syndrome, cramps and asthma.

NOTES FOR GARDENERS

Though one of the hardiest of passionflowers, and a weed in its native haunts, it is not necessarily the easiest to grow elsewhere, needing very sharp drainage, poor, sandy, slightly acid soil, full sun

PASSIFLORA INCARNATA

and hot summers for optimum growth, flowering and fruiting. The provenance of plants and seeds may determine hardiness, and those from its northernmost stations in Ohio are likely to be more resilient than those from southern states. Once established, it spreads by underground runners and may pop up at a distance from where it was first planted (which is not why it is called maypop – a word derived from the Powhatan *mahcawq*). Propagation is by seeds sown in spring at about 18°C (64°F), by semi-ripe cuttings in late summer, or by suckers, potted up and treated like cuttings, in spring or early summer. Plants can also be layered in late summer by removing leaves from a section of stem, bending it down to the ground, covering with soil and weighing down with a brick, leaving the end of the shoot to continue growing. By the following spring, the layer should have rooted and can be severed and transplanted.

Herbal Salads

ERUCA SATIVA VESICARIA SUBSP. SATIVA

EVERYONE KNOWS THAT SALADS ARE GOOD FOR YOU, but just how good depends on their ingredients and, in turn, on their freshness. As salad leaves are fragile and take several days to reach the consumer, it is not surprising that they are often past their best when eaten. For optimum flavour and nutrients, salad ingredients should also be organically grown and freshly harvested. Ideally, you should grow as many as you can yourself and harvest them at the last minute. Even without a garden, you can grow baby salad leaves in pots or trays, and sprout seeds in jam jars.

The perfect salad is based on a fairly bland main ingredient, such as lettuce, grated white cabbage, or non-leafy ingredients like grains or beans, to which stronger tasting herbal ingredients are added. This combination makes it easier to eat bitter or pungent herbs that would be fairly unpalatable on their own, and turns an ordinary salad into a revitalizing tonic. Chives, parsley, dill, fennel, tarragon or chervil all taste good enough to be used quite generously, and herb flowers are both beneficial and colourful. Chopped or finely sliced broccoli and other cabbage-type vegetables (see p.282) are also valuable when eaten raw. Many common weeds have herbal properties too (see p.302) and can be picked for salads. Harvest only tender young leaves or tips, and make sure they are free from pollutants (from vehicles, animals, mud-splashes, etc.) and wash them thoroughly.

We all vary in our tolerance of bitter, pungent flavours. If you are very sensitive, begin with small amounts until you acquire a taste for them.

The bitter leaves of chicory (*Cichorium intybus*) have a tonic effect on the liver and gall bladder. Bitter tastes prime the digestive system, triggering the secretion of bile and enzymes so that food is thoroughly processed. There are two main kinds of chicory: narrow-leaved Witloof or Belgian, with an elongated, compact head, known as a chicon, which is blanched white to reduce its bitterness; and red or raddichio types that form a cabbage-like head. Chicory is closely related to endive (*C. endivia*), a similarly bitter salad herb. Rocket (*Eruca vesicaria* subsp. *sativa*) is a traditional ingredient of *mesclun,* a mixed salad of baby leaves that originated in the south of France. Known also as arugula or rucola, it is a mustard-like annual and is extremely quick and easy to grow to leaf-picking stage, even in containers. Young leaves are best, becoming more pungent as the plant nears flowering. Flowers and buds are edible too. Like other members of the cabbage family (Brassicaceae), it contains sulphur compounds that have antibiotic properties and are vital for healthy skin, hair and nails.

NASTURTIUM OFFICINALE

TROPAEOLUM MAJUS

The pungent bite of mustard also occurs in watercress (*Nasturtium officinale*) and radish (*Raphanus sativus*). Both improve digestion, and clear toxins and congestion. They are particularly good salad ingredients in the winter to help shift catarrh. If you grow your own radishes, let the odd one go to seed. The flower buds are edible, as are immature seed pods which have a crisp, crunchy texture.

Dittander (*L. latifolium*) is similar to horseradish (see p.44) in pungency and flavour. New leaves of both can be added to salads for their stimulant, anti-bacterial effects.

Though not a cabbage relative, nasturtiums (*Tropaeolum majus*) are also rich in sulphur and antibiotic compounds. Nasturtium comes from an earlier name, *Nasturtium indicum*, 'Indian cress', which was given because of the pungent, watercress-like flavour. Growing nasturtiums is child's play, and all parts are edible, including flower buds, nectar spurs and unripe seeds. Just check them over and wash carefully in case of aphids. They will do you the power of good, conditioning skin and hair, increasing resistance to clearing excess mucus, and topping up vitamin C levels.

Alfalfa (*Medicago sativa*) has been called 'father of all herbs' and reputedly contains all known vitamins and minerals. It stimulates the digestion, detoxifies the system and has hormonal and diuretic effects. The sprouted seeds have a pleasant, pea-like flavour. Eat them, or young leaves, occasionally and in moderation; excess alfalfa increases sensitivity to sunlight, and may exacerbate auto-immune conditions. As is often the case, though a little may do you good, it does not follow that lots will do even more good.

MEDICAGO SATIVA

Purslane (*Portulaca oleracea*) was used medicinally by the Copts for inflammations and swellings, as it still is in Egypt today. The succulent leaves have a sour, refreshing taste and anti-bacterial effects that protect against gastric infections. Purslane is also rich in omega-3 fatty acids, which strengthen the immune system and maintain cardiovascular health.

Tasting like cucumber, the leaves of salad burnet (*Sanguisorba minor*) have a mild astringency that becomes more pronounced as they age. Pick when they are young and still soft, before the leaflets have unfolded. Salad burnet is a hardy perennial that comes into growth very early for winter and spring salads.

See also: *Allium schoenoprasum, A. tuberosum, Anthriscus cerefolium, Calendula officinalis, Centella asiatica, Petroselinum crispum, Rumex* species, *Sinapis alba, Trigonella foenum-graecum.*

PORTULACA OLERACEA

Perilla frutescens

PERILLA
SHISO. BEEFSTEAK PLANT

PORTRAIT

An erect, branched, strongly aromatic, frost-hardy annual, reaching up to 1.2m (4ft) tall, with broadly oval, pointed, green leaves 8–10cm (3–4in) long. Whorls of tiny white flowers appear in dense spikes, 4–8cm (1½–3in) long, in summer. Perilla grows wild in woods and grassland from the Himalayas to Japan and is widely naturalized in the United States.

HISTORY

Perilla has a long history of use as a culinary herb in Japan, and has been used medicinally in China since at least AD500. It was introduced to the United States in the nineteenth century and by the early twentieth century had become a common weed in many states. Where it has invaded pasture, there have been cases of poisoning in cattle. In Japan, oil extracted from the

PERILLA FRUTESCENS

seeds (*yegoma*) is used mainly for making synthetic leather and waterproof fabrics, and in the paper, printing and paint industries because it is fast-drying, resilient, water-resistant and glossy.

COOKING

Perilla is ubiquitous in Japanese cuisine. Almost all parts – leaves, seed leaves, flower spikes, seeds – are used in some way or other. The leaves are eaten raw or pickled, and used to wrap or garnish meat and fish. Chopped leaves mixed with grated horseradish appear as a garnish for steaks, which is perhaps why it is best known as 'beefsteak plant'. Immature flower spikes are used to garnish soup and tofu, and mature ones are fried. Purple leaves are a food colourant, notably in pickled *umeboshi* plums. Seeds are sprouted, and salted as a spice in pickles, tempura, miso and *shichimi* (Japanese seven-spice mixture, which also contains *sansho*, seaweed, chilli, orange peel, poppy and sesame seeds). Essential oil extracted from the foliage and flowering tops is used to flavour sauces, confectionery and tobacco. It contains a substance that is 2,000 times sweeter than sugar.

HEALING

In Chinese medicine perilla leaves and stems are a warming, anti-bacterial remedy that relaxes spasms and increases perspiration. They are used to treat colds, chills, nausea, food poisoning and allergic reactions, especially to seafood. Tea made from the stems is a traditional remedy for morning sickness, while the seeds have expectorant effects and relieve asthma, coughs and bronchitis.

NOTES FOR GARDENERS

Perilla is easy to accommodate in warmer areas, where it self-sows with great abandon in almost any conditions, but most freely in well-drained, light, rich, moist, slightly acid soil, in sun or part shade. In areas with cold winters it should be sown under cover in spring at 13–18°C (55–64°F). Sow seeds on the surface as they need light to germinate. The perillas most commonly in cultivation are the frilly-leaved green one and var. *crispa* which has metallic purple leaves with deeply toothed or crinkled margins. In addition to its herbal uses, the latter makes a spectacular plant for summer bedding and containers.

PERSICARIA BISTORTA

PERSICARIA ODORATA

Persicaria bistorta

P. odorata

BISTORT
VIETNAMESE CORIANDER

PORTRAIT

Persicaria bistorta is a hardy perennial with oval, pointed, unspotted leaves, reaching 15cm (6in) long. In summer it produces cylindrical spikes of tiny pale pink bell-shaped flowers. When flowering, the plant is about 50cm (20in) high. It forms large clumps in low-lying meadows and woods, often near water, in various parts of Europe and northern and western Asia. Vietnamese coriander is similar in appearance to the common European weed known as redshank (*P. vulgaris*) but there the resemblance ends, as *P. odorata* is from tropical south-east Asia and smells exactly like coriander. It is an evergreen perennial, some 45cm (18in) high, with jointed stems and narrow, pointed leaves about 10cm (4in) long, which have a maroon V-shaped marking near the base. The plant spreads far and wide by rooting wherever its stems touch the ground. Spikes of tiny pink flowers are produced from time to time but not commonly, at least not in cultivation.

History

Bistort has a penetrating, contorted rootstock that gave rise to various common names, such as serpentweed, adderwort and serpentary. The word bistort means 'twice-twisted', again referring to the appearance of the roots. Locally, in northern England the plant is known simply as dock, pudding dock or passion dock, from its traditional use as a potherb in spring around Easter. To keep this tradition alive, in 1971 an annual World Championship Dock Pudding Contest was started in the Pennines, around the Calder valley.

Cooking

In northern England, young bistort leaves and shoots were an ingredient of a traditional savoury herb pudding, known as Easter ledger or ledges, or Easter mangiant, which was often shortened to Easter giant. The leaves were finely chopped with nettles, blackcurrant leaves, parsley and chives, and mixed with barley and oatmeal, then steamed in a muslin bag. After a few hours, the mixture was turned out and mixed with a beaten egg and some butter. Though highly astringent, bistort roots are edible after soaking in water to remove some of the tannin. They are black on the outside, and red-fleshed. Vietnamese coriander is a vital ingredient of the sauerkraut-like dish *du'a cân*. In Vietnam the young leaves are also added to salads and used to flavour meat (especially fowl), fish and duck eggs. They can also be used to give a coriander-like flavour to any dish, especially of south-east Asian origin, such as the Malaysian *laksa*.

Healing

The astringent roots of bistort are a highly effective remedy for internal bleeding from the lungs, stomach or bowel. On a more day-to-day basis, they can be used to control diarrhoea (especially in babies), and externally to heal sore gums, mouth ulcers or haemorrhoids. Bistort root is available powdered, and as a tincture and liquid extract. If you grow your own, the roots can simply be decocted (boiled in water). Vietnamese coriander benefits the digestion. It is also supposed to lower the sex drive — an effect known as anaphrodisiac.

Notes for Gardeners

Wild bistort can be weedy and invasive. There is, however, a superior version, known as 'Superbum', which is taller and gives an impressive, long-lasting display of larger flower spikes. It tolerates dry soil but is in its element beside a pond or stream. Propagation is simply by division. Vietnamese coriander needs a minimum temperature of 7°C (45°F). In cool areas it can be grown as a pot plant, or over-wintered as such and planted out during the summer. The best way of propagating it is to detach a piece of stem that has already started to root (an 'Irishman's cutting'), and cut it back to about 10cm (4in) to focus its energies on further rooting.

Petroselinum crispum

PARSLEY

PORTRAIT

An aromatic, frost-hardy to hardy biennial, 15–20cm (6–8in) tall, reaching 1m (3ft) when flowering, with an off-white taproot and triangular, toothed leaves, divided into three main segments and again into smaller segments. Tiny yellow-green flowers are produced in flat-topped umbels in summer, followed by narrowly oval brown fruits. Parsley probably originated in south-eastern Europe and western Asia, and is now naturalized in many parts of Europe. There are three main kinds in cultivation: curly-leaved cultivars, derived from the species, which is the classic garnishing parsley; flat-leaved or Italian parsley (var. *neapolitanum*), a larger, hardier, more weather-resistant variety with a finer flavour; and Hamburg or turnip-rooted parsley (var. *tuberosum*), which is more a vegetable than a herb, with leaves reminiscent of parsley and celery in flavour, and parsnip-like roots.

PETROSELINUM CRISPUM 'MOSS CURLED'

PETROSELINUM CRISPUM

HISTORY

Both plain and curly parsleys were described by Theophrastus in his *Enquiry into Plants*, which dates from about 300BC. The curly variety gained favour during Roman times and remains the most popular by far. The scientific name *Petroselinum* comes from the Greek *petra*, rock, and *selinon*, parsley, which gave rise to the Old English *petersilie*, and Old French *peresil*, and eventually 'parsley'. There is a saying that parsley seed goes to the devil and back seven times before it comes up, and the devil likes it so much he always keeps some. This refers to the length of time it takes to germinate, and why germination is often patchy. Today parsley is probably the most widely cultivated and used herb in Europe and the United States. Oil extracted from the leaves and seeds is used in commercial food flavouring and in fragrances for men.

COOKING

Parsley leaves are used to garnish and flavour sauces, butter, dressings, stuffings, salads and a wide variety of meat, fish, egg and vegetable dishes. Chopped parsley gives colour and flavour to *chimichurri*, an Argentinian sauce for meat, and to *salsa verde* ('green sauce'), which is made from olive oil, vinegar or lemon juice, garlic, capers and anchovies in Italy, and from onion, garlic, chilli peppers and coriander in Mexico. It is also a vital ingredient of *tabbouleh*, a Middle Eastern salad of cracked wheat (bulgar), finely chopped tomatoes and onions. Parsley juice is added to mixed vegetable juices.

HEALING
Parsley is a diuretic herb that relaxes spasms, reduces inflammation, clears toxins and stimulates the uterus. Extracts of parsley roots are prescribed for cystitis, rheumatic and arthritic conditions, and menstrual problems, and to encourage lactation and contract the uterus after childbirth. The seeds are less often used but make a good substitute for celery seeds as a diuretic for gout, rheumatism and arthritis. Parsley should not be taken medicinally during pregnancy. The leaves are rich in vitamins (especially vitamins A and C) and minerals, such as boron and fluorine which strengthen bones. They help digestion and freshen the breath, so it is a good idea to eat your garnish.

NOTES FOR GARDENERS
Parsley likes moist, fertile, well-drained, sandy soil that is about neutral or verging on slightly acid (pH 5.3 at most), and a sunny or partly shaded position. Seed is best sown *in situ*, at any time during the growing season. A late summer sowing will crop through the winter and following spring, though in areas prone to hard or frequent frosts, plants may need the protection of a cloche. Seed normally takes three to six weeks to germinate but can be hastened by soaking in hot water before sowing.

Pinus species   PINE

PORTRAIT
Pumilio or dwarf montain pine (*Pinus mugo* var. *pumilio*) is a hardy shrub or rounded to spreading tree, about 3.5m (11ft) tall and 2–5m (6–15ft) wide, with thick, ascending branches, resinous buds and pairs of dark green needles, 3–8cm (1½–3in) long. After blooming, female flowers develop into egg-shaped brown cones up to 6cm (2½in) long. Pumilio pines are native to mountainous areas of central Europe. Scots pines (*P. sylvestris*) are much larger, reaching 15–25m (50–80ft) tall, with red-brown to purple-grey bark and grey-brown cones. They occur over both lowland and upland areas of Europe (excluding the far north) and temperate Asia. Longleaf or southern pitch pines (*P. palustris*) occur in dry, sandy areas of south-eastern United States.

HISTORY
Pines of many kinds have been used medicinally in various countries from earliest times. All are rich in resins and camphoraceous volatile oils, such as pinene, that are strongly antiseptic and stimulant. Among the pines used in traditional Chinese medicine is an extinct species, *P. succinifera*; the resin is extracted from buried trees that died thousands of years ago.

AROMATIC USES
Pumilio and longleaf pine oils are used in woody perfumes.

COOKING

Rather surprisingly, pine needle oil is used in the food industry for flavouring ice cream, baked goods, confectionery and soft drinks.

HEALING

Oil distilled from the needles of pumilio and Scots pines are common ingredients of cough and cold remedies, especially inhalants, and in ointments and liniments for muscular aches and pains, rheumatic and arthritic conditions. Scots pine seeds are used to treat bronchial and urinary infections, and tuberculosis. Resin from longleaf pines, known as colophony or rosin, is used externally for skin problems, as well as for bronchial and muscular complaints.

NOTES FOR GARDENERS

Pumilio pines are ideal for small gardens. They can be used with effect in pairs, or as a centrepiece, and are the right scale for rock gardens, Japanese-style gardens and containers. There are several named varieties with a compact or rounded habit that are even better than the species as ornamentals. Scots pines are much larger and faster growing, but for confined spaces there is 'Beuvronensis', a dwarf, rounded version that reaches only 1m (3ft), and 'Watereri', a slow-growing, upright little Scots pine, 4m (12ft) tall. Both pumilio and Scots pines need well-drained, neutral to acid soil in sun, though the latter will also tolerate alkaline soils. Longleaf pines are frost hardy; they contend with drought and poor soil but must have warmth and humidity. Propagate pines by seed sown in spring; otherwise by grafting, though pumilio pines can also be layered if there are conveniently low branches.

Piper nigrum # PEPPER

PORTRAIT

A tender, evergreen, perennial vine, climbing by means of aerial roots, with stout stems reaching 4m (12ft) or more, and pointed, leathery, deeply veined, oval leaves 10–15cm (4–6in) long. Tiny greenish-white flowers, often with males and females on different plants, are produced in spikes, 7–12cm (3–5in) long, followed by spherical berries which are green at first, turning yellow and then red when ripe. These constitute green peppercorns (fresh green berries, which are frozen or pickled) and black pepper (berries dried whole when yellow). Inside the red berries are grey-white seeds (white pepper), which are obtained by soaking in water for between seven and ten days, and rubbing to remove the outer layers, then drying. Pink peppercorns are from a quite different plant, *Schinus terebinthifolius*. Pepper vines are native to southern India, and are widely cultivated in the tropics.

HISTORY

Pepper has been traded since earliest times and has always been a valuable commodity. Today it accounts for a quarter of all spices in world trade. Attila the Hun demanded a huge quantity of pepper – 1,360kg (3,000lb) – as ransom during the siege of Rome in AD408, and its use as currency gave rise to the term 'peppercorn rent' for a nominal, very low rent.

COOKING

Pepper in its various guises adds flavour and piquancy to most savoury dishes, meat products, sauces, dressings, pickles and coatings for cheeses and cooked cold fish and meat. Ground white pepper is the least aromatic. Mignonette pepper (also called 'shot pepper' and, when finely ground, *poivre gris*, is a blend of ground white and black peppercorns. Green peppercorns are the least pungent, and are used in creamy sauces, pâtés, butter and sauces for duck or steak. They are also dried for stock, soups and casseroles.

HEALING

Pepper is a pungent, warming herb that lowers fever and improves digestion and circulation. In western herbal medicine it is used mainly with other herbs to relieve digestive discomfort. In Ayurvedic medicine it is regarded as a stimulating expectorant, mixed with *ghee* as a remedy for nasal congestion and sinusitis. The Indian patent medicine, *trikatu*, made from pepper, long pepper (*P. longum*) and ginger (*Zingiber officinale*), is taken for almost any 'cold' condition. Practitioners of traditional Chinese medicine consider it tranquillizing and anti-emetic, and use it to treat diarrhoea and vomiting caused by chills, food poisoning, cholera or dysentery. The essential oil helps relieve rheumatic pain and toothache but should not be taken internally.

NOTES FOR GARDENERS

Pepper vines need rich, well-drained soil in light shade and high humidity, with ample moisture during the growing season, and a minimum temperature of 16°C (61°F). Propagate by seed sown when ripe at 20–24°C (66–75°F) or by semi-ripe cuttings in summer. In areas outside the tropics they can be grown under glass if sufficiently high temperatures and humidity can be provided, and may fruit as container plants. They are unlikely to succeed as houseplants.

Plantago major
P. psyllium

GREATER PLANTAIN
SPANISH PSYLLIUM

PORTRAIT

A small, low-growing perennial with long-stalked, oval leaves up to 15cm (6in) long and dense 'rat-tail' spikes of minute green flowers in summer, greater plantain is a tough little plant that adopts a flattened position on well-beaten tracks and survives the passing of a ten-ton truck. Originally from Europe and temperate Asia, this common weed spread during colonial times – often in trouser turn-ups – to many other parts of the world, and earned the name 'white man's foot'. Rather different in appearance, though still fairly obviously a plantain, is psyllium or fleaseed, an annual with whorls of small, narrow, grey-green leaves and brown bobble flower heads. It too is a weed, though Mediterranean in origin, and sows itself merrily wherever it is cultivated for medicinal purposes.

HISTORY

Greater plantain was known as 'waybread' – the seeds were once ground into meal – and was one of the nine sacred herbs of the Anglo-Saxons. Its importance as a medicinal herb has held firm through the ages: it was mentioned by Chaucer and Shakespeare, as well as in classic herbals, and was well-researched during the twentieth century. Plantain seeds readily absorb moisture and become mucilaginous. This property is utilized in several species (notably *P. indica*, *P. ovata*, and *P. psyllium*) to produce an effective, gentle bulk laxative, known as ispaghula. In earlier times, this gelatinous substance was used for stiffening muslin and other fabrics. The name 'fleaseed' arose because the seeds resemble fleas in size and colour.

COOKING

Greater plantains are edible, though their leaves are fibrous, due to the tough veins that serve to reinforce the foliage against wear and tear. The youngest leaves, perhaps briefly blanched in boiling water or deep-fried, are the best bet. Psyllium seeds are palatable and are produced in such quantity that they can be sprouted for salads. Commercially, they yield an oil rich in linoleic and alpha-linolenic acids, and the outer coat provides a mucilage used as a thickener and stabilizer in the frozen food industry.

PLANTAGO PSYLLIUM

HEALING

Greater plantain is a potent healing herb. Leaf extracts reduce inflammation, dilate the bronchiole tubes and are diuretic. They soothe and heal mucous membranes, making an excellent remedy for sore, irritated or ulcerated tissues. It is mainly used to treat cystitis, haemorrhoids, ulcers (including gastric ulcers and varicose ulcers), ear and eye infections, bronchitis, catarrh, sinusitis, asthma, dry coughs and hay fever. Combined with agrimony, St. John's wort, German chamomile and peppermint, it helps to heal and relieve the pain of gastric ulcers. Seeds of ispaghula plantains produce bulk laxative materials and also soothe the digestive tract in gastro-enteritis, dysentery and diarrhoea. Ribwort plantain (*P. lanceolata*) has exactly the same properties as greater plantain.

NOTES FOR GARDENERS

No sane gardener would regard greater plantain as an ornamental, but its cultivars have quite a following. Most popular is the beetroot-coloured 'Rubrifolia', which can be used to great effect in borders, though is a menace if it gets into the lawn (it comes true from seed and sows with abandon).

More for connoisseurs, 'Rosularis' bears flower heads resembling green roses. Surprisingly, it too comes reasonably true from seed. The Chinese *P. asiatica*, which looks like greater plantain and is used in similar ways, has a variegated form with white-marbled leaves. Greater plantain and its kin are extremely easy to grow, revelling in heavy, moisture-retentive loam in full sun. Psyllium is easy too but prefers lighter, well-drained soil. Sow it once and you will have it forever.

Platycodon grandiflorus

BALLOON FLOWER
CHINESE BELLFLOWER

PORTRAIT
A clump-forming perennial with thick roots, oval, bluish green leaves up to 5cm (2in) long, and clusters of five-petalled blue flowers, 5cm (2in) across, which open from large, inflated buds. Balloon flowers grow wild on grassy slopes in hilly areas and mountains of east Asia.

PLATYCODON GRANDIFLORUS

HISTORY
This ancient Chinese herb was first mentioned in the Shen Nong herbal, which dates from the Han Dynasty (206BC–AD23). It reached European gardens in the nineteenth century, largely due to the efforts of Robert Fortune, who collected it on a four-year plant-hunting expedition to China that began in 1843.

COOKING
Balloon flower is grown as a vegetable in parts of Asia, especially in Korea. The white, crunchy roots are seasoned with vinegar, soy sauce and sesame oil, and eaten in salads or added to soups. They are often sold fresh, dried or frozen in oriental stores.

HEALING
The roots of balloon flowers are expectorant and dilate the bronchial tubes. They are also effective against a number of disease-causing organisms. Sold in the form of 'platycodi tablets' and as an

ingredient of various patent remedies, balloon flower is one of the most popular Chinese remedies for coughs and colds, pleurisy and bronchitis.

NOTES FOR GARDENERS .

Wild balloon flowers can reach 1m (3ft) tall, and these are the species grown for medicinal and culinary use. More common as ornamentals (though they also have perfectly usable roots), are dwarf varieties derived from the Japanese form *apoyama*, which is only 20cm (8in) high but has the same size flowers. Compact forms make excellent container plants and are ideal for the rock garden and other confined spaces. Double-, white-, and pink-flowered forms are available too. All need light, moist, well-drained soil in sun or part-shade. They are easy to grow from seed sown in spring. Named varieties may not come true, but there is no such thing as an unlovely balloon flower. The best in terms of habit and flowers can also be propagated by carefully removing basal shoots – with some root if possible – and potting up until they are well established.

PLECTRANTHUS AMBOINICUS

Plectranthus amboinicus

CUBAN OREGANO
SPANISH THYME

PORTRAIT

An evergreen perennial with thick, succulent, pale green leaves 4–8cm (1½–3in) long, which have a velvety, strangely oily texture and neatly scalloped margins. They have a powerful aroma, reminiscent of thyme – or could it be oregano? In summer, long spikes of small lavender flowers are produced. Left to its own devices outdoors it reaches 30–90cm (1–2ft) high and has a spreading, almost shrubby habit. As a pot plant it stays smaller.

HISTORY

No one quite knows where Cuban oregano came from originally – probably from India or Africa, but certainly not from Cuba (that name is explained by its common use in the Caribbean today). Its Latin name suggests Ambon, an island in the Moluccas, though most likely it was taken to the East

Indies at an early date. Apparently it reached the American continent from Spain, presumably during colonial times, which is where the name 'Spanish thyme' came from. Today it is most popular in warm, humid countries that are anathema to Mediterranean herbs such as thyme and oregano.

COOKING

Cuban oregano can be used with discretion in any strongly flavoured fish or meat dish. In Vietnamese cuisine it is a vital ingredient of the sour soup known as *canh chua*.

HEALING

The pungent oils of Cuban oregano have decongestant properties that may help relieve coughs and bronchial infections. They also benefit the digestion, relieving griping spasms in the digestive tract, and having a mildly laxative effect. There is evidence too of antibiotic and anti-inflammatory effects that improve healing of minor injuries, such as insect bites, cuts and grazes, and minor burns.

NOTES FOR GARDENERS

This is a rewarding herb to grow. It makes an attractive specimen, especially if you can track down its variegated forms – 'Variegated' has white-edged leaves and 'Wellsweep Wedgewood' has dark green margins. Outdoors, it needs well-drained soil and full sun, and temperatures above 10°C (50°F) – any lower and the leaves turn to mush. In cool climates, Cuban oregano can be grown as a houseplant on a sunny windowsill. Although it enjoys humidity, it shows no signs of ill effects from central heating. What it does dislike is over-watering, so let the pot dry out between drinks. Propagation is easy at almost any time of the year provided that the cuttings are kept fairly dry.

Primula veris

P. vulgaris

COWSLIP

PRIMROSE

PORTRAIT

Cowslips are small, clump-forming perennials with oblong-oval, deeply veined leaves up to 20cm (8in) long. They produce nodding clusters of yellow flowers, protruding from pale green, tubular calyces. Primroses are similar in habit, with narrower, longer leaves and solitary, pale yellow flowers, about 3cm (1½in) across, held upwards on slender pale green stalks – often so generously that the plant looks like a posy. The flowers of both have a delicate fragrance. Primroses are essentially hedgerow and woodland plants, preferring rich, moist soil and dappled shade. They can be in flower soon after Christmas in mild winters. Cowslips like a more open grassland habitat, usually on chalky soil, and are later, very definitely spring flowering. The two species are mainly European in distribution, extending into western Asia. In many areas their numbers decreased dramatically during the latter half of the twentieth century through loss of habitat and changes in farming practices.

HISTORY

Primula veris was once known as *herba paralysis, radix arthritica* and palsywort because it was much used in medieval times to treat conditions involving cramps, spasms, paralysis and arthritic pain. Its present-day name comes from the Old English *cuslyppe,* meaning cow dung, as cowslips grow in meadows where cattle graze, thus appearing to spring from cowpats. Primrose flowers, mixed with nutmeg, were prescribed by Culpeper in the seventeenth century for 'all infirmities of the head'. He noted that the leaves were used in cosmetics 'by our city dames' to improve the complexion and remove 'spots and wrinkles of the skin, sun-burning and freckles'. Cowslips were also a favourite cosmetic herb. According to William Turner, the sixteenth-century herbalist, 'Some weomen…sprinkle ye floures of cowslip with whyte wine and after…wash their faces with that water to…make them fayre in the eyes of the worlde rather than in the eyes of God, whom they are not afryd to offend'. Both cowslips and primroses are harbingers of spring; *Primula* comes from *primavera,* the Latin word for spring.

COOKING
Young leaves of cowslips and primroses are good in springtime salads. Flowers can be added too and are pretty as a garnish. It is best to remove the flowers from the calyxes; a process called 'pipping'. As

PRIMULA VERIS

can be imagined, many hundreds of 'pips' are needed for candying or making wine. The old-fashioned dessert known as primrose pottage is a mixture of ground rice, white wine, honey and flaked almonds, to which are added a few strands of saffron and the chopped yellow petals of primroses.

HEALING
Primroses and cowslips have very similar properties but the latter are favoured by herbalists today. The root eases bronchial congestion and catarrh; the leaves have a similar action but are weaker. Cowslip flowers are mildly sedative, relaxing and anti-inflammatory, helping to relieve sleeplessness and allergies. They were traditionally made into cowslip wine, which was taken as a nervine. Cowslip tea is another option.

NOTES FOR GARDENERS
Even the smallest garden has room for a primrose or cowslip. They make perfect container plants too. For culinary or medicinal use plant the true species, but keep them well apart or they will

Primula vulgaris

hybridize and produce polyanthus. They can be grown from seed, sown when ripe and left over winter in a cold frame. Alternatively, buy 'plugs' from a wildflower centre that supplies plants of known provenance – so that you can find out from the grower exactly where the seed came from. In this way, you can avoid introducing unsuitable strains into your area.

Prunella vulgaris   SELF-HEAL

PORTRAIT

A creeping, aromatic perennial, reaching 20cm (8in) high, with four-angled stems and small, dark green, oval leaves. From summer into autumn it sends up squat spikes of two-lipped purple flowers that emerge over several weeks from brownish bracts. Self-heal is a grassland plant that occurs in meadows and woodland clearings, and in more urban settings in grass verges. It has a wide

PRUNELLA VULGARIS

distribution in Europe and many temperate areas of Asia and North Africa, so is a familiar herb in many different cultures. Either deliberately or by chance, it was introduced to North America and Australia, where it has joined ranks with the native flora. The closely related *P. grandiflora* (large self-heal), another European species, is less common and, though little used as a herb, probably has similar properties.

HISTORY

According to John Gerard, whose *Herball* dates from 1597, 'There is not a better Wound herbe in the world than that of Self-Heale', and in the seventeenth century, in a matter-of-fact way, Culpeper explained that it is called self-heal because 'when you are hurt, you may heal yourself'. Other versions of the name, all-heal and cure-all, convey the same message. Though self-heal has a very long history of use as a wound herb in European herbal medicine, it is used quite differently in China. First recorded in Chinese medical literature during the Han Dynasty (206BC–AD23), self-heal – or *xu ku cao* as it is known to Chinese herbalists – is used for conditions associated with 'liver fire'. The name *Prunella* is an alternative spelling of *Brunella*, from the German *Bräune*, quinsy – a throat infection for which self-heal was once the standard treatment.

COOKING

Self-heal's little leaves are perfectly edible in a salad of mixed greens. They can also be used fresh or dried as a herb tea, either on their own, or blended with other herbs.

HEALING

Though undoubtedly an effective herb, self-heal has fallen by the wayside in western herbal medicine. It is nevertheless a useful first-aid herb for healing cuts and bruises, and minor burns. Another way of using it is as a gargle for sore throats, and as a mouthwash for bleeding gums or mouth ulcers. In China it is a different story. There it remains an important medicinal herb for treating acute conjunctivitis, swollen glands in the neck, mastitis and various other manifestations of weak liver energy. In addition, research has shown that self-heal goes some way to lowering blood pressure, and has antibiotic effects against certain organisms that cause enteritis and urinary infections.

NOTES FOR GARDENERS

In moist conditions, whether in borders, gravel paths, or between paving stones, self-heal tends to take over, rooting as it goes and sowing itself far and wide. A better place for it is in the wildflower meadow, where companion grasses will keep it in check. Propagation is very easy from seed sown in either autumn or spring, or by division. There is a white-flowered form that is less commonplace and would make a good foil for wild strawberries or primroses.

Pueraria lobata   JAPANESE ARROWROOT
KUDZU VINE

PORTRAIT

A rampant, deciduous, twining climber, up to 20m (70ft) or more, with huge tuberous roots, densely hairy new shoots and trifoliate leaves. Each leaflet is slightly angular in shape, the centre one reaching 18cm (7in) long. Purple pea-like flowers, 2cm (1in) long, are produced in erect clusters in late summer and early autumn. They are showy and fragrant, smelling rather like grapes. After flowering, flat hairy pods, about 5cm (2in) long, start to form. Kudzu is native to China, Japan, and Korea, where it occurs in sparse woodland and thickets. It is frost hardy and often survives outdoors in cold areas if given a sheltered spot or some protection at ground level.

HISTORY

This extremely useful plant has an unfortunate history. It was introduced to the United States from Japan in the 1870s, following its promotion as a high-yielding food, fodder and fibre crop. Another potential role was in erosion control, and for this purpose it was widely planted by the Soil Erosion Service in 1933. Ten years later, kudzu had spread over some 500,000 acres of south-eastern America. Battles to eradicate, or at least control it, continue to this day. On the other hand, kudzu has an ancient and distinguished record as a culinary and medicinal herb, long used in Japanese cuisine and first mentioned in Chinese medical literature some 2,000 years ago.

COOKING

Kudzu root is the source of a very fine starch, known as Japanese arrowroot, that is used in Japanese cuisine for thickening sauces and soups, making noodles and crispy coatings for tempura, and as a gelling agent. It is easier to make fruit jellies using kudzu than with gelatin, as the powder is simply sprinkled into boiling fruit juice; it dissolves readily and sets quickly as the liquid cools – and of course it is vegetarian. The actual roots are sometimes eaten as a vegetable, or used to make a sweetish stock for soups. Young leaves and shoots are also eaten in a variety of ways.

HEALING

Known in Chinese herbal medicine as *ge gen*, kudzu root is a classic remedy for measles, headaches due to high blood pressure and for the aches associated with fever. It also has a long history of use in China, and in traditional Vietnamese medicine, as a cure for inebriation and alcoholism. Research has shown that it contains chemicals, daidzin and daidzein, which appear to suppress the

PUERARIA LOBATA

craving for alcohol. In traditional Chinese medicine it was prescribed with chrysanthemum flowers to treat hangovers and alcohol poisoning, as well as alcoholism itself. Clinical trials in China have also shown that extracts of kudzu roots lower blood pressure and help control angina.

NOTES FOR GARDENERS

Gardeners in parts of the United States will never accept that any sane person would want to grow a kudzu vine. However, sensibly sited and in the right conditions, controlled by winter chill and a cool growing season, it is more attractive as a fast-growing climber than the Russian vine (*Fallopia baldschuanica*), and though it's just as likely to drive you to drink, at least it provides a hangover remedy for the 'morning after'. Propagating kudzu is done by seed, sown in spring after soaking it in water for 24 hours, or by layering, or by dividing the rootstock. Once planted, stand back, as it can grow 10m (35ft) a year. It tolerates most soils, and drought, and is at its most rampant in a rich sandy loam. Growing it strictly as an annual is a good strategy; moving or eradicating an established plant is difficult, as any pieces of the root left in the ground will sprout.

Punica granatum POMEGRANATE

PORTRAIT

A large deciduous shrub or small tree, sometimes spiny, with glossy, narrowly oblong leaves up to 8cm (3in) long. It can reach 6m (20ft) tall and 5m (15ft) wide, but is commonly half this size. Scarlet funnel-shaped flowers, about 4cm (1½in) across, with rumpled petals and matching scarlet calyxes, appear over a long period in summer, followed by spherical, often red-flushed fruits some 12cm (5in) in diameter, which have a thin, yellow-brown, shell-like rind and numerous seeds, each enclosed in a bead of juicy pink flesh. Pomegranates grow wild from south-east Europe to the Himalayas.

HISTORY

The legendary apple that tempted Adam in the Garden of Eden was probably a pomegranate. This round, mouth-watering, seed-filled fruit has been a symbol of fertility since earliest times in

PUNICA GRANATUM

Mediterranean regions and especially among Jewish people. In the Temple of Solomon it represented the future. In ancient Egypt, five pomegranate trees were planted in the garden of Ineni, chief builder to the pharoah Tuthmosis I (1528–1510BC), at Thebes, and pomegranates feature in tomb paintings. The first mention of pomegranate rind as a remedy for tapeworms was made in the Ebers papyri, dating from around 1500BC. The pomegranate reached China from Kabul, the capital of Afghanistan, in 126BC and, being the auspicious colour red, soon became a popular fruit for ceremonies and festivals.

COOKING

Pomegranate fruits, separated into individual fruitlets, are a favourite Middle Eastern ingredient of salads and desserts. The juice is equally important, both as the syrup grenadine, and as a thick paste or molasses, which is often used in Middle Eastern cooking as a flavouring for meat dishes. Even the dried seeds have their uses as an ingredient in stuffings and chutneys. Dried with the surrounding aril, seeds of the western Himalayan variety 'Daru' are used as a condiment known as *anardana*.

HEALING

Pomegranate bark and fruit rind contain very poisonous alkaloids that cause tapeworms to detach from the gut wall. If the dose is followed promptly by a strong laxative, such as cascara, the parasites are then voided. This remedy was know to the ancients – the Greek physician Dioscorides described it in the first century AD – and then inexplicably fell into disuse in Europe until the days of the British Empire, when an Indian herbalist successfully cured an Englishman of tapeworms and attracted the interest of doctors serving in India. Roundworms and pinworms are similarly susceptible. The bark and rind are also highly astringent, and in carefully measured doses have been used to control diarrhoea. Even more carefully calculated doses are needed for worming treatments.

NOTES FOR GARDENERS

Pomegranates need long hot summers and warm autumns for successful fruiting, and a cool winter in which to become dormant and lose their leaves. In areas with a Mediterranean climate, they can be grown outdoors as specimen trees or as hedging; where they are grown commercially there are many different varieties to choose from. Elsewhere, full-sized pomegranate trees are not a realistic proposition for the garden. Having said this, older trees are hardier than youngsters, so an imported mature specimen – perhaps as a centrepiece for a sheltered courtyard garden – might be worth the extra expenditure. Failing this, more modest-sized specimens can be grown as container plants and kept frost free in winter. The dwarf variety, *nana*, is ideal for pots and especially for bonsai techniques, slowly reaching 90cm (3ft) or more. At the other end of the scale, try growing your own pomegranate using seeds, cleaned and dried, from a supermarket fruit; sow in spring at 13–18°C (55–61°F). Faster results are from semi-ripe cuttings.

Rheum palmatum — CHINESE RHUBARB

PORTRAIT

A robust perennial with a huge rootstock and stout red-green stalks, bearing umbrella-sized palmate leaves, jaggedly cut into between three and nine pointed lobes. In summer a tall spire of tiny star-shaped, greenish-cream to dark red flowers is produced, reaching 2.5m (8ft) in height. Chinese rhubarb is native to north-western China and north-east Tibet, where it grows in damp areas on the edges of woodland.

HISTORY

In the days before antibiotics, the cure for most ills was a purgative, such as rhubarb root. Chinese rhubarb was a major item in world trade by ancient Greek times, and was often called Turkey rhubarb because it came overland via Turkey. Trade was controlled by the Chinese and Russians through the Kiakhta Rhubarb Commission on the border between Siberia and Mongolia. The monopoly was so successful that it took until 1762 for Europeans to obtain living plants and begin cultivating their own supplies. Such importance was attached to the plant that large acreages were devoted to its cultivation; eighteenth-century plans of the Royal Botanic Garden in Edinburgh, then a physic garden, show a greater area devoted to Chinese rhubarb than to any other medicinal herb. As the Commission lost its stranglehold, it was finally abolished in 1782.

A.M. 3267ᶻ -'56.

V.A.M.

HEALING

Rhubarb roots have been used as a laxative for 2,000 years and remain important in medicine generally, prescribed by both herbalists and mainstream doctors alike. *Rheum palmatum* is the most important species but *R. officinale* is also used; the hybrid rhubarb grown for its edible stems is not used medicinally. The roots contain laxative anthraquinones and tannins; in small doses the latter have a constipating effect, so, as with any herb, the correct dose is most important. In addition to its laxative effect, rhubarb root, in the form of a decoction or tincture, is a good digestive stimulant and makes a useful lotion for burns.

NOTES FOR GARDENERS

Rheum palmatum is an outstandingly handsome plant for a large border or beside a pond. In spring the tightly crumpled new leaves emerge from bulbous red bracts and unfurl like a giant butterfly, almost before your eyes, and for weeks in summer the flower spikes provide an architectural feature. The only disadvantage may be its size, as mature plants need a good 2m (6ft) of elbow room. For

RHEUM PALMATUM

an even more spectacular effect, plant the variety 'Atrosanguineum', which has bronze new leaves and cherry-red flowers. Chinese rhubarb is a very hardy and tolerant plant but does best in moist, deep, humus-rich soil and a sunny position. Propagation is easiest by division in spring, though seed can be collected and sown when ripe.

Rosa species

ROSE

PORTRAIT

Rosa canina (dog rose) is a scrambling hedgerow shrub, reaching 3m (10ft), with very thorny, arching stems, small, single, shell pink to white flowers, and scarlet, egg-shaped hips. Sweetbriar (*R. rubiginosa*) is similar, with apple-scented foliage and brighter pink flowers. Both grow wild in Europe, western Asia and North Africa. The Middle Eastern damask rose, *R.* x *damascena*, is a vigorous shrub with grey-green leaves and semi-double pale pink flowers. The French rose, *R. gallica*, is an upright shrub, found from southern and central Europe to the Caucasus. It bears leathery, dark green leaves, and single or semi-double, pink to deep pink flowers. The variety *officinalis*, known as the apothecary's rose, has semi-double crimson flowers. The Japanese rose (*R. rugosa*), from eastern Asia, is a densely prickly shrub with deeply veined leaves, and single, magenta-pink to white flowers, followed by bright red, globose hips. All are fragrant.

ROSA CANINA

ROSA GALLICA 'VERSICOLOR'

HISTORY

The rose was first described as 'queen of flowers' by the Greek poetess Sappho in 600BC, but long before this roses were cultivated in ancient Persia and Egypt. A bunch of roses was found in the tomb of Tutankhamun, possibly placed there by his young wife as a symbol of love. Just as they are today, roses were worn by Roman brides and bridegrooms, and used to adorn images of the gods Cupid and Venus. Rose water was first made by the Persian physician Avicenna (AD980–1037), and distillation of roses, to produce otto or attar of roses, began in Persia in the late sixteenth century. The apothecary's rose probably reached France from Syria in about 1240 and was named *officinalis* as it was grown mainly for medicinal purposes (an *officina* was an apothecary's shop).

During the fifteenth-century Civil War ('War of the Roses') in England, the red rose was adopted by the House of Lancaster and the white rose by the House of York. The striped York and Lancaster rose, *R.* x *damascena* var. *versicolor*, dates from around the time that Henry VII ascended the throne in 1485, uniting the two factions.

COOKING

Rose petals are used to flavour tea, wine, vinegar and sugar, are made into jelly, and crystallized. Middle Eastern cuisine is especially fond of rose-flavoured desserts and treats, such as Turkish delight, and rosebuds are an ingredient of the spice mix known as *ras el hanout.*

BEAUTY

Rose oil and rose water are soothing, exquisitely scented astringents, widely used in skin-care products; old-fashioned 'cold cream' originally contained both. It takes a thousand roses to produce a pint of rose water, and 1 tonne (0.98 tons) of petals yields a mere 300g (11oz) of essential oil. Two of the finest roses for perfumery are 'Professeur Emile Perrot' (to which the names 'Kazanlik' and *R. x damascena* 'Trigintipetala' are also applied), and 'Gloire de Guilan'. Bulgarian rose attar is distilled mainly from *R. x damascena* and *R. alba.* Almost all women's perfumes contain rose oil, as do a surprising 42 per cent of men's fragrances. Seeds of sweet briar and the South American *mosqueta* (*R. rubirinova*) contain an oil rich in essential fatty acids (EFAs) that encourage tissue regeneration; it has anti-wrinkle and hydrating properties and reduces scarring.

HEALING

Red rose petals were listed in the British Pharmacopoeia until 1934 as an astringent and flavouring for medicines but are little used today. In traditional Chinese medicine, *R. rugosa* flowers (*mei gui hua*) are sometimes used as a tonic for liver energy, and as an antidote to antimony poisoning. Rose oil is important in aromatherapy as a tonic for the womb and sexual organs, and to tone the circulatory and digestive systems. It has sedative, anti-depressant and, of course, aphrodisiac effects. In practice, any rose can be used medicinally, though the most fragrant deep pink varieties are preferred. Rose hips (mainly from *R. canina* and *R. rugosa*) are very rich in vitamin C and widely used in food supplements and remedies for coughs and colds.

NOTES FOR GARDENERS

Though many roses prefer heavy, even clay soils, some thrive in light, sandy soils. *Rosa gallica* occurs in sandy meadows and dunes, and *R. rugosa* grows wild on seashores, tolerating very sandy, saline conditions and salt spray. For medicinal purposes, plant *R. gallica* var. *officinalis*, but for culinary purposes any very fragrant pink or red rose will do. *Rosa gallica* retains its fragrance well, even when dried, and is excellent for teas and pot-pourris. The climbing, flesh-pink tea rose 'Belle Portugaise' has a particularly good flavour for desserts and confectionery. *Rosa rugosa* is multi-purpose, with superb flowers and hips for all uses.

Rosmarinus officinalis   ROSEMARY

PORTRAIT

Rosemary is a very variable, conifer-like shrub with intensely aromatic, evergreen, needle-shaped foliage and pale blue flowers that appear in spring, or earlier in mild climates. Wild plants on Mediterranean coasts reach about 1.5m (5ft) and fill the air with fragrance. Some botanists consider there are two species: *R. officinalis*, common rosemary; and *R. eriocalyx*, also known as

Rosa Gallica Aurelianensis.   *La Duchesse d'Orléans.*

P. J. Redouté.   *Langlois.*

R. lavandulaceus or Prostratus Group, which has small leaves and a sprawling or creeping habit. The latter is confined to southern Spain and North Africa, and is consequently more tender.

HISTORY

Traditionally associated with memory and fidelity – in the words of Shakespeare's Ophelia: 'There's rosemary, that's for remembrance; pray, love, remember' – rosemary has featured in both weddings and funerals since ancient Egyptian times. The word *Rosmarinus* means 'dew of the sea', an apt name for a coastal plant dedicated to Venus or Aphrodite, the goddess of love who rose from the sea. According to John Evelyn, the seventeenth-century diarist, the flowers 'are credibly reported to give their scent above 30 leagues off at sea'. Hungary water made from rosemary dates from medieval times when, so the story goes, a hermit divulged the recipe to the elderly Queen Izabella of Hungary who was crippled with rheumatism and gout. After a year of use, she was restored to such health and beauty that the King of Poland proposed to her. More simply, according to Banke's herbal, dated 1525, 'smell of it oft, and it shall keep thee youngly'.

ROSMARINUS OFFICINALIS

COOKING

Rosemary is a strongly flavoured herb and the leaves are quite tough, so care is needed in its use. A sprig is usually sufficient, placed on top of the dish or as a bed for grilled or barbecued meat and removed before serving. Its pungency is a match for roasted Mediterranean vegetables, lamb and any dish in which red wine and garlic predominate. Finely chopped rosemary works well as a flavouring in biscuits, both sweet and savoury. Most bouquet garnis contain rosemary and in Italy sprigs are often included with meat from the butcher. The flowers have a much more delicate flavour and are good in salads accompanying smoked meats. Different kinds of rosemary can vary considerably in flavour. Choose varieties with an appetizing aroma, such as 'Arp', 'Gorizia' and 'Tuscan Blue'; those with a high camphor content are better suited to medicinal use.

BEAUTY

The camphoraceous oils in rosemary stimulate the skin's circulation, ensuring that tissues are well supplied with nutrients and cleansed of waste products. It is particularly good for the scalp and

America *R. fruticosus* and *R. idaeus* are replaced by a range of indigenous species that were similarly important as food and medicine for native people. These include *R. laciniatus*, the evergreen or cut-leafed blackberry that gave rise to the popular cultivated blackberry, 'Oregon Thornless'. The berries of all kinds are nutritious, being rich in vitamins A, C and BI, fruit acids, sugars and pectin, while the roots and foliage contain astringent tannins that have many different applications medicinally.

COOKING

Apart from the obvious uses as fresh, cooked or preserved fruits, raspberries provide the basis for a raspberry liqueur, and are used to flavour wine vinegar and fruit-flavoured Belgian and German beers. Blackberries are less widely used as a flavouring, but are a favourite colouring for red wine; they also make an excellent red country wine, either on their own, or mixed with elderberries. The leaves of both can be dried for tea; blackberry leaves are widely used in blended herb teas.

RUBUS FRUTICOSUS

HEALING

Blackberry and raspberry leaves and roots are good general astringents that have a tightening effect on mucous membranes and help to dry up discharges and excess fluids. The kinds of problems that benefit from astringent remedies are diarrhoea, haemorrhoids, eye, mouth and throat inflammations, minor wounds and burns, sores and ulcers. In addition, raspberry leaves are a traditional tonic, taken during the last ten weeks of pregnancy to strengthen the uterine muscles so that they contract more forcefully during labour. Raspberry juice or syrup is a traditional flavouring for medicines, and blackberry juice, with lemon and honey, is a good cold remedy.

NOTES FOR GARDENERS

Raspberries and blackberries need moisture-retentive, humus-rich soil to give of their best, and may need netting during the fruiting period if you are to beat the birds; otherwise they are undemanding and can be grown in either sun or part-shade. Give some thought to the choice of varieties, and plant and prune according to the advice of the grower or gardening manual; if neglected, they become an impenetrable and less productive thicket. There are numerous varieties of raspberry that, chosen judiciously, will keep you in fruit from early summer until the first frosts, together with yellow- and purple-fruited kinds to provide novelty. The choice of blackberries is increasing yearly as more selection and breeding takes place. 'Merton Thornless' is particularly good for small spaces, being compact as well as thornless and producing very large, well-flavoured fruits.

Rumex species   SORREL & DOCK

PORTRAIT

Sorrel (*R. acetosa*) is a clump-forming perennial with bright green, oval leaves up to 14cm (5½in) long, which are arrow-shaped where they join the stalk. In summer, tall flowering stems appear, terminating in loose spikes of small, red-green flowers. It reaches 60cm–1.2m (2–4ft) when

RUMEX SCUTATUS

RUMEX ACETOSA

flowering. French sorrel (*R. scutatus*) is smaller and mat-forming, no more than 50cm (20in) tall, with heart-shaped to arrow-shaped leaves 1–5cm (½–2in) long. The flowers are typical, but smaller and more delicate in effect than those of common sorrel. Sheep's sorrel (*R. acetosella*) is even more slender, with narrow, arrow-shaped leaves and rusty red flowers. It forms large colonies on dry, bare, acid soil. Curled dock (*R. crispus*) is a coarse, very variable perennial with a stout taproot and narrowly oblong leaves up to 30cm (12in) long. The leaves are four to five times as long as broad, and have noticeably wavy or crinkled margins. Small green flowers are produced in simple spikes that bear small, very crinkled leaves where they branch. Sorrels and docks occur widely in most temperate regions.

HISTORY

In the British Isles, dock or docken leaves have been picked and held to the skin to soothe nettle stings since time immemorial. Eating dock leaves apparently cured Julius Caesar's soldiers of scurvy; they knew the plant as *herba britannica*. Sorrel has always been known as a cleansing herb.

463

RVMICIS
TERTIVM GENVS.

Guter Heinrich.

q 4

Martin Martin, the seventeenth-century physician and author of *A Description of the Western Isles of Scotland*, recorded how he advised St Kildan to lose weight by eating sorrel – a remedy that apparently had dramatic results within a few days.

COOKING

Sorrel leaves add a pleasant acid flavour to salads, soups, sauces and omelettes. Pureed, they can be used to stuff oily fish or to make a tangy, green mayonnaise. French sorrel and sheep's sorrel are more acidic and therefore used in smaller quantities for the same purposes. Young dock leaves are edible though may need boiling in two changes of water to reduce bitterness. Docks and sorrels contain oxalic acid which is toxic in excess, encouraging the formation of kidney stones; they should be avoided by anyone with a history of this problem.

HEALING

Curled dock is a key medicinal herb; the roots are used to cleanse the tissues of toxins that build up through poor digestion and elimination. An overburden of toxins is implicated in many chronic conditions, from arthritic and rheumatic complaints to skin problems and fungal infections. Curled dock has a laxative effect and stimulates the bile ducts, removing toxins and improving the digestive process from start to finish. Common sorrel and French sorrel are not much used medicinally. Far more important is sheep's sorrel, which is an ingredient of essiac, a native American cancer remedy that also includes burdock (*Arctium lappa*), Chinese rhubarb (see p.244), and slippery elm (*Ulmus rubra*). It too is a detoxifying, laxative herb that also has diuretic effects.

NOTES FOR GARDENERS

Rather than plant wild sorrel, which goes to seed rapidly after its first flush of tender new leaves, search for improved varieties, such as 'Profusion', a non-flowering clone that can be harvested right through the growing season, and even in mild spells during the winter. French sorrel is more ornamental as a garden plant, especially in the silver-leafed form, 'Silver Shield', although it is still invasive. Sheep's sorrel is available as seed or plants from wildflower specialists. Sorrels can be multiplied by dividing in autumn or spring. Curled dock is a pernicious weed; some herbalists grow it to ensure good quality, organic roots, but it has no virtues (and plenty of vices) as a garden plant. Never let it self-seed.

Ruta graveolens   RUE

PORTRAIT

Rue is a rounded, evergreen shrub with blue-green leaves up to 15cm (6in) long, which are neatly dissected into tiny oval lobes. They have a powerful aroma that is hard to describe but bears some resemblance to wet paint. The foliage is far prettier than the small, drab yellow, four-petalled flowers that appear in summer. Rue bushes grow wild in dry sunny, often rocky hillsides, and even in walls, in Mediterranean regions. Egyptian or fringed rue, R. chalapensis, is similar in appearance, but with more finely divided foliage and a more southerly distribution into north-eastern Africa and south-western Asia.

HISTORY

Mithridates, a member of the Alexandrian School of Medicine which was established in Egypt in about 300BC, regarded rue as one of the most effective antidotes to poisons. Rue has also been revered as a protection against evil since classical times; in particular, it was thought to safeguard the eyesight. These beliefs were long-lived; John Gerard, the sixteenth-century English herbalist, wrote: 'When the Weesell is to fight with the Serpent, she armeth her selfe by eating Rue', and John Milton, in *Paradise Lost*, refers to the Angel cleansing Adam's sight with 'Euphrasy and Rue' (euphrasy or eyebright, *Euphrasia officinalis*, was another important herb for the eyes).

During the Great Plague of London (1664–5), court rooms were strewn with rue to protect judge and jury against infection and it was an ingredient of Four Thieves Vinegar, which allowed a notorious band of robbers to plunder plague victims without catching the disease. Well into the eighteenth century, posies of rue were carried against jail fever and fleas. Another of rue's common names is 'herb of grace' or 'herbygrass', because sprigs of rue were once used to sprinkle holy water over the congregation during services. Shakespeare mentions it a number of times in this context.

RUTA GRAVEOLENS

COOKING

There is some equivocation about the use of rue as a culinary herb. The strong, bitter flavour is difficult to match with foods, though the chopped leaves are sometimes recommended as an addition to salads. Traditionally, sprigs of rue are steeped in *grappa*, the Italian grape spirit, and the seeds are used to flavour palm wine and various spice mixes in North Africa. Egyptian rue is less bitter. it is added to *merguez* (lamb and beef sausages).

HEALING

Rue is a very poisonous plant and no longer much used in herbal medicine. It contains alkaloids, volatile oil and flavonoids, including rutin, which is well known for its effectiveness in strengthening capillaries and reducing blood pressure – so rue may well be good for the eyes. A less beneficial effect is that it stimulates the uterus and in the past has been used to induce abortion; fatalities have occurred as a result. Records show that over the ages rue has been used to treat a wide range of conditions, from dyspepsia to multiple sclerosis and hysteria, but the present consensus is that the risks outweigh the benefits. A homeopathic preparation of rue was used in 1818, perfectly safely, by Samuel Hahnemann to treat varicose veins, neuralgia and rheumatism.

NOTES FOR GARDENERS

Rue is grown more for its beauty than its uses, being very tidy in habit and remaining colourful all year. 'Jackman's Blue' is particularly fine, and easily propagated from semi-ripe cuttings in summer (it even roots in water). 'Variegata' is pretty too, with white-splashed foliage and, unusually for variegated plants, comes true from seed. The only note of warning comes with regard to pruning, which is best done as an all-over trim in early spring. Rue is particularly irritant to the skin, sensitizing it to sunlight; the slightest contact on a sunny day will cause blistering. Always wear gloves whenever handling rue; bare legs are vulnerable too, so take care if wearing shorts. Otherwise, rue is undemanding and rewarding as a garden plant, needing nothing much more than well-drained soil and sun.

Salix species

WILLOW

PORTRAIT

White willow, *S. alba*, is a fast-growing tree with deeply fissured, grey-brown bark, and slender, pointed, fish-shaped leaves up to 10cm (4in) long. In spring, as the new leaves open, flowers appear in the form of yellow male catkins about 5cm (2in) long, and smaller, yellow-green female catkins. After flowering the females elongate, releasing fluffy seeds as they ripen in summer. Mature trees reach 25m (80ft) high, with a spread of 10m (30ft). They grow throughout Europe to central Asia and North Africa, mainly in wet ground by rivers, and are brittle, often splitting as a result of storms and lightning strikes.

HISTORY

The use of willow for relieving pain and lowering fever was recorded by Dioscorides in the first century AD when the practice was well established. Clay tablets from the Sumerian period in the fourth millennium BC indicate that willow was a remedy for rheumatism. Likewise in North America, many different tribes used willows medicinally, seldom differentiating between the various species. Willows contain salicylates that have analgesic and anti-inflammatory properties. Work on these compounds began in the early nineteenth century, culminating in the development of acetyl salicylic acid, better known as aspirin, in 1897. Aspirin is the top-selling pill of all time, and probably the cheapest; some 60 billion doses are swallowed every year.

HEALING

Herbalists still use decoctions and tinctures of willow bark to ease aching muscles and joints, and to relieve fevers, headaches and menopausal symptoms, such as hot flushing and night sweats. Poplars (*Populus* species) contain salicylates too, and are used in similar ways. Aspirin meanwhile is enjoying a new lease of life as a wonder drug that reduces the risk of heart attack and strokes. There is evidence too that it may protect against certain kinds of cancer, and Alzheimer's disease.

ALTERVM SALI-
CIS GENVS.

Eeel Weiden.

NOTES FOR GARDENERS

The white willow is less often planted in gardens than its varieties, which are grown for their colourful winter stems. Golden willows (subsp. *vitellina*) have yellow-orange shoots, and in 'Britzensis' the stems are bright orange-red. To get the best from these plants, cut the stems back every year or alternate year in spring (or at least every three years), and feed with well-rotted manure to ensure vigorous new growths. This pruning regime keeps plants at the shrub stage – a manageable size for pond-side planting or as a winter feature, perhaps under-planted with early spring bulbs, in the border.

Salvia species   SAGE

PORTRAIT

Common sage, *S. officinalis*, is a shrubby plant, about 60cm (24in) in height, with velvety oval leaves up to 8cm (3in) long, which are the colour described as sage green. In summer, it produces whorls of purple-blue flowers that prove irresistible to bees. Narrow-leafed sage (*S. lavandulifolia*) and Greek sage (*S. fruticosa*) are closely related and used like commn sage; all are Mediterranean in origin. Clary sage (*S. sclarea*) is a large, sticky-hairy, Eurasian biennial or short-lived perennial, some 1m (3ft) tall. It has oval, grey-green, deeply veined leaves up to 23cm (9in) long, and branched panicles of cream and lilac flowers, accompanied by mauve-pink bracts. Red sage (*S. miltiorhiza*) is a hardy, herbaceous perennial from north-east China, with red roots, dark green leaves divided into three to seven ovate, toothed leaflets, and large, purplish-blue, claw-shaped flowers. It reaches 80cm (32in) high.

HISTORY

Though most familiar as a culinary herb, common sage has been revered as a cure-all and longevity herb since classical times, when it was known as *Salvia salvatrix*, 'sage the saviour'. This reputation gave rise to proverbs, such as 'He that would live for aye [ever] must eat sage in May'. The word 'sage' is synonymous with 'wise', though its origin is more likely the Latin *salvere*, to be safe and well, or saved. Historically, clary or 'clear eye' was important for eye problems; the mucilage obtained from the seeds when soaked in water was used to remove foreign bodies and reduce inflammation. The Chinese, renowned for longevity and sagacity, used to import sage for tea, in exchange for China tea. Red sage, also known as red ginseng, has been used in Chinese medicine for more than 2,000 years.

COOKING

Common sage is a variable species and it is worth comparing the aromas of different plants before using them in cooking. Arguably the best for culinary purposes is not common sage, but narrow-leafed sage, which has a more balsamic flavour. Sage is a good partner for strongly flavoured foods, such as pork with apples and/or mushrooms, liver and bacon, sausages, and stuffings for meat. It goes well with some cheeses too, the classic example being Sage Derby, which is marbled with ground sage leaves. Sage also makes a very pleasant herb tea. On the subject of teas, several Mexican sages, such as *S. hispanica* and *S. columbariae*, are used to make *chia*, a refreshing drink based on the seeds, which are soaked in water to form a gelatinous mass, to which lemon juice or other flavourings are added.

HEALING

Common sage contains volatile oils that are strongly antiseptic, anti-inflammatory and anti-microbial. It is also astringent and relaxes spasms. Used as a gargle or mouthwash, sage tea is a good home remedy for sore throats, mouth ulcers and gum infections. Taken as a tea, sage has a tonic effect on the nervous and digestive systems. For women, its oestrogen content helps regulate hormonal imbalances, especially during the menopause. Sage also has the unusual property of reducing perspiration. Clary sage is less used for eye problems now than for its tonic, relaxing and oestrogenic effects, which are similar to those of common sage. Red sage has hormone-regulating effects, and contains strongly anti-bacterial substances that control infections caused by *Staphylococcus* organisms, such as tonsillitis and infected wounds. In addition, it tonifies the circulatory system, and is specifically used to treat angina. Sages are powerful herbs, toxic in excess, and not to be taken internally during pregnancy. The antioxidant effects of sage are of interest to researchers. Apparently sage inhibits an enzyme that breaks down acetylcholine, a compound that may protect against, or even treat, Alzheimer's.

SALVIA OFFICINALIS

SALVIA OFFICINALIS 'BERGGARTEN'

NOTES FOR GARDENERS

As a garden plant, the most versatile is common sage. It remains neat and colourful all year, and has a wide range of varieties to inspire planting schemes and attractive containers throughout the seasons. Favourites for colour include the purple-leafed 'Purpurascens', yellow-variegated 'Icterina' and 'Tricolor', which has white and pink variegation. White- and pink-flowered forms are available too. For flavour and habit, the robust, large-leafed 'Berggarten' is a winner, and for containers, there is a dwarf form. Clary is a striking ornamental and though short-lived, often self-sows obligingly. The form known as *turkestanica* produces a colourful, long-lasting display of pink-bracted flowers, while 'Vatican White' is an ethereal plant for dark backgrounds and shafts of early or late sunlight. A well-grown flowering plant of red sage attracts attention; when not in flower you would be hard-pressed to recognize it as a sage. All sages like well-drained soil; red sage seems to need more moisture than most. The species are easily propagated from seed sown in spring, while varieties should be increased by softwood or semi-ripe cuttings, early or late in the growing season, respectively.

Herbal Seeds

Oryza sativa

Hordeum vulgare

SEEDS ARE A MIRACLE OF PACKAGING. However small, they contain all the genetic information and nutrients needed for the growth of a new plant, together with a programme that maintains dormancy until conditions are right for germination.

It is no coincidence that many animals, ourselves included, rely on seeds for food. By definition seeds store well, and are powerhouses of complex nutrients — starches, proteins, vitamins, minerals, fats and oils. Every major human civilization has been founded on a successful agricultural system that produced surplus grain — rice, wheat, oats, maize (corn) — to sustain the population through periods of scarcity.

Seeds also contain various chemicals, such as volatile oils. In some cases these compounds have healing properties that give seeds added value in our diets.

Seeds of pumpkin (*Cucurbita maxima*) and orange-fleshed winter squash (*C. moschata*) are rich in vitamin E, which stops their oils turning rancid. By eating them, we can utilize this anti-oxidant effect to prevent the formation of free radicals that accelerate ageing, especially of the skin. Pumpkin seeds are also a good source of zinc, which is vital for glossy hair, resilient skin and, in men, for prostate health. On the medicinal side, pumpkin seeds contain cucurbitacins that rid the body of intestinal parasites — a traditional remedy for tapeworms, safe for children and pregnant women.

At the green grass stage, barley (*Hordeum vulgare*) has been described as the perfect food, containing all the necessary nutrients to sustain life. Fortunately, it is available juiced, or dried and ground as a tonic supplement, so we do not have to much our way through barley grass like a cow. This humble grain has been cultivated since 4000BC, and though more often fed to animals or malted and brewed into beer, it is a superb food for the human body. Roman gladiators were nicknamed *hordearii*, 'barley eaters', because they ate barley for strength and stamina. Research in the 1990s showed that it can help regulate blood sugar and cholesterol levels, prevent cancer and degenerative conditions, and control *Candida* infection.

Nuts may be high in calories, but they contain calories with a difference. Regular consumption of nuts is linked with lower rates of circulatory disorders, diabetes, cancer and Parkinson's disease. For optimum value, buy nuts that have been shelled but left whole (the oils in slivered, chopped or damaged nuts soon become rancid) and store them in the fridge or freezer. Walnuts (*Juglans nigra*) are a rich source of omega-3 fatty acids, which are anti-inflammatory and reduce the risk of heart disease. Walnut oil, pressed from the seeds, tastes wonderful in salad dressings, and even small amounts maintain coronary health. Almonds (*Prunus dulcis*) contain mono-

SIMMONDSIA CHINENSIS

unsaturated fat, rich in oleic and linoleic acids that lower cholesterol levels. Almond oil is almost odourless, and is used extensively in cosmetics and skin-care products. It conditions the skin and is readily absorbed.

Macadamia nuts (*Macadamia* spp.) contain 80 per cent mono-unsaturated fats and palmitoleic acid, a substance found in skin that maintains moisture and elasticity, making macadamia oil a valuable ingredient of moisturizers and anti-wrinkle creams. Being edible, it is often used in lip balms.

Jojoba (*Simmondsia chinensis*) is a shrub of American deserts with olive-shaped seeds that yield a unique liquid wax. A high proportion of products for dry skin and hair, as well as soaps, sunscreens, massage oils and pharmaceutical creams contain jojoba oil, which has exceptional conditioning properties.

Sesame (*Sesamum indicum*) is a tropical annual that bears very small, shiny, cream to brown seeds, which contain 45 per cent protein and 55 per cent oil. Sesame oil is rich in vitamin E and extremely resistant to oxidation. Consumption of seeds and oil is associated with longevity and the oil is also used as a conditioner in hair and skin products.

Some seeds are important as spices, containing essential oils that give them a supercharged flavour and aroma. Anise (*Pimpinella anisum*) is an unspectacular plant with tiny seeds that contain between 70 and 90 per cent anethole. Though now in competition with synthetic anethole and cheaper sources of aniseed flavours, such as star anise (*Illicium verum*), anise is still essential for liqueurs such as anisette, and aperitifs like pastis, ouzo, raki and arak. Anise extracts are warming, stimulant, reputedly aphrodisiac (for women), and good for indigestion, liver function and respiratory tract infections. They are often added to herbal cough remedies and laxatives.

SESAMUM INDICUM

Cocoa 'beans' (*Theobroma cacao*) have a complex chemistry, containing more than 300 compounds, including stimulant alkaloids, such as caffeine and theobromine, and substances known as tetrahydro-beta-carbolines, which are also found in alcohol and may be responsible for 'chocoholism'. Today, chocolate is probably the world's favourite flavour. The beans are fermented, roasted and ground to make a solid, which is then hot-pressed to remove the 'butter', leaving cocoa powder. Cocoa butter is important in cosmetics (especially lipsticks), skin products and various pharmaceutical preparations, such as suppositories. It is non-irritant and combines particularly well with powders to make pastes and creams.

See also: *Anethum graveolens, Carum carvi, Coriandrum sativum, Cuminum cyminum, Daucus carota, Foeniculum vulgare, Linum usitatissimum, Oenothera biennis, Papaver* species, *Piper nigrum, Silybum marianum, Sinapis alba, Trigonella foenum-graecum, Zanthoxylum piperitum.*

ILLICIUM VERUM

Sambucus nigra   ELDER

PORTRAIT

Elder bushes occur widely in Europe, North Africa, and south-west Asia. They are upright shrubs or multi-stemmed small trees, reaching about 6m (20ft) high, with arching, corky grey-brown branches and strong-smelling, pinnate leaves up to 25cm (10in) long, divided into five, sometimes seven, oval, pointed leaflets. Tiny cream flowers, with a scent similar to muscatel wine, are borne in flattened umbels up to 20cm (8in) across, in early summer, followed by small, spherical black berries.

HISTORY

The elder is a tree of contrasts. It was once planted in the courtyards of synagogues in Israel, possibly for use in rituals of the Jewish cabbala, while in the British Isles, before the days of indoor sanitation, it was traditionally grown next to the privy to deter flies. The young wood is brittle and

filled with soft pith that can be hollowed out to make blowpipes or simple musical instruments. Old wood is almost as hard as metal, and was once used by cobblers to make nails for the soles of shoes. According to Scandinavian folklore, one should never harvest or cut an elder without first asking the elder tree mother, Hylde-Moer. This is just one of the many superstitions connected to this important plant that has been called 'the medicine chest of the people'.

BEAUTY

Elderflowers are the basis for soothing anti-inflammatory lotions and creams that are especially good for chapped and irritated skin, or as an aftershave. Cold elderflower tea bags can be used to soothe tired or sore eyes, and sunburn.

COOKING

Fresh elderflower clusters make delicious fritters. Stripped from their stalks, the blossoms are made into cordials, wine, and 'champagne', and are used to flavour desserts and jams (they go very well with both gooseberries and rhubarb). The dried flowers make a classic herb tea. Raw elderberries should not be eaten as the seeds contain an unpleasant-tasting, poisonous alkaloid. When cooked and sieved, elderberries are superb as ingredients for wine, chutneys, ketchups, sauces, jams, jellies and syrups. They are also mixed with other fruits to make pies and desserts. The juice has often been used to colour red wine and port.

HEALING

All parts have medicinal uses: roots and bark are purgative; an ointment of the leaves heals chilblains and bruises; juice from the vitamin-rich, mildly laxative berries, mixed with lemon juice and honey, is a detoxicant for rheumatism, skin diseases and respiratory infections; and the flowers lower fever, and relieve symptoms of colds, flu and catarrh. Herbalists use mainly the flower heads in infusions and tinctures to strengthen the respiratory system in catarrh and hay-fever sufferers.

NOTES FOR GARDENERS

Elders are easy to please, needing only moist soil in sun or dappled shade. There are some wonderful varieties for the garden, such as 'Aurea', one of the best of all golden-leaved shrubs, 'Black Beauty', which has black-purple foliage and pink flowers, and the finely cut parsley-leafed form, *laciniata*. Others include the yellow-variegated 'Aureomarginata', white-margined 'Marginata', and 'Pulverulenta', which has white-dotted leaves. The only drawback to elders as foliage plants is that they produce the largest, showiest leaves after hard pruning, which is at the expense of flowers and fruit. It is, however, a balance worth achieving, as these are some of the most attractive, useful shrubs you can plant.

Sanguinaria canadensis

BLOODROOT
PUCCOON

PORTRAIT

A small woodland perennial from eastern North America, with red-fleshed rhizomes and grey-green, heart-shaped to kidney-shaped, scalloped leaves 15–30cm (6–12in) across. Solitary cup-shaped white flowers, about 8cm (3in) across, sometimes pink-tinged, emerge in early spring as the new leaves unfold.

HISTORY

Bloodroot is a member of the poppy family, Papaveraceae, and in common with many poppies contains a number of toxic alkaloids. It was traditionally used by various North American tribes to induce therapeutic or ritual vomiting. When the rhizomes are cut or broken, they ooze blood-like juice that was used for body painting and to dye implements red. The name 'puccoon' is of Algonquian origin; other common names include redroot, bloodwort and Red Indian paint. This interesting herb was listed as an expectorant in the *United States Pharmacopoeia* from 1820 to 1926. In *The Housekeeper's Guide*, 1854, it was recommended as a 'Preventive of Bilious Fever', pounded in equal quantities with mandrake root and mixed with molasses.

HEALING

The alkaloids in bloodroot include sanguinarine, which acts as an antiseptic and local anaesthetic, and is a powerful expectorant. It also inhibits formation of dental plaque and is used in oral hygiene products. In herbal medicine, this potent herb is now used mainly to relieve congestion in chronic bronchitis, asthma and whooping cough. It also makes an effective gargle for sore throats, and can be applied in the form of a lotion or ointment to skin infections, such as athlete's foot. The dried, powdered root is a remedy for nasal polyps. As bloodroot induces vomiting in even small amounts, it is not a herb for self-medication, and is not prescribed during pregnancy and lactation, or to patients suffering from glaucoma.

NOTES FOR GARDENERS

This delightful woodlander needs reliably moist, humus-rich soil in shade or dappled shade, or even in deep shade. The flowers of the wild species are delicate and short lived; those of the double form, 'Plena', are larger and last longer. By the time that the flowers have faded, there is more to

SANGUINARIA CANADENSIS

enjoy as the elegantly lobed leaves unfurl. Bloodroot is a good companion for other woodland herbs, such as ginseng, goldenseal, birthroot and blue cohosh, planted perhaps above a ground-hugging mat of bugle. Grouping them together also helps to remind you where they are planted during their long summer dormancy. The best way of propagating bloodroot is by dividing the rhizomes in winter, or immediately after flowering. It can also be grown from seed, sown in pots when ripe and left outdoors to chill, before germinating the following spring.

Saponaria officinalis　　　　　　　　SOAPWORT

PORTRAIT

An upright perennial, reaching 60cm (2ft) high, with narrowly ovate, stalkless leaves 4–7cm (1½–3in) long. From summer to autumn it bears clusters of pale pink flowers, 2cm (1in) across, that resemble miniature single pinks. Plants spread rapidly by rhizomes, forming large, long-lived colonies. Soapwort is native to Europe.

HISTORY

Soapwort is one of many plants worldwide that are rich in saponins (soap-like substances) and were used for cleaning purposes before commercial production of soap began in the 1800s. Saponins are soluble in water and lower the surface tension, producing a lather. Crushing soapwort roots or foliage and shaking them vigorously in warm water creates this effect. Before soap was readily available, housewives made their own cleaning materials, either by using soap-like plants, or by boiling together a basic mixture of grease and wood ash to make soap. Colonies of soapwort or 'fuller's herb' can still be found near old woollen mills, where the plants were originally grown for washing wool. They have also been found on the sites of Roman baths. Soapwort is not, however, a plant of the past; it is still used by museums for cleaning and restoring furniture, pictures and tapestries.

SAPONARIA OFFICINALIS

BEAUTY

Soapwort is used in natural skin and hair-care products for sensitive skin.

HEALING

When swallowed, saponin-rich plants are highly irritant to the gut, which in the right dose has the useful effect of stimulating the coughing reflex. In excess saponins are very poisonous as they destroy red blood cells. Soapwort's main use as a medicinal herb is as an expectorant for bronchial congestion. It is also used as a wash or bath additive for scaly skin eruptions or dry, itchy skin conditions. Homeopaths use soapwort for skin problems too.

NOTES FOR GARDENERS

Growing soapwort is very easy indeed in almost any soil and in sun or semi-shade. Stopping it from taking over the border is more of a challenge, especially if given ideal conditions – moist but well drained, neutral to alkaline soil in a sunny position. Ruthlessly removing runners is the only way to control it. Otherwise, provide stiff competition by way of shrubs or robust perennials. The single-flowered wild soapwort is very pretty, but prettier still are the doubles, in pale pink ('Rosea Plena'), white ('Alba Plena'), or deep pink ('Rubra Plena'), which have showier, longer-lasting flowers. There is a variegated form, 'Dazzler', but it readily reverts, leaving you with the wild species. If soapwort exceeds its bounds in the border, take note of another of its names, hedge pink, and let it naturalize in a hedgerow or wildflower area.

Sassafras albidum   SASSAFRAS

PORTRAIT
A suckering, deciduous tree, reaching 20m (70ft), and broadly columnar in shape, with very attractive, aromatic, roughly oval leaves up to 15cm (6in) long, mostly cut into three nearly equal,

SASSAFRAS ALBIDUM

rounded lobes, and sometimes with a single lopsided lobe on one half of the leaf. In spring, yellow-green flowers about 1cm (½in) across, are produced in clusters as the new leaves unfold, followed – on trees approximately ten years old – by red-stalked, oval, dark blue fruits, 1cm (½in) long. Sassafras trees are native to eastern North America. They are characteristically multi-stemmed, and in autumn turn bright yellow or orange-gold, with red tints.

HISTORY
For perhaps thousands of years sassafras was one of the most important medicinal plants to every native American tribe that lived within its natural range. It was probably the first North American medicinal herb to reach Europe and commercially, after tobacco, was the single most important plant to come out of the New World. Sassafras was first sent from Florida to Spain and was in use there by about 1560. Ironically, this ancient and valuable herb was banned in the United States in 1960 and by the Council of Europe in 1974. The reason is that sassafras root contains safrole, which causes liver cancer in laboratory animals. Safrole is quite a common substance in plants; it

also occurs in nutmeg, star anise and black pepper, to mention but a few herbs, and there is no indication that it is dangerous in the amounts normally used in food. Having said this, safrole-free sassafras products have been developed that pose no threat and are perfectly legitimate in foods.

COOKING

The roots are traditionally made into a tea with maple syrup which if strong enough sets into a jelly. Sassafras leaves are dried and powdered to make 'filet', which is used in Cajun cooking to thicken gumbo (spicy chicken or seafood soup), and the wood is used for smoking dry-cured country hams in the southern states of the USA.

HEALING

Sassafras is a stimulant, alterative herb that was traditionally taken as a spring tonic and 'blood purifier'. Other than that, it was used to treat almost any kind of complaint you can think of, especially venereal diseases and eruptive fevers, such as measles and scarlet fever, as well as being considered an aphrodisiac. In particular, it induces sweating, which cools the body in fever and eliminates toxins. The oil and root bark were used externally, for problems such as rheumatism, gout, skin diseases and lice infestations. Essential oil of sassafras is very toxic (as are all essential oils if swallowed in sufficient quantity); just a few drops would cause death in a small child, and a teaspoonful might kill an adult. Many herbalists no longer prescribe sassafras, though it is still popular in its homelands.

NOTES FOR GARDENERS

Though hardy, sassafras needs a warm climate to reach its full potential. In cooler northern areas, it is more of a shrub and appreciates a warm, sunny spot. Fertile, well-drained, sandy, neutral to slightly acid soil is ideal, but even poor dry soils are tolerated. Patient gardeners can grow sassafras from seed, which may take two years to germinate, or beg a sucker from someone with a tree. Fast-track gardeners should buy the largest specimen they can find from a specialist tree nursery.

Satureja species   SAVORY

PORTRAIT

Summer savory (*S. hortensis*) is a bushy, summer-flowering annual, reaching 35cm (14in) high, with very narrow leaves up to 3cm (1½in) long. Winter savory (*S. montana*) is similar in appearance but shrubby and later flowering. Both have white to lilac or purple flowers. Creeping savory (*S. spicigera*) is a prostrate shrublet, 6–15cm (2½–6in) high, with tough narrow leaves only 2cm (¾in) long and white flowers in autumn. Thyme-leaved savory (*S. thymbra*) is a dense shrublet, about 40cm (16in) tall, with very short, narrow, almost bristly leaves and pink flowers in summer. All are from Europe, but from different regions. Savories occur in the New World too: *yerba buena* or Oregon tea (*S. douglasii*), from coniferous woods in western North America, has creeping stems, rounded, evergreen leaves and white or purple flowers; Jamaican peppermint (*S. viminea*) is an evergreen West Indian shrub with narrow, bright green leaves and tiny white flowers. There is an African savory too – *S. biflora* – which has lemon-scented foliage.

HISTORY

The name *Satureja* is from *satyrus*, a satyr – a drunken, lustful woodland god – as these plants are supposed to have aphrodisiac effects. Given their unassuming appearance and rather sharp aromas, this seems rather surprising. Further confusion follows over their identities. This group of plants has led botanists a merry dance, and most of them at some time or other have been classified as *Micromeria*, *Clinopodium*, *Calamintha* or even *Thymus*. Though long used as herbs, they are modest in terms of history too. Perhaps the only one with a claim to fame is *S. douglasii*, named after the great explorer of the American West, David Douglas. Its common name, *yerba buena*, is distinguished too – it was adopted by the Mexican village that we now know as San Francisco.

COOKING

The minty American savories are used more for tea than flavouring, while the European savories are first and foremost culinary herbs. Though savory is known as 'the bean herb', complementing and aiding the digestion of pulses, the various kinds can be used with any meat or vegetable dish,

SATUREJA MONTANA

or soup that would otherwise call for oregano or thyme. They are particularly good in marinades for grilled meat or in dressings for salads of roasted Mediterranean vegetables or for piquant olives. The oregano-like *S. thymbra* is used in the Middle Eastern spice mixture known as *za'tar*.

HEALING

As you might guess from their pungent aromas, savories are rich in volatile oils, similar to those in oregano and thyme (summer, winter, creeping and thyme-leaved savories) or mint (*S. douglasii*, *S. viminea*). These have anti-bacterial, anti-fungal and anti-oxidant properties, but neither the herbs nor their essential oils are much used medicinally. In general, they improve digestion and relieve indigestion, but could equally be used as a warming, decongestant remedy for chest infections.

NOTES FOR GARDENERS

Savories are niche plants rather than taking centre stage in the garden. Winter savory can be planted as a dwarf hedge or edging, kept tidy by clipping over in early spring. Creeping savory makes a good companion for thyme borders, usefully extending the flowering season to the first frosts. European savories come from dry grassland or stony hillsides, so need well-drained soil and full sun. *Yerba buena* prefers moist, sandy, slightly acid loam and is borderline hardy. Though at home as ground cover in humus-rich soil, it is often grown as a trailing plant in hanging baskets or the front of window boxes that are in shade for some of the day. Jamaican peppermint is tender, needing a temperature of at least 10°C (50°F) throughout the winter.

Scrophularia nodosa   FIGWORT

PORTRAIT
A large perennial with square stems and oval, pointed leaves up to 12cm (5in) long, which have toothed margins and heart-shaped bases. Small maroon-brown, hooded flowers, pollinated by

SCROPHULARIA NODOSA

wasps, are borne in well-spaced panicles throughout the summer and autumn. Figwort is found in damp woods and hedgerows in many parts of Europe. In good soil it can reach 1.5m (5ft) tall.

HISTORY
According to Culpeper in *The English Physician Enlarged* (1653), 'a better remedy cannot be found for the kings evil' – a term that refers to scrofula or tuberculosis of the lymphatic glands. *Scrophularia* was the classic remedy for this condition, in which the lymph glands in the neck swell into nodules that resemble those of figwort roots. As such, it is an example of the Doctrine of Signatures, where the appearance of a plant indicated its medicinal use – the symbolic shape or colour ('signature') having been given by God as a guide to which herb to use. For hundreds of years this theory, which was developed by the sixteenth-century Swiss alchemist and physician Paracelsus, had a major influence on European herbalism. Similar theories are found in different cultures, perhaps because all human beings associate form with meaning. However fanciful such theories may seem, many of the herbs in question – including figwort – work well for the conditions they symbolize.

HEALING

To this day, figwort is used by herbalists to treat swollen lymph nodes (as in mononucleosis or glandular fever), chronic skin diseases, mastitis and various lumps, swellings and tumours. It contains similar substances to those found in devil's claw (*Harpagophytum procumbens*), which have anti-arthritic effects. Basically, figwort is a detoxicant, improving excretion through bladder and bowels, and stimulating the liver and circulation, all of which helps to reduce levels of toxins that cause so many health problems. Applied externally, it is a good healing herb, both for the complaints already mentioned, and for minor injuries, haemorrhoids, abscesses, ulcers and the like. Various other figworts are similarly used as cleaning, healing herbs for deep-seated infections, including water figwort (*S. aquatica*), the North American *S. marilandica* and the Chinese *S. ningpoensis*.

NOTES FOR GARDENERS

Scrophularia nodosa can look interesting when spot-lit by a shaft of sunlight, but most gardeners would agree that the only place for it really is in the wild garden. *Scrophularia aquatica* is rather better looking, especially in its variegated form ('Variegata'), which is a handsome waterside plant. The latter does not come true from seed, so needs dividing in spring, but the species are easy from seed sown when ripe or in spring. In fact, figwort usually needs no such encouragement and will sow itself generously.

Scutellaria species   SKULLCAP

PORTRAIT

Virginian skullcap (*S. lateriflora*) is a rhizomatous perennial, reaching 30–70cm (12–28in) high, with oval, toothed leaves up to 8cm (3in) long and small tubular, blue flowers in the axils in summer. It is North American, mainly found in moist lowlands in the north and west. European skullcap (*S. galericulata*) is smaller, 15–50cm (6–20in) tall, and likes wetter places, often beside ponds and canals; it has smaller leaves and larger, more vivid blue flowers. Baikal skullcap (*S. baicalensis*) is a hardy woodland perennial from Mongolia, China and Japan. It reaches 30–38cm (12–15in) high, and has tapering, purple-tinged, lanceolate leaves up to 5cm (2in) long and one-sided spikes of densely hairy, bright purple-blue flowers 2.5cm (1in) long.

HISTORY

Skullcaps were so named because the shape of the flowers resembled the leather helmet (*galerum*) worn by Roman soldiers. European skullcap was once given to control fits in 'tertian ague' or malaria. Virginian skullcap was originally a native American remedy for women's problems. It is also known as mad dog skullcap, a name that dates back to the late eighteenth century when a Dr. Vandesveer apparently used it with great success to prevent '400 persons and 1000 cattle from becoming hydrophobus after being bitten by mad dogs . . .' In the nineteenth century, Physiomedicalists (followers of the Anglo-American school of herbal medicine founded by Samuel Thomson) used it not only to treat rabies, but also for other serious disorders, such as epilepsy and schizophrenia. The earliest descriptions of Baikal skullcap were found in the *Ming Yi Ben Lu* (AD500), and on wooden tablets in a grave in north-western China, dated to the second century AD.

COOKING
In central Asia, whole plants of Baikal skullcap are dried for making tea.

HEALING
Virginian skullcap has a pronounced sedative and tonic effect on the nervous system. It is used mainly to relieve tension headaches, insomnia, anxiety and nervous exhaustion, which are so prevalent in the western world. European skullcap can probably be used for the same purposes but is less potent. Baikal skullcap is a bitter, cooling herb, used in Chinese medicine for conditions caused by 'excess heat and damp'. Research has demonstrated that it has strong anti-inflammatory and anti-allergenic effects.

NOTES FOR GARDENERS
Medicinal skullcaps are easy to grow in sun or dappled shade. Baikal skullcap is undoubtedly the most handsome of the bunch and is often grown as an ornamental in its own right. European skullcap is at home in the bog garden, while its American cousin prefers woodland conditions.

SCUTELLARIA BAICALENSIS

SCUTELLARIA LATERIFLORA

All are propagated from seed sown in autumn, or by division in either autumn or spring. Basal and softwood cuttings, taken in late spring, root readily.

Senna species — SENNA

PORTRAIT
The true senna, *S. alexandrina*, is a small shrubby perennial, no more than 1m (3ft) high, originally from Nubia (an ancient region of southern Egypt and northern Sudan, now mostly beneath the reservoir of Lake Nasser). It has long spreading branches and pinnate leaves up to 15cm (6in) long, divided into five to eight pairs of narrow pointed leaflets. Bright yellow, five-petalled flowers appear in erect, open clusters, followed by more or less straight pods, 5–7cm (2–3in) long and 1–2.5cm (½–1in) wide. There has been much confusion over its identity. It was classified under another genus and as two different

species, *Cassia angustifolia* (Tinnevelly senna) and *C. acutiloba* or *C. senna* (Alexandrian senna). These are now regarded as the same plant and go by the name *Senna alexandrina*. The so-called wild or American senna, *S. marilandica*, is from damp places in woodland and prairies in the mid-western United States. It is a larger plant, about twice the size, with longer leaves, divided into more oval, yellow-green leaflets, and similar yellow flowers, which produce narrow black pods up to 11cm (4½in) long.

HISTORY

In many different cultures and for many centuries, purging has been a first line of defence in treating almost any ailment. As a consequence, laxative herbs have been held in very high esteem and traded since earliest times. Senna was mentioned in a Coptic prescription for flatulence (Copts were the early Christian descendants of the ancient Egyptians), and probably reached Europe through Arabian physicians in about AD600. It was cultivated in England by about 1640, though often failed to produce pods. American senna reached Europe in 1723. It was packaged in large quantities by the Shakers. Being an indigenous, wild-collected herb, it was a much cheaper commodity than Alexandrian senna.

SENNA SPECIES

HEALING

To this day, senna is an ingredient of most laxative preparations – a testimony to its safety and efficacy. It is a stimulating laxative, ideal for acute constipation associated with feverish illnesses and other conditions, or as a way of clearing the bowel before and after surgery. Taken regularly for chronic constipation, it makes the bowel lazy – 'laxative dependent' – causing as many problems as it solves. Both leaves and pods are used; they are usually combined with other herbs, such as ginger or coriander, to allay the unpleasant griping that they cause when taken alone. American senna is milder and slower acting.

NOTES FOR GARDENERS

Growing your own senna may be something to which few gardeners aspire, but the American wild senna would not look out of place among shrubs and tall perennials in a damp woodland area or beside a pond. It is a pretty plant, quite hardy, and available from some specialist nurseries. The true senna is more problematic, being tender and difficult to come by. If you can find seeds of either kind, sow them at 18–24°C (64–75°F) in spring. Plants can also be propagated by division in spring, or by semi-ripe cuttings in summer.

Silybum marianum MILK THISTLE

PORTRAIT

Milk thistle is a robust hardy biennial, 1.2–1.5m (4–5ft) tall, found in fields and waste ground from southern Europe to southern Russia and down into North Africa. In the first year it forms a rosette of deeply lobed, spine-edged leaves 50cm (20in) or more in length, beautifully marked with a dribble-like pattern of white variegation. The following year stout flowering stems develop, topped by bright purple thistles, about 5cm (2in) across, which are surrounded by a ring of fearsome spines. As a finale, large brown-black seeds are blown away by a parachute-like tuft of silky white hairs.

SILYBUM MARIANUM

HISTORY

Dioscorides knew this plant as *silybon* or 'thistle-like', hence its generic name. Its other names, *marianum* and milk thistle, come from the story that the plant's unusual variegation was caused by the Virgin Mary's milk, which splashed on to the leaves and ran down the veins. Culpeper called it Our Lady's thistle and regarded the seeds and distilled water as an effective remedy for jaundice and other liver-related problems. He also recommended cooking young plants as a vegetable to cleanse the blood in spring, adding in his inimitable way 'but cut off the prickles unless you have a mind to choak yourself'. Milk thistle was once grown as an artichoke-like vegetable but after research in Germany during the 1970s it became far more important as a medicinal plant and is now a best-selling herbal remedy. It contains unique substances, collectively referred to as silymarin, which protect the liver against toxins and help to detoxify and regenerate liver cells. There has been an impressive amount of research done on the effects of silymarin. If taken promptly in cases of poisoning, say by death cap fungi or carbon tetrachloride (dry-cleaning fluid), it can prevent the severe and often fatal liver damage that normally follows.

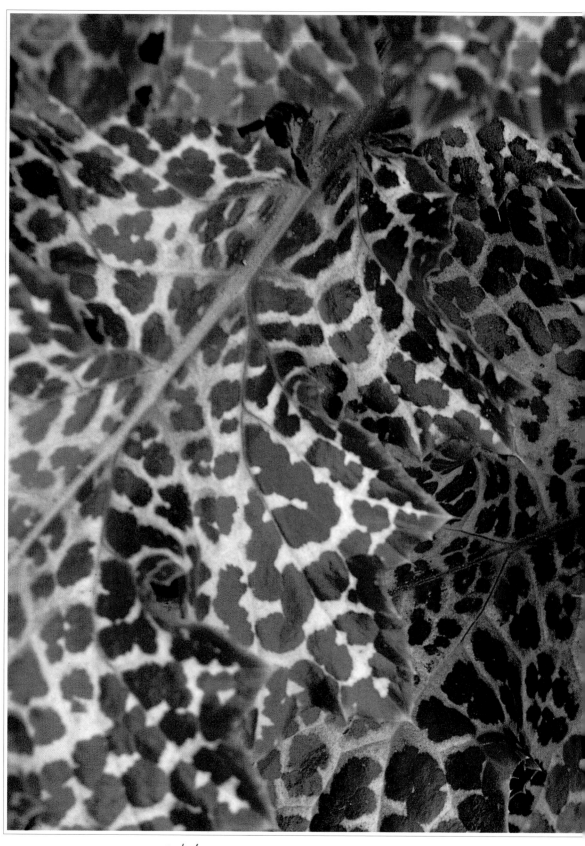

Silybum marianum

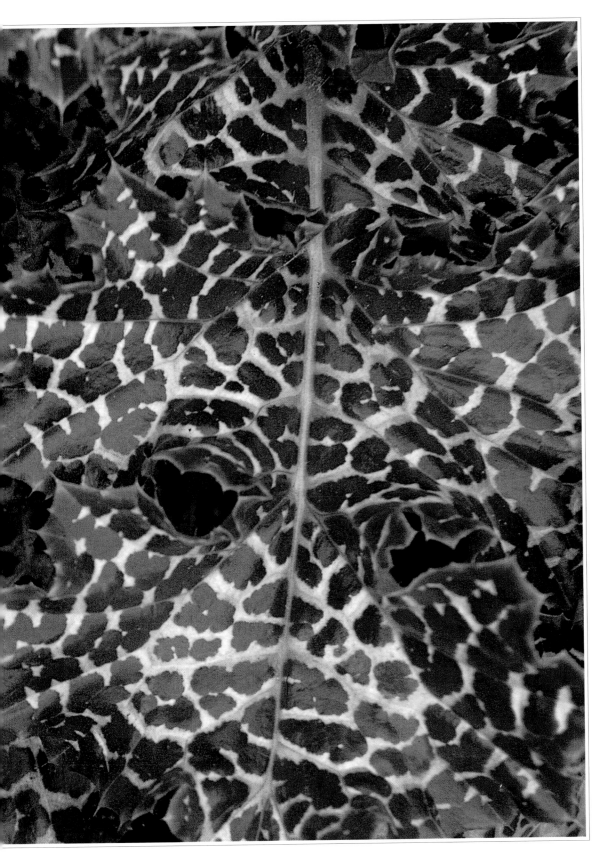

257

COOKING

All parts are edible and have the same benefits to digestion as artichokes. After carefully removing the spines, young leaves make a pleasant vegetable, raw or cooked, and unopened flower buds can be served like mini-artichokes. The roots are good too, especially if grown in rich moist soil, and the seeds can be roasted to make a kind of herbal coffee that acts as a liver tonic.

HEALING

In addition to its valuable role in arresting the course of certain kinds of poisoning, silymarin has also been shown to improve liver function in cases of hepatitis and cirrhosis, and to reduce side effects from cancer chemotherapy. And on a lighter note, it takes its place alongside raw eggs and 'the hair of the dog' as a hangover cure.

NOTES FOR GARDENERS

Even better news is that milk thistle makes a magnificent garden plant, combining architectural presence with fine ornamentation. It is also remarkably easy to grow in either good soil or poor, dry conditions. All it needs is sun. For a normal biennial sequence, sow seeds in late spring or early summer, either directly into the ground, or two to a pot, thinning to the strongest. Alternatively, grow as an annual by sowing in pots in late winter and planting out in spring. Some plants may reach flowering size the first year but will not achieve the size of those raised as biennials.

Sinapis alba	WHITE MUSTARD
Brassica juncea	BROWN MUSTARD
B. nigra	BLACK MUSTARD

PORTRAIT

Mustards are all annuals of the cabbage family, Brassicaceae, which originated in various parts of Europe and the Near East. They look rather similar, with irregularly lobed leaves, bright yellow, four-petalled flowers and erect pods containing small round mustard seeds. Where they do noticeably vary is in the colour and pungency of their seeds, and in the size of the plants. Black mustard has very dark brown, highly pungent seeds but can grow to 3m (10ft) tall, making it less popular than its smaller relatives, which at 1–1.2m (3–4ft) are better for mechanical harvesting.

HISTORY

The word 'mustard' comes from the Latin *mustum*, grape must, and *ardens*, burning, as the Romans made this hot, spicy condiment by mixing the ground seeds with must (fermenting grape juice). The use of mustard for culinary purposes spread with the Roman Empire to northern Europe. Mustard was used medicinally in ancient times. It is mentioned in an Assyrian herbal as a mouthwash for toothache, and the Copts used it in a poultice for headaches.

COOKING

Flavour and strength in mustard depends on the kind of seeds used, and the method of preparation. Chemically, mustard seeds contain a substance known as sinigrin and an enzyme, myrosin. When cold liquid is added to ground mustard seeds, the enzyme reacts with the sinigrin to form a sulphur compound that has the burning taste and aroma we enjoy so much as a condiment. The reaction takes 10–15 minutes. Hot liquids, vinegar and salt inhibit the enzyme, producing a milder, more bitter mustard.

There are three main kinds of mustard: American uses mild-flavoured white mustard; English is made from a mixture of white and black or brown; and French, which originally used black but today is more often made from brown mustard. Mustard seeds can also be sprouted. Traditionally, white mustard seeds were sown in punnets with those of *Lepidium sativum* as peppery tasting 'mustard and cress' for salads and egg sandwiches; the mustard seeds grow more quickly so were sown three days later. Today, real mustard and cress is a rarity, having been superseded by the milder tasting salad rape (*Brassica napus*). Increasingly popular are young mustard leaves, grown for the 'baby salad leaves' market. These are produced from various strains of brown mustard.

SINAPIS ALBA

HEALING

In medicinal terms, mustard is known as a 'counter-irritant', causing inflammation of the tissues, which dilates the blood vessels and results in increased blood flow. This in turn has a warming effect, raises perspiration rate and speeds the excretion of toxins. Applied as a poultice, mustard helps to relieve bronchitis, pleurisy and neuralgia. It is also used in a foot bath or rubbing oil for chilblains, joint pains or a sprained ankle. Care should be taken when using it topically, as too much mustard or mustard left for too long can cause blistering of the skin.

NOTES FOR GARDENERS

Growing your own mustard for seeds is too fiddly a proposition for most gardeners. However, mustard plants are worth growing for their tasty young salad leaves; red-leaved and curly varieties are visually attractive too. Plants that escape being eaten at an early stage go on to produce flower buds, which can also be added to salads or briefly steamed like broccoli. Sow seeds from early spring to autumn, according to instructions on the packet.

Herbal

Used wisely, stimulants can enhance functions that have become sluggish. Instinctively we choose the refreshing taste of lemon or lime to invigorate us in a hot, torpid climate, and ginger or other warming spices when temperatures are low.

In the nineteenth century, patients suffering from tuberculosis would be sent to a sanatorium in the mountains, surrounded by pine forests. The essential oils in pine are strongly antiseptic and decongestant, but most of all they trigger inhalation, which expands the lungs and clears the airways. A similar effect happens with minty aromas, as everyone recognizes when they clean their teeth or use a mouthwash.

Some of the oldest herbs in the world are digestive stimulants. We begin meals with bitter aperitifs to rev up the liver and gall bladder, ensuring the flow of bile and enzymes that are needed to break down and assimilate the nutrients in foods. And we often end a meal with peppermints or mint tea to give the digestion one last boost.

Any kind of stimulant can be used to excess. Too much menthol (an essential oil in mint) can cause thickening of the mucous membranes which makes bronchial congestion worse, not better, and over-exposure to warming herbs like mustard can actually blister the skin. The stimulant herbs that get the worst press are not kitchen cupboard familiars like mint and mustard, though – the real villains, we are told, are those that increase alertness and raise our 'feel-good' factor. Surely it is a question of balance? There is nothing intrinsically 'bad' about the stimulants described below. Problems occur only when we overuse or abuse them.

Every culture has its daily stimulant drink. In parts of South America the usual tea is maté, made from the non-prickly leaves of Paraguayan holly (*Ilex paraguariensis*). It contains stimulant compounds, such as caffeine and theobromine, which increase alertness and give a feeling of well-being. Guaranà (*Paullinia cupana*), from the seeds of an Amazonian liana, is preferred in Brazil. It makes a coffee-like drink that contains a stimulant almost identical to caffeine.

Coffee drinking originated in Africa and caught on in Europe during the seventeenth century. High consumption of coffee (*Coffea arabica*) results in rapid heart beat, raised blood pressure, anxiety and wakefulness. Persistent high intake has been linked to numerous other conditions. On the positive side, coffee – like tea – is irreplaceable as an occasional 'pick-me-up'. It even saves lives as an antidote to narcotic poisoning.

Khat or qat (*Catha edulis*) is an East African tree with glossy oval leaves that are chewed fresh in Afro-Arabian cultures. It contains alkaloids similar

Ilex paraguariensis

Coffea arabica

Stimulants

in effect to those in *Ephedra* species, which relieve fatigue, improve mental performance and communication skills, and induce mild euphoria. Vast areas, including up to half the fertile land in Yemen, are devoted to khat cultivation, as the leaves have to be harvested daily and consumed within 24 hours. Khat is a permissible stimulant for Muslims, air-freighted daily to Arab communities worldwide, though increasing concerns about its abuse have prompted several countries to ban it.

The chewing of betel nut – the seed of a tropical Asian palm, *Areca catechu* – has been part and parcel of everyday life in the Indian subcontinent for hundreds, if not thousands of years. The large, woody seed is sliced, mixed with lime and spices, and wrapped in a leaf of betel pepper (*Piper betle*). Betel nuts contain tannins and alkaloids that stimulate saliva flow, raise heart and perspiration rates, and suppress hunger. On the plus side, betel chewing protects against dysentery, malaria and intestinal parasites, but in the process turns the saliva red, blackens teeth and encourages spitting. These and other negative affects on health are behind moves to discourage betel chewing.

The use of coca (*Erythroxylum coca*) as a stimulant in South America goes back at least 1,500 years. The Incas took a *cocada*, the equivalent to a tea or coffee break, to chew coca leaves, which helped them adapt to high altitudes and work harder on the meagre rations provided by their Spanish conquerors. Coca reached Europe in the nineteenth century and became very popular as a stimulant tonic in the form of tea, wine and elixirs. Many eminent people of the time, from the Pope to Sigmund Freud and the fictional Sherlock Holmes, partook of the substance extolled as a 'brain tonic and cure for all nervous affections, from sick headache to melancholy'. There was even a museum devoted to coca on the banks of the Seine in Paris. Coca contains various alkaloids, the most notorious being cocaine, which was first isolated in 1860 and revolutionized eye surgery, before becoming a major social problem.

Coca-Cola was first produced in 1886 as one of many alcoholic tonics or patent medicines of the era that contained coca. At the onset of prohibition the recipe was modified and promoted as an alcohol-free 'Intellectual Beverage and Temperance Drink'. Coca extracts were removed following the ban imposed on coca and its derivatives in 1902. Cola, the other half of the equation, is a pleasantly flavoured stimulant obtained from the large seeds of the African cola tree (*Cola nitida*). Cola nuts contain significant amounts of caffeine, and sweeten other foods and drinks.

See also: *Camellia sinensis*, *Capsicum* species, *Lobelia inflata*.

CATHA EDULIS

PIPER BETLE

ERYTHROXYLUM COCA

261

Smilax species # SARSAPARILLA

PORTRAIT

Sarsaparilla plants are prickly vines that climb by means of tendrils, positioned in pairs at the base of each leaf stalk. The name comes from the Spanish *zarza*, bramble, *parra*, vine, and the diminutive *illa* – in other words, a small bramble-like climber. The leaves are commonly oval to heart-shaped, prominently veined and often patterned. Tiny male and female flowers are produced separately and are usually yellow-green to brown; females develop into small black, blue or red berries. Sarsaparilla vines occur in woodland and thickets in many parts of the world, from temperate to tropical regions, and are especially common in the Americas and Asia. One of the main species used is Honduran sarsaparilla, *S. regelii*, which has also been known as *S. ornata* and *S. officinalis*.

HISTORY

Sarsaparillas were used in folk medicine in their homelands before entering international trade in the 1530s. They came initially from Mexico, Guatemala and Honduras. Until it went out of favour in the late nineteenth century, sarsaparilla was in widespread use as a cure-all and tonic, especially for syphilis. In 1831, 176,854lb (80 tonnes) were imported into England alone. It provided the basis for many patent medicines, such as *Ayer's Sarsaparilla* that claimed 'Disorders of the liver, stomach, and kidneys, as well as tuberculosis, tumors, rheumatism, female weaknesses, sterility, pimples, and syphilis, could be cured by just one remedy'. It also acquired a reputation for enhancing the male body and virility; in the early days, it was taken as root beer, and more recently as a supplement for bodybuilders.

COOKING

Sarsaparilla root has a bitter, liquorice-like flavour that is characteristic of root beers. Commercially, extracts are also used in flavouring soft drinks, ice cream, confectionery and baked products. The tender young shoots can be eaten like asparagus.

HEALING

Long-established uses of sarsaparilla for urinary and kidney complaints, rheumatism, skin diseases, digestive and reproductive problems have been largely substantiated by research. The roots are rich in hormonal substances that may indeed help women with menstrual or menopausal problems, and have gentle anabolic effects in men. Extracts have shown pronounced diuretic action, increasing excretion of uric acid, a toxin associated with gout and joint pain. Impressive results have also been reported in clinical tests using sarsaparilla in treating such serious conditions as leprosy and syphilis.

NOTES FOR GARDENERS

Several species are grown for their ornamental foliage. Italian sarsaparilla, *S. aspera*, is quite widely available. It has narrowly heart-shaped, shiny, mottled leaves, clusters of fragrant cream flowers and red berries that turn black when ripe. Though Mediterranean in origin, it is reasonably hardy and undemanding in northern regions, thriving in well-drained soil in sun or partial shade, and scrambling around among shrubs or against a wall. Established plants are multi-stemmed, and can be divided in spring.

Plate 393.

Sarsaparilla of America. ⎰ 1. Flower. 3. Fruit open. ⎱ *Smilax aspera Peruvana.*
⎱ 2. Fruit. 4. Seed. ⎰
Eliz. Blackwell delin. sculp. et Pinx. 5. Part of the Root.

Symphytum officinale

COMFREY

Portrait

This large perennial has tapering, narrowly oval leaves up to 25cm (10in) long and mauve-purple to pink or creamy white, pendent, tubular flowers, produced in clusters in summer. The whole plant is covered in minute bristles, giving it a rough, abrasive texture. Comfrey grows in damp grassland and near water in many parts of Europe and western Asia.

History

In the seventeenth century, Culpeper described comfrey as being 'special good for ruptures and broken bones; yea, it is said to be so powerful to consolidate and knit together, that if they be boiled with dissevered pieces of flesh in a pot, it will join them together again'. This belief in the extraordinary healing power of comfrey goes back centuries. The Romans knew *S. officinale* as

SYMPHYTUM X UPLANDICUM 'VARIEGATUM'

conferva or join together, from which the word 'comfrey' is derived, and another common name is knitbone. Its reputation as a healing herb was sullied in the early 1990s when its use internally was banned in several countries following research into isolated comfrey alkaloids that indicated liver damage in laboratory animals.

Cooking

Young leaves can be eaten as a vegetable, or added to soups and sauces in much the same ways as spinach. Comfrey leaf fritters are good too. When dried, the leaves make a bland-tasting tea that can be mixed with other herb teas or with Indian tea. The leaves are exceptionally high in protein and are eagerly consumed by livestock.

Beauty

Comfrey extracts are added to skin-care products, especially to rejuvenating face creams. The extracts are often in the form of allantoin, either natural or synthesized.

HEALING

It is debatable whether the alkaloids in comfrey cause liver tumours when extracts of the whole herb are used, but to err on the safe side, herbalists no longer prescribe comfrey root in tablet or capsule form. There is no perceived danger in using the leaves as tea, or in external use of the herb. More important than alkaloids, comfrey contains astringent, soothing, and anti-inflammatory compounds, and a remarkable healing substance called allantoin that stimulates the growth of new cells. Allantoin is so effective that it is synthesized by the pharmaceutical industry for use in dermatological products. Research has also shown that when comfrey is applied to the skin, allantoin penetrates as deep as bone, so the name 'knitbone' may not be so far-fetched after all.

NOTES FOR GARDENERS

Its high protein content makes comfrey very useful for composting and mulching. The leaves can be crammed into a barrel of water to make an excellent, if smelly, liquid fertilizer that matches or betters commercial products. Plants can be cut to the ground several times a year for these uses. Comfrey is easier to grow than to get rid of, so think carefully where to plant it. The roots can go over 1.5m (5ft) deep and any bit left in the ground will sprout. As it is not particularly ornamental, an ideal position is near the compost heap, stable or vegetable plot, or in a wild or woodland area. The sterile clone 'Bocking' is best for garden areas, being productive in terms of foliage, but guaranteed not to self-seed. For borders or pond margins, choose the white-flowered form, *ochroleucum*, or a colourful Russian comfrey, such as *S. x uplandicum* 'Variegatum' or 'Axminster Gold'.

Tabebuia species

LAPACHO
PAU D'ARCO, IPÊ-ROXA

PORTRAIT

Tabebuias are large, handsome tropical American trees with simple to palmate leaves and large, brightly coloured, funnel-shaped flowers in spring. In deciduous species, flowering commonly takes place when the trees are leafless, making a spectacular display. Trees can reach 50m (150ft) tall, with trunks 2m (6ft) in diameter. The most widely used species is *T. impetiginosa* (formerly known as *T. avellanedae*), with pink flowers. Also used are *T. rosea* (pink poui), which may have white, pink or lilac flowers, and the yellow-flowered *T. serratifolia* (yellow poui).

HISTORY

These magnificent trees first received media attention after research in Brazil during the 1960s showed that their bark may have potent anti-cancer effects. In traditional medicine, lapacho is regarded as a cure-all and used to treat various conditions, from dysentery to snakebite, as well as cancer. The trees are so revered and so popular as ornamentals that a number of South American countries have adopted one or other as a national symbol; *T. serratifolia* is the national flower of Brazil. Tabebuias are also in great demand for their timber, which is extremely hard and durable. Native tribes once made arrows from the wood, as indicated by the name *pau d'arco*, which means 'bow stick'. Felling for timber is having a serious impact on wild populations. Medicinal uses are less likely to have a further detrimental effect as the inner bark can be stripped from felled timber.

Tabebuia serratifolia

COOKING

The bark is brewed into a tonic tea that Gandhi was reputed to have drunk.

HEALING

The inner bark and wood of *Tabebuia* trees contains lapachol, a unique quinone that has anti-cancer properties, and a number of other complex constituents that are anti-inflammatory, antibiotic, anti-fungal and immunostimulant. A decoction or tincture of lapacho can therefore relieve chronic fungal infections such as candidiasis, recurrent bronchial and urinary tract infections, pelvic inflammatory disease and other chronic conditions, such as ME (myalgic encephalomyelitis or chronic fatigue syndrome). In the form of an ointment it can also help slow-healing wounds and ulcers.

NOTES FOR GARDENERS

Being tropical, tabebuias need minimum temperatures of 10–15°C (50–59°F). In temperate regions it is probably feasible to grow them in pots, though unlikely that they will flower as well as plants in the open ground – and in any case they rarely flower before reaching about 3m (10ft) tall. Seeds germinate readily at 16°C (61°F) and young plants have attractive foliage to make up for the lack of flowers.

Tagetes lucida
T. patula

MEXICAN TARRAGON
FRENCH MARIGOLD

PORTRAIT

Mexican tarragon is a woody-based perennial with narrow, finely toothed leaves up to 10cm (4in) long and bright golden-yellow flowers 1cm (½in) across. It grows in dry areas of Mexico and Guatemala, and reaches 30–80cm (12–32in) tall. French marigold, also from Mexico, is a small, bushy annual, reaching 30cm (12in) high, with deeply divided, toothed leaves about 8cm (3in) long and yellow to orange or brown-red flowers up to 5cm (2in) across.

HISTORY

Tagetes patula (French marigold), the familiar bedding plant, reached European shores in 1573 and is still one of our best-known half-hardy annuals, with numerous varieties grown in temperate gardens. *Tagetes lucida* was introduced to cultivation in the Old World in 1798 but, by contrast, has never been very widely grown. It is an ancient plant and was used to flavour *chocólatl*, the cocoa-based drink of the Aztecs. Though both species are primarily culinary herbs, they do have medicinal uses.

COOKING

Tagetes lucida is one of several closely related species that have an anise-like flavour and are used for flavouring in countries where true tarragon (*Artemisia dracunculus*) is difficult to grow or little known. They include *T. anisatum* (anise marigold) and *T. filifolia* (Irish lace marigold or *hierba anis*). Also closely related are: *T. erecta* (Aztec marigold) with fairly pungent leaves and yellow flowers that are dried as a saffron-like food colouring; *T. lemmonii* (Copper Canyon daisy), which has a strong lemon-mint

Tagetes maximus rectus, flore luteo, maxima, multiplicato.

A. CALAVAS, PARIS

NICOLAS ROBERT. — *Tagetes erecta.*

aroma; and *T. tenuifolia* (lemon marigold, signet marigold), with lemon-scented foliage and flowers. In spite of its Central American origins, *T. patula* has become a popular flavouring in parts of Africa and in Georgia, where the dried flowers are an important ingredient of beef soup (*kharcho*). They are also used in Georgian recipes that include walnuts and vinegar, as they stop the walnuts turning black.

HEALING
Both species have diuretic properties and relieve indigestion. *Tagetes lucida* is probably the more potent of the two, as it reputedly lowers blood pressure, brings down fever and has hallucinogenic and anaesthetic effects.

NOTES FOR GARDENERS
Mexican tarragon is very easy to grow as a border plant. Though far less showy than French marigolds, it can still be in flower in December in a mild autumn. Plants are reasonably easy to propagate from cuttings of non-flowering shoots in spring or summer. They can also be raised from

TAGETES LUCIDA

seed, though it is slow to germinate. In cold areas, over-winter plants in the same way as geraniums. Finding seed of wild French marigolds, the true *T. patula*, is not so easy; instead, grow a variety with smallish flowers in mixed colours, such as 'Favourite', which is closer to the original. Named varieties can sometimes have a very good flavour; the 'Gem' series of *T. tenuifolia* is delightfully citrus scented.

Tanacetum balsamita   ALECOST

T. vulgare   TANSY

PORTRAIT
Alecost is a rhizomatous, woody-based perennial with oblong, silver-green, mint-scented leaves up to 20cm (8in) long and daisy-like flowers 1cm (½in) across in summer. It forms large clumps

on stony ground and waste places in many parts of Europe and central Asia, reaching 90cm (3ft) tall when flowering. Tansy is also Eurasian and similar in habit, with strongly aromatic, feather-cut leaves up to 15cm (6in) long, and divided into deeply toothed leaflets. Long-lasting yellow, button-like flowers appear in late summer and autumn; flowering plants can be nearly 1.2m (4ft) tall.

HISTORY

Little used today, alecost was one of the most popular herbs during the sixteenth and seventeenth centuries, both as a flavouring, a medicine and a strewing herb for earthen floors; it was even grown for export in Spain. Another of its names is costmary. The 'cost' part in costmary and alecost has a very ancient origin: it comes from the Sanskrit word *kustha*, meaning an aromatic plant. The other parts, 'mary' and 'ale' refer to its dedication to the Virgin Mary, and to its use in medieval times as a flavouring for ale. Alecost leaves make good bookmarks, hence another name, bible-leaf.

The history of tansy charts a similar decline in popularity. In the British Isles it was traditionally used in cooking at Easter, partly as a symbol of the bitter Passover herbs, and also 'to drive away

TANACETUM BALSAMITA

TANACETUM VULGARE

the wyndenes [windiness]' after eating peas and beans in Lent. Tansy cakes ('tansies') – a kind of omelette – were given as a prize for the victor in a handball game played at this time between clergy and congregation. The word tansy is from the Greek *athanasia* or immortality, as corpses were once packed with tansy leaves to keep bugs and vermin away, and help preserve them until burial.

HEALING

Alecost was once used for liver and gall bladder complaints, and made into ointment for bruises, infestations of parasites and 'scorching of gunpowder blasts'. Its uses are obsolete now. Tansy is out of favour too, as it contains thujone and camphor, which are potentially very toxic; the use of tansy as a medicinal herb, especially in the form of essential oil, is actually illegal in some countries. In the past it was commonly used to expel intestinal worms. It is also strongly insecticidal. One effect of tansy is to stimulate the uterus. This may help with menstrual problems but would be dangerous during pregnancy.

NOTES FOR GARDENERS

Alecost is the better behaved of the two, though in time it will form very large clumps. The subspecies *balsametoides* (camphor plant) is to all intents and purposes identical, apart from its camphor scent. Tansy is downright invasive – ideal for a hedgerow or meadow area but often a nuisance in borders. The variety *crispum,* known as fern-leaf tansy, is prettier and not quite as much trouble, as are the variegated 'Silver Lace' and yellow-leafed 'Isla Gold'. Propagation of all but the last two cultivars can be done by seed sown in spring at 10–13°C (50–55°F); otherwise divide or take basal cuttings in spring.

TANACETUM PARTHENIUM

Tanacetum parthenium   FEVERFEW

PORTRAIT

Feverfew is a wasteland plant, originally found from south-eastern Europe to the Caucasus, and now widely naturalized elsewhere in Europe, North America and Australia – wherever, in fact, it has been taken as a medicinal herb or ornamental. It is a short-lived perennial, 45–60cm (18–24in) tall, with long-lasting, daisy-like flowers, 2.5cm (1in) across, and chrysanthemum-like leaves up to 8cm (3in) long, which are cut into irregular toothed segments.

HISTORY

In the seventeenth century, Culpeper stated that feverfew was 'very effective for all pains in the head', and in *A Welsh Botanology* (1813) there is a description of how a woman who was driven almost insane by migraine was cured by infusions of feverfew. Then the use of feverfew in relieving severe headaches was forgotten about until the late 1970s when a doctor's wife, Mrs Ann Jenkins, started taking a leaf a day for her migraine attacks on the recommendation of a friend who was taking it for arthritis. After ten months she was free from attacks. The news travelled quickly among migraine sufferers, and in the 1980s clinical trials confirmed feverfew as a highly effective remedy for this debilitating complaint. Feverfew gets its name from the Latin *febris*, fever, and *fugare*, to drive away, as it was once used as a febrifuge, lowering temperature by increasing perspiration rate, which cools the body.

HEALING

No remedy, herbal or otherwise, works for everyone, but the success rate of feverfew in reducing migraine attacks is very high if taken in the correct dose for the prescribed time (it does not work instantly). The daily dose of leaves is best eaten in a sandwich to mask the taste (and to prevent mouth ulcers – a common side effect); an easier alternative is a few drops of tincture diluted with water. Feverfew may also help arthritic and rheumatic conditions, especially if taken in conjunction with other herbs and dietary changes as prescribed by a medical herbalist.

NOTES FOR GARDENERS

Feverfew is a variable species that in the course of cultivation has thrown up some fine ornamental varieties. They vary greatly in size, from tall, double-flowered varieties, such as 'Rowallane', which are excellent as border plants and cut flowers, to the tiny 'Golden Moss', a favourite for edging and 'carpet' bedding at only 10cm (4in) high. Some are in between; 'Snowball' and 'Golden Ball' have pompom flowers and reach about 30cm (12in). The all-time favourite is 'Aureum', golden feverfew, which has luminous yellow foliage and the typical daisy flowers. Feverfew and its variaties are remarkably easy from seed sown in seed compost in spring. They tend to self-sow generously but unwanted seedlings are easily spotted and removed.

Taraxacum officinale   DANDELION

PORTRAIT

Dandelion is one of the commonest weeds in the world, found in grassland throughout temperate regions. It is a very variable hardy perennial with a taproot and rosette of saw-toothed leaves, 15–20cm (6–8in) long. In spring a succession of primary yellow, slightly domed flower heads are produced atop fleshy, hollow stems. These are followed by globes of silk-tufted seeds, known as dandelion clocks because of the children's game of telling the time by blowing the seeds away. All parts ooze milky sap when bruised.

HISTORY

The use of dandelion as a medicinal herb was recorded in a Chinese herbal dated to around AD659, and in Arabic medicine in the eleventh century. The earliest mentions in Europe were made by the Welsh physicians of Myddfai in the thirteenth century, and in the *Ortus Sanitatis* in 1485. The name dandelion also goes back to the fifteenth century, originally from the French *dent-de-lion* and Latin *dens leonis*, lion's tooth, which describes the leaves. A more vernacular name, pissabed, is a graphic description of their diuretic effects. This too has a French version, *pissenlit*.

COOKING

Traditionally, drinks such as dandelion coffee and 'dandelion and burdock' were made from the roots, while the flowers provided the basis for dandelion wine. Perhaps more appealing to today's tastes are the leaves, which are a healthful addition to salads and stir-fries. The common or garden dandelion does, however, have very bitter leaves, and for culinary use should be blanched like chicory (as is discussed below).

HEALING

Dandelion leaves are the perfect diuretic, efficiently relieving fluid retention associated with premenstrual tension, kidney problems or high blood pressure, and containing high potassium levels to compensate for the amounts lost in the urine. The roots act more on the liver and gall bladder, improving both digestion and elimination, which in turn sees an improvement in chronic health problems such as skin diseases, gout and arthritic complaints. All in all, dandelion is one of the best, cheapest and most readily available detoxicants in the herbal repertoire.

TARAXACUM OFFICINALE

TARAXACUM OFFICINALE

NOTES FOR GARDENERS

For all its variability, the dandelion has failed to throw up much in the way of ornamental variaties, though variegated and white-flowered forms do occur. Connoisseurs of salad leaves may like to track down improved varieties, such as '*Amélioré à Coeur Plein*' and 'Broad Leaved' (also known as as 'Thick Leaved' or 'Cabbage Leaved'). For growing as a salad crop, sow seeds in trays first, rather than in the open ground, to encourage branching of the taproot, which increases leaf production. Plant out into fertile soil – a moist, sandy loam is ideal – and pick young leaves before flower buds appear. If growing as a root crop, harvest in autumn, and at all costs, do not let your crop go to seed. You can also blanch dandelions that appear as weeds in the garden by inverting a plant pot over each one and covering the drainage holes with stones. After a few weeks the leaves turn pale and lose their bitterness. For winter use, dig the roots in autumn, remove all but the growing point and replant close together in containers of moist compost. Keep them in total darkness at 10°C (50°F) for four weeks and they will sprout tender blanched leaves.

Leontodon Taraxacum.

Herbal Tonics

Tonic herbs have been used for centuries to restore and maintain vitality, and increase longevity. They differ from stimulants (see p.60), which have more immediate, short-term effects and are often used for limited periods to treat an acute problem. Tonics bring about more profound changes in the metabolism, are taken for longer, and usually for a chronic condition. Tonic herbs are often part of a formula or prescription, compiled by a skilled and experienced herbalist.

A term often used in connection with tonic herbs is 'adaptogen'. This means that the herb gives greater resistance to stress and enables us to adapt more readily to demands and changes. In this context, adapt means being able to take things in our stride and recover our equilibrium quickly after dealing with challenging situations or physical traumas. Adaptogenic herbs, such as ginseng (see p.112) have complex effects, supporting the functions of the nervous, immune and endocrine (hormone) systems, which work together to maintain balanced responses to the demands of daily living.

Most of us could do with a tonic at some time or other. Traditionally, tonics were taken in spring to clear away toxins that build up through the winter when we are often less active and more prone to infection. Different parts of the world use different herbs for this purpose; in the British Isles, nettle soup was a great favourite. Tonics are also important after illness or surgery, and can help women through difficult times after childbirth and during the menopause. Adaptogenic herbs are useful for preparing the body for a period of increased stress or, taken from time to time in later life, can help to keep the system in good order, protecting against cancer and degenerative diseases.

In Chinese medicine a number of fungi are used as tonic herbs and the majority are now cultivated for culinary and medicinal purposes. Maitake (*Grifola frondosa*) appears at the base of deciduous trees, such as beech and oak. It smells like mice but tastes delicious, and is a gourmet ingredient of soups and Japanese tempura. As a herb, maitake is a powerful immune stimulant, used to strengthen defences against cancer, AIDS and late-onset diabetes.

Reishi (*Ganoderma lucidum*) is a glossy cinnamon-brown bracket fungus that is made into a kind of candy rather than eaten as a vegetable. Used for 2,500 years in Chinese medicine, reishi is one of the great Taoist longevity herbs, and today is of interest for improving immunity, reducing allergic responses and strengthening heart and liver function.

Shiitake mushrooms (*Lentinus edodes*) are now widely available in supermarkets. Again used for ages – more than 2,000 years – in Chinese medicine, shiitake is now tackling twenty-first-century health problems,

LENTINUS EDODES

such as cancer, AIDS, viruses, allergies, *Candida* infections, environmental pollutants and any conditions involving depressed immune function. Eaten regularly, shiitake has a rejuvenative effect on older people and helps younger ones maintain vitality.

Perhaps the strangest Chinese herb is the caterpillar fungus (*Cordyceps sinensis*), which parasitizes the larvae of a rare Himalayan moth. The fungus can now be cultured on grain, but, traditionally, infected caterpillars were collected by the Yung people in western China and tied in bundles for the herb trade. The caterpillar fungus serves as a tonic for lungs and kidneys, and has anti-cancer effects. It is added to soups, stews, ginseng elixir and other herbal tonics.

Wolfberry is an ancient Chinese herb that comes from either *Lycium barbarum* or *L. chinense*, closely related spiny shrubs of the potato family (Solanaceae). The oval red fruits, which have a sweet, liquorice-like flavour, are eaten fresh or dried as a tonic for the liver, kidneys and blood. They lower blood pressure, improve eyesight and protect the liver from toxins and are added to tonic soups, stews, teas, and 'designer' soft drinks.

Schisandra (*Schisandra chinensis*), a red-berried climbing shrub, is an all-round tonic and adaptogen. In Chinese it is known as *wu wei zi*, 'five-flavour fruit', because the berries have all the elemental flavours – sweet, sour, acrid or pungent, bitter and salty. They have a reputation for increasing bodily fluids, thereby rejuvenating the skin and also having an aphrodisiac effect. Traditionally between three and ten grams of berries are chewed daily for 100 days as a tonic for the kidneys, sexual organs and nervous system.

Chinese foxglove (*Rehmannia glutinosa*) is another very famous oriental tonic. The roots are either chewed raw or dried and cooked in wine. Traditionally used to 'cool the blood' in over-heated conditions, Chinese foxglove is regarded as a longevity herb that keeps mental faculties sharp into old age. It is a potent liver and kidney tonic with cardiotonic effects, and is used in many Chinese herbal tonics. As a boost for women after childbirth it is often combined with Chinese angelica (see p.38).

For centuries native Brazilians have used the roots of suma (*Pfaffia paniculata*), a shrubby Amazonian vine, as a tonic, especially during convalescence and the menopause. It is also known as *para toda*, 'for everything' – in other words, a cure-all. Research has shown wound-healing, pain-killing, anti-inflammatory and anti-diabetic effects and derivatives have been patented as anti-tumour drugs.

See also: *Angelica polymorpha* var. *sinensis*, *Astragalus membranaceus*, *Codonopsis* species, *Eleutherococcus senticosus*, *Fallopia multiflora*, *Glycyrrhiza* species, *Panax quinquefolius*, *Smilax* species, *Withania somnifera*.

Thymus species

THYME

PORTRAIT

Thymes are small evergreen perennials and shrubs that grow wild in Europe and Asia, mainly in calcareous grassland. They have very small, oval to linear, highly aromatic leaves, and whorled clusters of tubular, two-lipped flowers, which are pink, purple, or white in colour. There are about 350 different species, varying greatly in aroma: *T. herba-barona* has caraway-scented foliage; *T. mastichina* smells like eucalyptus; and *T. capitatus* is a source of oregano oil. The three most useful species are: common thyme, *T. vulgaris*, which forms a dense bush, 15–30cm (6–12in) high, with tiny grey-green leaves and pale purple to almost white flowers; lemon thyme, *T. x citriodorus*, which is similar in habit, with slightly larger, lemon-scented green leaves and mauve-pink flowers; and wild thyme, *T. serpyllum*, a creeping shrublet with minute green leaves and rounded heads of purple flowers.

THYMUS VULGARIS

THYMUS SERPYLLUM

HISTORY

Thyme's medicinal uses go back to Assyrian times (the end of the second millennium BC). In terms of folklore, thyme is associated with death; the souls of the dead were said to rest in the flowers, and sprigs of thyme were worn or added to a ritual drink when communing with the departed. In England, bringing wild thyme into the house is said to bring death or serious illness to a member of the family. Apparently the scent of thyme has been detected at haunted sites.

COOKING

Common thyme gives a rich, savoury flavour to robust soups, gravies and *jus*, marinades, stuffings and casseroles. It is the perfect companion for strong flavours, such as red meat and game, garlic, anchovies, olives, virgin olive oil and red wine, and retains its flavour well in slowly cooked dishes. Dried thyme is an essential ingredient of *bouquet garni* and *herbes de Provence.* Lemon thyme has a lighter note, better suited to white meat, fish and pale-coloured or creamy sauces and soups. You can use the flowering tops as well as the leaves.

HEALING

All thymes are rich in volatile oil that consists mainly of thymol, which is strongly antiseptic, anti-fungal and an important ingredient of oral hygiene products. Thyme is also expectorant and relieves spasms. Its main use in herbal medicine is as an infusion (tea) for coughs and colds, and other throat and chest infections. Thyme tea does not taste as nice as might be expected from the plant's invigorating aroma but it is worth drinking occasionally, as research indicates it has a tonic effect that retards the ageing process. A strong infusion can also serve as a gargle for throat and gum infections, and thrush. Thyme is also applied in the form of diluted essential oil to skin problems, such as athlete's foot and scabies, and to relieve rheumatic pain.

NOTES FOR GARDENERS

Thymes need sharp drainage and full sun but are otherwise undemanding. Their small size makes them ideal for containers, crevices in paving, and for planting in gravel at the side of a path. The main enemy is winter wet and encroaching vegetation or fallen leaves, which cause rotting. To avoid this, plant thymes in an open situation, away from overhanging plants, and mulch directly under the plant with gravel. Frequent propagation pays dividends too, as most thymes become woody and sparse with age. Common and wild thymes can be raised from seed but if anything are easier from cuttings in summer. Thymes are as ornamental as they are useful. To ring the changes, there are golden forms of lemon thyme, a variegated common thyme called 'Silver Posie' and many varieties of creeping thyme with white, pink or magenta flowers, and/or variegated foliage.

Tilia species

LIME
LINDEN

PORTRAIT

Lime trees, which are also known as linden or basswood trees, have smooth grey trunks, glossy twigs and deciduous, oval to rounded, heart-shaped, pointed leaves. In summer they produce small, pale, scented flowers in pendulous clusters, with their stalks fused to papery, pale green bracts that help carry the seeds away on the wind. The flowers are rich in nectar and attract hordes of bees: after pollination they develop into little ball-shaped capsules. Botanists reckon that there may be between 20 to 45 species, occurring in woodland in Europe, Asia and North America. The main species used medicinally are the European white lime or silver linden (*T. tomentosa*), small-leafed lime (*T. cordata*), and large-leafed lime (*T. platyphyllos*), together with the hybrid common lime (*T. x europaea*), which is a cross between *T. cordata* and *T. platyphyllos*. All are large trees, reaching 25–35m (90–120ft).

HISTORY

According to Greek myth, the nymph Philyra was raped by the god Saturn, who was disguised as a horse. She gave birth to Cheiron, the centaur, and was so horrified that she begged the gods for help and was turned into a lime tree. According to John Gerard, whose herbal was first published in 1597, 'The floures are commended by divers [various people] against paine of the head . . . against dissinesse, the Apoplexie [stroke], and also the falling sicknesse [epilepsy] . . .' In folklore, simply sitting beneath a flowering lime tree was said to cure epilepsy. Lime blossom tea (*tilleul*) is very popular in France and harvesting the flowers is carried out on a large scale in northern areas.

Places in the British Isles that begin with 'lin' or 'lynd', such as Lincolnshire and Lyndhurst, indicate that limes are or were common in the area.

COOKING

Lime trees often have obligingly low branches, making it easy to gather large quantities of flowers quickly and easily. The only problems are likely to be the bees, and timing; lime flowers develop narcotic properties as they age, so harvesting must take place when the flowers first open, avoiding any in which the stamens are falling or that show signs of a developing seed capsule. In the spring, young lime leaves can be added to salads and sandwiches. Hives in areas with large numbers of lime trees produce linden honey — one of the best for sweetening herb teas.

HEALING

Lime flowers are rich in flavonoids and also contain tannins, mucilage and volatile oil. They have soothing, sedative and expectorant effects, and increase perspiration rate, which cools the body in

TILIA X EUROPAEA

fever. Taken as a tea, liquid extract or tincture, lime flowers relieve feverish colds and flu, and are often combined with anise and thyme for catarrh and dry coughs. They can also ease tension and reduce episodes of insomnia, panic and nervous palpitations. Flavonoids benefit the circulatory system, strengthening blood vessels and lowering blood pressure.

NOTES FOR GARDENERS

Lime trees thrive in moist, well-drained, neutral to alkaline soil and need plenty of space; traditionally, they have often been planted in avenues. They can be coppiced, but re-growth is unlikely to flower. For confined spaces, choose a less vigorous cultivar, or one with an upright habit. Both *T. cordata* 'Greenspire' and 'Rancho' are conical, as is *T. platyphyllos* 'Princes Street', which also displays bright red twigs in winter. *Tilia platyphyllos* 'Laciniata' is slow growing, reaching 15m (50ft) eventually; it has attractive, deeply cut leaves and flowers profusely. Avoid planting limes near garden seats and parking areas, as they tend to drop sticky honeydew during the summer.

TILIA. Off.
Tilia europæa. Bot.
Die Linde

33

Herbal

MANY PEOPLE DISLIKE THE IDEA of taking pills and potions. What better way then of maintaining and improving health than by eating herbal vegetables, salads (see p.202) and fruits (see p.126). A herbal vegetable is one that has benefits over and above its basic food value. In traditional Chinese medicine, healing vegetables have always played an important role. An ancient medical book found in a grave from the Han Dynasty (206BC–AD220) described the therapeutic use of vegetables. Even in western culture there is a saying that 'food is the best medicine', and we are all familiar with the story of Popeye and spinach, or the fact that carrots help you see in the dark. Increasingly, scientific research is focusing on exactly what our foods contain, and how these compounds behave when digested.

Another advantage of using vegetables to invigorate and tone the system is that, for the most part, they are easily recognized, readily available and cheap. There are no anxieties about consuming rare herbs that have been collected from the wild, and probably look and taste unappetizing into the bargain.

Members of the onion family (Alliaceae) offer many benefits to health. They contain allicin, which rids the body of cancer-causing toxins, and have anti-bacterial, anti-viral and anti-inflammatory effects. In addition, they lower blood pressure and blood sugar, and clear bronchial congestion. Regular consumption of onions (*Allium cepa*) reduces the risk of heart attack, stroke and stomach cancer.

ALLIUM FISTULOSUM

Celery (*Apium graveolens*) is a herbal remedy for rheumatic and arthritic disorders, gout and inflammations of the urinary tract. It is alkaline and diuretic, increases excretion of uric acid, and has an antiseptic effect on the urinary tract. In addition, celery is rich in apigenin, a substance that dilates blood vessels and guards against high blood pressure. Cultivated celery has been bred to remove much of the bitterness, and is blanched to make it milder still. It is an excellent cleansing vegetable, especially when juiced with other vegetables. Celery seeds are even more potent.

Vegetables of the cabbage family (Brassicaceae), such as broccoli, cabbage, Brussels sprouts and kale, contain anti-cancer compounds. These include sulphorophane, which destroys carcinogenic substances in the gut, and indoles and isothiocyanates (ITCs) that protect against cancer-causing synthetic hormones, such as xeno-oestrogens. Eating brassicas significantly reduces the risk of developing cancer, especially of the colon, and benefits are directly related to the amount you eat. In China, juice of Chinese cabbage or pak choi is taken to cleanse the system

BRASSICA OLERACEA

Vegetables

of environmental toxins, such as petrol and paint fumes. The sweet, mild flavour of Chinese cabbage makes it ideal for juicing with other vegetables.

When tomatoes (*Lycopersicon esculentum*) first reached Europe from South America in the sixteenth century, they were declared poisonous, and it was well into the nineteenth century before many people would eat them. Tomatoes contain lycopene, which protects against cancer, and is one of the most potent anti-oxidants known. P-coumaric acid, another anti-cancer compound, is found in tomatoes and peppers; it inhibits the formation of nitrosamines – carcinogenic compounds formed from nitrates in foods.

Sea vegetables are less familiar than most, but seaweeds (Algae) have long been used for culinary and healing purposes by coastal communities the world over. Their underwater foliage contains about twenty times more minerals than land vegetables, together with gels that are easily digested. Kombu (*Laminaria japonica*) is a kelp with leathery blades that contain a natural form of sodium glutamate. In Japan, kombu is the main ingredient of the soup stock known as *dashi*, and is eaten in hundreds of different ways. Many benefits are attributed to kombu; it cleanses the colon, lowers blood pressure, and has a tonic effect on mucous membranes and the lymphatic system.

Nori (*Porphyra tenera*) has translucent, purple-black, lettuce-like foliage that is dried in thin sheets to wrap sushi, flavour soups or to crumble as a seasoning. It is protein- and vitamin-rich, equalling carrots in vitamin A and tomatoes in vitamin C. Eating nori lowers cholesterol levels and improves digestion, especially of fried foods. Laver (*Porphyra umbilicalis*), a closely related species, was a popular food in the British Isles in the eighteenth century and is now enjoying a revival. Traditionally it was coated with oatmeal and fried as 'black butter', or cooked to a gelatinous consistency, known as 'laverbread' and served with mutton.

Dulse (*Rhodymenia palmata*) contains more iron than any other food, and has a high protein, potassium and magnesium content. It is a traditional food in many northern coastal communities, where it is added to soups and chowders, fried as a chewy snack, and used to thicken sauces. Dulse is a traditional Icelandic remedy for seasickness, while research shows it is effective against the *Herpes* virus.

See also: *Allium sativum, Asparagus officinalis, Capsicum* species, *Cynara cardunculus* Scolymus Group, *Daucus carota, Dioscorea* species, *Foeniculum vulgare, Zea mays.*

ALGAE

TRIFOLIUM
PRATENSE.

Trifolium pratense

RED CLOVER

Portrait

A very variable, short-lived sprawling perennial with long-stalked, trefoil leaves, divided into three oval leaflets up to 3cm (1½in) long, which are often marked with a grey-green V-shape in the centre. Stems can reach 40cm (16in) – even 60cm (24in) long – but unless supported by surrounding vegetation they tend to collapse, leaving the plant semi-prostrate. Purple-pink tubular flowers are produced in dense globose heads, about 2.5cm (1in) long, in late spring and summer. Red clover is a grassland species, found throughout Europe, except in the extreme north and south, and naturalized in North America and Australia.

History

Three-leafed clovers of various kinds are regarded as symbols of the Holy Trinity, and it was a plant of this kind that St Patrick used to demonstrate this point of Christian teaching. The shamrock – from the Irish *seamróg*, the diminutive of *seamar*, clover – went on to become the emblem of Ireland, and has been worn to celebrate St Patrick's Day since 1681. Exactly what shamrock is remains a mystery. Red clover is one of perhaps a dozen possible candidates; in an appeal for examples of the true shamrock in 1988, 7 per cent of specimens submitted were red clover.

Red clover is extremely efficient at fixing nitrogen through nodules on the roots, thus improving pasture. The use of clover for this purpose was introduced to the British Isles from Flanders by Sir Richard Weston, pioneer of crop rotation, in the mid-seventeenth century. On the medicinal side, around the same time, Culpeper mentioned white clover, *T. repens*, as a poultice for 'hard swellings and imposthumes'. Red clover has a reputation for curing cancer and was at the height of popularity for this purpose in the 1930s.

Cooking

Fresh or dried flower heads make a pleasant herb tea. Young leaves and flower heads, broken into florets, can be added to salads. They are rich in vitamins and minerals.

Healing

Present-day herbalists definitely prefer red clover to white. It acts as an expectorant and reduces spasms, so is useful in clearing congestion and calming the coughing reflex in bronchial infections. The other main use is for skin problems, such as psoriasis and eczema. Red clover is an alterative or cleansing herb, which speeds the breakdown and excretion of wastes, and improves vitality. In addition, it has hormonal effects and is an ingredient in formulae to relieve menopausal symptoms. Though there is no clinical evidence for its effectiveness in cancer therapy, it is often used in the background treatment of breast and skin cancers. Two minor uses of red clover are as a tea to suppress appetite in dieters, and as an ingredient of herbal substitutes for chewing tobacco.

Notes for Gardeners

Red clover is an essential component of seed mixes for a perennial European wildflower meadow. Seed can also be bought separately from merchants who stock wildflowers and green manure crops.

Varieties such as 'Kenland' and 'Red Merviot' enrich the soil and produce dense foliage that can be mown for compost. To add red clover to existing grassland, buy 'plugs' from a wildflower centre and plant in bare patches, from where they will grow into surrounding areas. Keep well watered until established, and then they should self-sow. Red clover can also be grown as an ornamental. The variety 'Susan Smith' has yellow-veined leaves and is often sold as a bedding plant.

Trigonella foenum-graecum FENUGREEK

PORTRAIT
An aromatic annual with trefoil leaves, divided into oblong, toothed leaflets up to 5cm (2in) long. Yellow-white, violet-flushed flowers, about 1cm (½in) long, are produced singly or in pairs in spring and summer, followed by narrow, upward-pointing pods up to 11cm (4½in) long, containing between

TRIGONELLA FOENUM-GRAECUM

10 and 20 almost rectangular, yellow-brown seeds that are aromatic when heated. Fenugreek reaches 15–50cm (6–20in) in height, and is native to southern Europe and western Asia.

HISTORY
Fenugreek has been used since the Early Bronze Age in the Near East; plant remains have been found in Iraq that date back to 4000BC, and it is described in the Ebers papyrus (*c.*1500BC) as an aid to childbirth. In the first century AD, Dioscorides knew it as *telis*, and recommended it as a decoction or mixed with goose grease as a pessary for gynaecological problems. It also has a long history of use in Ayurvedic medicine, and first appeared in Chinese medical literature in 1061. Fenugreek is often grown as a fodder crop; the word fenugreek is a contraction of *foenum-graecum*, Greek hay.

COOKING
Roasted, ground fenugreek seeds are one of the main ingredients of curry powder. The seeds can be sprouted too and eaten in salads or stir-fries. In the Middle East, sprouted seeds are added to

lamb stews, and in northern Yemen a dish called *helba* is made from the cooked, pureed seeds, garnished with meat and fried onions. The aromatic leaves, known as *methi*, are cooked as a pot herb or dried to use for flavouring root vegetables in Middle Eastern and Indian dishes. Seed extracts are used in the food industry to make maple, vanilla, caramel and butterscotch flavours.

HEALING
In North Africa, fenugreek is still an important herb for women, used to induce labour and increase milk flow, and often made into a sitz-bath for uterine problems. It contains hormonal substances and can be grown as a source of diosgenin for the contraceptive pill. Chinese medicine prescribes fenugreek for period pains and as a pessary for cervical cancer. Research has shown that fenugreek has anti-tumour effects for cancer of both the cervix and the liver. Western herbal medicine regards fenugreek more as a tonic for convalescence and loss of appetite, and as a soothing remedy for gastric inflammation. Applied externally, fenugreek poultices and creams can also alleviate skin inflammations. Fenugreek should not be taken medicinally during pregnancy and may interfere with various prescription drugs. In particular, it lowers blood sugar levels, so should be avoided by diabetics on hypoglycaemic therapy.

NOTES FOR GARDENERS
Fenugreek is easily grown from seed sown in spring in well-drained, fertile soil. Seeds remain viable for four years and germinate in a week. In frost-prone areas, wait until late spring before sowing as it is not hardy. When established, fenugreek is drought tolerant. Though not particularly ornamental, it can be added to an annual meadow mix, along with poppies, cornflowers and marigolds.

Trillium erectum   BIRTHROOT

PORTRAIT
A very variable, hardy perennial with upright stems, bearing three stalkless, broadly oval leaves up to 20cm (8in) long. In spring an outward-facing, unpleasant-smelling flower, coloured maroon, or occasionally yellow or white, is produced from the centre of the whorl of leaves. It is composed of three elliptic, pointed, curved petals, up to 8cm (3in) long, and three narrower, purplish-green sepals. Birthroot reaches 50cm (20in) high and occurs in moist woodland in eastern North America.

HISTORY
Also known as purple or red trillium, stinking Benjamin, wake robin and Indian balm, *T. erectum* was used by native tribes to induce labour and control post-partum haemorrhage, hence its most common names, birth (or beth) root. White-flowered plants were preferred. The rhizomes were also chopped and added to food as an aphrodisiac, and settlers believed that chewing the root would cure palpitations. The first detailed description of the uses of birthroot appeared in *Medical Flora* by Constantine Rafinesque, which was published in two volumes from 1828 to 1830. It was listed in the American Pharmaceutical Association's *National Formulary* between 1916 and 1947.

Healing
Birthroot is an astringent, warming herb that controls internal haemorrhage and discharges. To this day it is regarded as an extremely useful remedy for heavy periods, uterine bleeding caused by fibroids, and for vaginal infections such as thrush. It can also be used to check bleeding from the urinary tract and lungs. Needless to say, this is not a herb for self-medication.

Notes for Gardeners
Once established, trilliums are long-lived, very rewarding garden plants that will increase slowly and surely to form impressive clumps. They associate well with ferns and other woodland herbs, such as ginseng, goldenseal and blue cohosh, and like them need the right conditions – moist, neutral to slightly acid, humus-rich soil in dappled shade. Seeds take two to three years to germinate, then you have to wait another five to seven for young plants to reach flowering size, so it is well worth starting with divisions or decent-sized plants. The white-flowered form, *albiflorum*, shows up well in shady places.

TRILLIUM ERECTUM

Tussilago farfara   COLTSFOOT

Portrait
A robust, creeping perennial with long-stalked, rounded, indented leaves up to 30cm (12in) wide, which emerge with a woolly, cobweb-like covering on both surfaces, and when mature have downy undersides. Yellow, dandelion-like flowers, about 4cm (1½in) across, are borne on purple-tinged, woolly, scaly stalks before the new leaves in early spring, followed by a seed head resembling a dandelion clock. Coltsfoot is a widespread weed of damp, heavy soil in bare areas or grassland in Europe, western Asia and North Africa.

History
In the first century AD, the ancient Greek physician Dioscorides described burning coltsfoot leaves to cure dry coughs; around the same time, Pliny likewise recommended that the smoke was

Tuffilago Farfara.

swallowed rather than inhaled. *Tussilago* is from the Latin *tussis* or cough, and the name has been used for the plant since classical times. The word *farfara* is from the Greek word for a white poplar, whose leaves have similarly downy undersides.

COOKING

Young leaves, flower buds and newly opened flowers have all been eaten in salads and soups by country folk, and made into tea. The flowers have been used for wine making, and the rhizomes candied as a medicinal sweetmeat. Alarm has been raised about the pyrrolizidine alkaloids in coltsfoot, which are toxic to the liver. These are mostly destroyed by heat, but perhaps it is best to err on the side of caution and limit the intake of fresh plant material.

HEALING

Coltsfoot is a classic herbal remedy for coughs, often combined with horehound (*Marrubium vulgare*) and mullein (*Verbascum thapsus*, see p.293) for irritating coughs, and with liquorice (see p.138),

thyme (see p.278) and wild cherry (*Prunus serotina*) for spasmodic coughs. It reduces inflammation, relaxes spasms, soothes irritation, expels mucus and stimulates the immune system, making an excellent remedy for upper respiratory and chest infections, and residual catarrh, and also helps to relieve asthma and wheezing in bronchitis. Some herbalists no longer prescribe coltsfoot because it contains pyrrolizidine alkaloids that may damage the liver. In Chinese medicine the flowers are preferred to the leaves. The dried leaves are an ingredient of herbal tobaccos.

NOTES FOR GARDENERS

Coltsfoot is an extremely invasive weed and, though cultivated in controlled conditions as a medicinal crop, it is an unwise choice for the herbaceous border. Given some competition from fellow wildflowers and grasses, it is less troublesome – at the edge of a meadow or hedgerow area, or other wild part of the garden, or on a patch of builders' rubble, subsoil or some other spot where little else will grow. In Victorian times there was a variegated form, with creamy white margins and blotches, but it has disappeared without trace.

Vaccinium species   CRANBERRIES & BLUEBERRIES

PORTRAIT

The American or large cranberry (*Vaccinium macrocarpon*) is a mat-forming evergreen shrub, no more than 15cm (6in) high, with wiry branches and dark green, elliptic to oblong leaves up to 2cm (¾in) long. In summer, pendent pink bell-shaped flowers, about 1cm (½in) long, are produced, followed by spherical red berries up to 2cm (¾in) across. It occurs in marshes in eastern North America, from Canada to the Carolinas. Similar but smaller all round, and with light purple flowers, is the European or small cranberry, *V. oxycoccos.* There are two main kinds of blueberry also. The American or high bush blueberry, *V. corymbosum,* is a deciduous shrub, 1–4m (3–12ft) high, with narrowly oval leaves 3–8cm (1¼–3in) long, which turn orange and scarlet in autumn. It has white, sometimes pink-tinged flowers, followed by globose blue-black berries, 1cm (½in) across. The European bilberry, *V. myrtillus,* is a creeping shrub which again is smaller all round, reaching 60cm

VACCINIUM CORYMBOSUM

(2ft) high, with pink flowers and berries 6–12mm (¼–½in) across. They too are found in moist to wet acid soils.

HISTORY

Nutritious cranberries and blueberries have been eaten by human beings since hunter-gatherer times. They were an important harvest for North American tribes, who dried the surplus to use like raisins, or cooked and made them into a paste that was dried into a fruit 'leather'. *Vaccinium myrtillus* was recorded as a medicinal herb by Abbess Hildegarde in Germany in the twelfth century. In Scotland it has been known as a cure for kidney stones since the fourteenth century when a cattle drover turned doctor, Fearchar Lighich, first used them for this purpose. Cranberries have likewise long been used in folk medicine. Changes in urine after eating cranberries were observed by physicians in Germany in the nineteenth century, and in New England, a mixture of boiled cranberries and seal oil was prescribed for gallstones. Research into the medicinal uses of cranberries and blueberries intensified during the 1990s, and consumption of fresh and dried fruits, juice and extracts increased accordingly.

Plate. 3.

3

1

2   2

1

Mullein

Hig Taper

Eliz Blackwell delin sculp et Pinx.

1 Flower
2 Fruit
3 Seed

Verbascum

Tapsus barbatus

COOKING

There are countless ways of using cranberries and blueberries: fresh or dried, in salads, sauces, desserts, jellies, jams, muffins, pies etc., or as juice. They dry well, and are readily available as 'craisins' and 'braisins'.

HEALING

Bilberries are laxative when fresh and anti-diarrhoeal when dried. They have a high anthocyanin content that strengthens blood vessels, making the berries an important item in the diet for those who suffer from vein problems. Blueberries are rich in anti-oxidants that improve neurological function and retard ageing. Cranberries contain a substance that prevents bacteria from invading the lining of the urinary tract; they also reduce numbers of bacteria and increase the acidity of the urine. Consuming cranberries in some form or other is a simple, effective way of maintaining urinary health and resisting attacks of urinary tract infections, such as cystitis.

NOTES FOR GARDENERS

The basic requirement for growing any of these plants is moist, acid, peaty or sandy soil. Gardeners with other conditions will have to grow them in containers, or in a bed or border filled with acid (ericaceous) compost. They can be grown from seed sown in autumn, or from greenwood cuttings in early summer for blueberry species, or from semi-ripe cuttings later on in summer for cranberries. For the two main commercial species, *V. corymbosum* and *V. macrocarpon,* it is worth looking for the heavier-cropping, larger-fruited varieties that are now available from specialist fruit nurseries.

Verbascum thapsus   MULLEIN

PORTRAIT

Mullein is a hardy biennial that in its first year has a rosette of bluntly oval, woolly grey leaves up to 50cm (20in) long. The following summer, a stout felted flowering stem develops, reaching 1.2–2m (4–6ft) tall and terminating in a dense, usually unbranched spike of yellow flowers, each about 2.5cm (1in) across. It grows wild from Europe to western Asia, and is naturalized in North America, usually on dry, sunny banks and disturbed ground.

HISTORY

According to Homer, the Greek poet who lived in the eighth century BC, Ulysses took mullein (*moly*) on his travels to protect him evil. When he landed on the island of Aeaea, where the enchantress Circe lived, his men were turned into pigs but he was unaffected and, armed with the plant, forced her to restore them to human form. Medicinally, mullein has been used as a cough remedy since classical times. It was a useful plant in other respects: Roman women mixed an infusion of mullein flowers and lye to dye their hair; the woolly leaves were put inside stockings to keep the feet warm in winter, dipped in tallow to make candle wicks (a practice still prevalent in seventeenth-century England), and wrapped round figs to preserve them. In sixteenth-century Britain, mullein was carried to prevent 'the falling sickness' (epilepsy), a belief dismissed by John Gerard as 'vaine and superstitious'.

HEALING

Mullein is a relaxant herb that lubricates tissues and has antiseptic, healing properties. An infusion of the flowers or leaves curbs mucus production and makes coughing more productive; it can be used for almost any respiratory complaint, but is specifically used for bronchitis, often combined with horehound (*Marrubium vulgare*), coltsfoot (see p.288), *Lobelia inflata* (see p.165) or thyme (see p.278). The Quinlan cure was an Irish remedy for tuberculosis; it consists of a decoction of mullein leaves in milk. Oil of mullein, made by steeping the flowers in olive oil, makes a soothing remedy for earache, haemorrhoids, chilblains and rheumatic pain, and can be used as a chest rub for bronchial complaints.

NOTES FOR GARDENERS

This common wildflower makes quite a statement as a garden plant. Its huge woolly leaves and towering flower spikes have an architectural grandeur and in good soil it can reach impressive proportions. Once introduced, it will always be around, self-sowing generously and often in places where you would never have planted it, but where it looks just right. To start from scratch, sow seed in late spring or early summer for normal biennial behaviour, or in early spring at about 15°C (59°F) as an annual. Any well-drained soil in sun will suit. Around flowering time, plants are invariably visited by mullein moths, whose caterpillars rapidly devour every leaf. Picking them off one by one is the best solution.

Viola tricolor   HEARTSEASE

PORTRAIT

Heartsease has oval to heart-shaped, toothed leaves up to 3cm (1¼in) long, becoming narrower higher up the stems, and little pansy flowers, about 2.5cm (1in) long, which are tri-coloured lavender-blue, yellow and white, usually with a dark spot and lines on the lower petal and deep purple-black upper petals. It may be an annual, biennial or a short-lived perennial, and anything from 8–35cm (3–14in) tall, depending on conditions. Heartsease grows wild in Europe on disturbed ground and acid, sandy grassland, especially after a fire. Hybrids between *V. tricolor* and the field pansy, *V. arvensis*, are common, resulting in more variable flowers.

HISTORY

There are references to heartsease in literature through the ages: in his herbal published in stages between 1551and 1568, William Turner called it banwurt [bonewort] 'because it helpeth bones to knyt again'; John Gerard, whose *Herball* was published in 1597 reckoned it was good for bronchial complaints, itching skin problems, and feverish illnesses, convulsions, and epileptic fits in children and infants. In the seventeenth century Culpeper recommended it for venereal disease and Shakespeare wrote in *A Midsummer Night's Dream*, 'The juice of it on sleeping eyelids laid Will make or man or woman madly dote Upon the next live creature that it sees'. Over the centuries this appealing wildflower with its face-like flowers has acquired innumerable common names, such as love-in-idleness (i.e. in vain), trinity violet, cuddle-me, bird's eye, call-me-to-you, Jack-jump-up-and-kiss-me, tittle-my-fancy, herb constancy and kit-run-about.

La Pensée.

Viola tricolor

Viola tricolor (<small>WITH</small> *Linaria vulgaris*)

HEALING

Today heartsease is mainly used as a detoxifying herb for skin diseases, arthritis and rheumatism, and for acute bronchitis and whooping cough in children, often combined with red clover for the former, and with mouse-ear hawkweed (*Pilosella officinarum*) for the latter. It is also the standard herbal remedy for capillary fragility in patients on steroid medication. The whole herb is taken as an infusion, or is available in the form of liquid extract or capsules. An infusion can be applied externally to soothe itching skin conditions, such as eczema and nettle rash. Heartsease oil, made by steeping the herb in vegetable oil, is effective for cradle cap in babies.

NOTES FOR GARDENERS

Heartsease is one of the most delightful itinerant members of the garden plant community, sowing itself obligingly in nooks and crannies, and never looking out of place, even in the vegetable plot. It is a good subject for containers too, mixing well with foliage herbs such as chives and parsley. To found a dynasty of wild pansies, sow seeds when ripe or in spring or buy a few plants from the local herb nursery. Named varieties derived from *V. tricolor*, such as 'Bowles' Black', and the yellow-flowered 'Prince John' will add to the gene pool, giving even more variation in colours and markings.

Viscum album   MISTLETOE

PORTRAIT

Mistletoe is an evergreen parasitic shrub, growing mainly on apple, hawthorn, lime, maple, poplar and rowan trees in Europe and east to the Caucasus. It has pendulous, symmetrically branched stems, and pairs of yellow-green narrow leaves about 5cm (2in) long. Clusters of inconspicuous yellow flowers in the spring are followed by globose, white, sticky berries 6–12mm (¼–½in) across.

HISTORY

No doubt because of its unusual mode of growth, mistletoe has always been held in awe. According to Pliny (AD23–79), nothing was more sacred to the Druids than mistletoe when found on oak. It was gathered with great ceremony; two white bulls were sacrificed, and a priest wearing white vestments would climb the tree and cut the mistletoe with a golden sickle, catching the sacred plant in a white cloak so that it never touched the ground.

Kissing under the mistletoe supposedly originated in Norse legend, though by all accounts was not a common practice until the nineteenth century. The story goes that Balder, god of peace, was killed by an arrow made of mistletoe, which was then entrusted to the goddess of love, so that anyone passing beneath it should receive a kiss. Though mistletoe is regarded as good luck in a house, often kept through the year to protect against lightning and ensure love, it is often banned from churches because of its pagan associations. Medicinally, mistletoe was recorded as a remedy for epilepsy and tumours before the birth of Christ.

HEALING

Mistletoe has an interesting chemistry, containing substances that inhibit tumours, stimulate the immune system, slow the heart rate and have tranquillizing effects. As such, it is a very potent and,

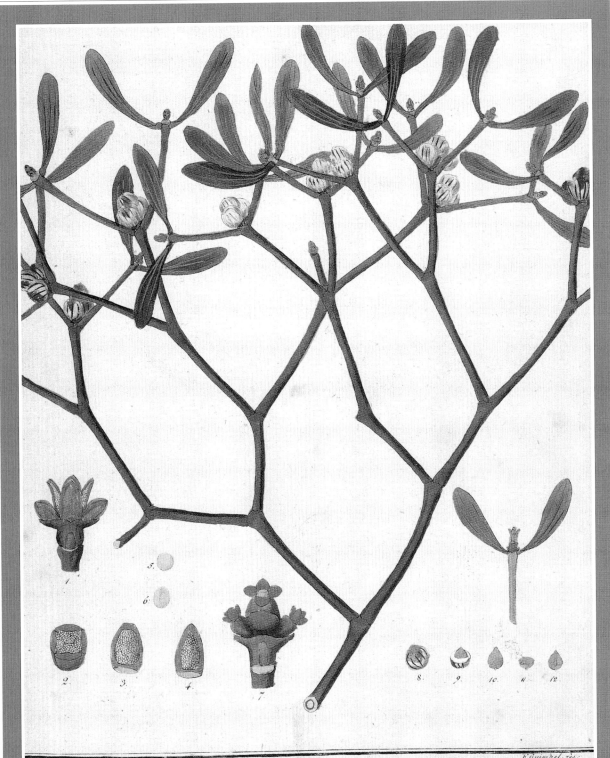

Viscum album

in the case of the berries, a highly toxic herb, not suitable for self-medication. Herbalists prescribe it for cardiac and circulatory disorders, epilepsy, tinnitus, rabies, insomnia, hyperactivity, and withdrawal from benzodiazepine tranquillizers. It is also used in cancer therapy.

NOTES FOR GARDENERS

Berries from Christmas mistletoe usually fail to germinate because they are immature. Better results are obtained from berries collected in spring. Do not remove the seed from the berry but squash the whole fruit in a crevice of bark on a suitable host tree that is at least fifteen years old – preferably the same species as the berries were harvested from. The best site is the crook of a young, high branch where the resulting plant will receive enough light. You can tell if germination has taken place by swelling of the branch. Seedlings are very slow growing, often putting out only two small leaves in the first year. Fruiting may take five years, and only female plants produce berries, so aim to create a colony on several trees in the same area. An apple orchard is ideal; little harm is done to the trees, and the mistletoe is a convenient height for harvesting.

VISCUM ALBUM

Vitex agnus-castus {.handwritten}
V. negundo {.handwritten}

CHASTE TREE
CHINESE CHASTE TREE

PORTRAIT

The European chaste tree, *V. agnus-castus*, is an aromatic deciduous shrub or small tree, reaching 5m (15ft), with hand-shaped leaves, divided into five to nine narrow, pointed leaflets up to 11cm (4½in) long, with grey-white undersides. In summer, small, sweetly scented, tubular lilac flowers, emerging from downy calyxes, are produced in dense spikes up to 30cm (12in) long, followed by tiny red-black, peppercorn-like berries. It is native to southern Europe and central Asia, growing beside streams and in damp coastal places, but is widely naturalized. The Chinese chaste tree, *V. negundo*, is more of a shrub, with leaves divided into three to five leaflets, and spikes of pale violet flowers in summer and autumn. It comes from East Africa and East Asia, and is very variable, with at least seven distinct forms.

HISTORY

The association of *V. agnus-castus* with chastity goes back into the mists of time; it is mentioned in this connection in the *Iliad*, an epic poem written by Homer in the eighth century BC. Centuries later, the ground seeds were used as a condiment by monks to lower their sex drive, hence the name 'chaste tree', and white-flowered plants became symbols of virtue in southern Europe. The Chinese chaste tree makes its first appearance in medical literature in the *Tu Jing Ben Cao* by Su Song in about 1061.

HEALING

Just how the seeds of *V. agnus-castus* made the monks lose interest in sex is unclear but research has shown a marked hormonal effect and today it is one of the most used herbs for adjusting female hormones. It appears to balance levels of oestrogen and progesterone, and is used to treat problems of the menstrual cycle, and infertility. It also encourages milk production in nursing mothers. Chinese chaste tree has different uses, mainly for lowering fever. It also has analgesic and sedative

VITEX AGNUS-CASTUS

effects and in traditional Chinese medicine is given for colds, migraines, arthritis and certain eye problems. Hormonal effects may be present too, as it is known to stimulate beard growth, and is also used for breast cancer.

NOTES FOR GARDENERS

Chaste trees are worth growing for their elegant foliage and attractive, scented flowers quite late in the season when most other trees and shrubs are past their best. Given a sunny, well-drained spot, they cope with quite poor dry soil. Both kinds are frost hardy only, so need a sheltered position, perhaps against a wall, in areas with cold winters. Young specimens can be grown in containers and moved under cover in winter; they do not need much in the way of light when leafless, and could even be kept in a garage. Prune them like buddleia, cutting back hard to the required shape and size — even to ground level — in the spring before new growth begins. Propagation is straightforward too, from seeds sown when ripe or in the spring at about 10°C (50°F), or from semi-ripe cuttings before flowering begins.

ALLIARIA PETIOLATA

ALLIUM URSINUM

ARCTIUM LAPPA

Herbal

A WEED IS JUST A WILD PLANT growing in the wrong place. Usually this means it is common on cultivated land and competes with crops or ornamentals. As plants go, weeds are successful entrepreneurs that we unwittingly invite along. They quickly take advantage of bare ground, germinating and growing rapidly, and reproducing prolifically. Perennial weeds gain even more ground by sending out runners and offsets that form dense colonies. Because the word 'weed' is used in a derogatory way, we automatically take a negative attitude towards weeds. Learning to recognize and destroy them is part of a gardener's expertise.

Yet one person's weed is someone else's garden plant; American weeds include many popular European ornamentals, such as sunflowers (*Helianthus annuus*) and teasels (*Dipsacus fullonum*). Many important herbs are actually weeds too: agrimony (see p.20), dandelion (see p.273) and red clover (see p.285), to mention just a few.

Weeds can be useful. They arrive unbidden on our doorsteps – even sprouting through paving and walls – and are both abundant and free. Many are edible in salads or as vegetables, and some have valuable health-giving and healing properties. Using your weeds, whether as food, medicine, or simply as compost material, is far better than merely disposing of them. It also makes them allies, rather than enemies, which makes for happier gardening.

Garlic mustard (*Alliaria petiolata*) is a member of the cabbage family. It has a mustard-like flavour and garlicky aroma – the pungency associated with anti-oxidant sulphur compounds. Young leaves and flower buds are delicious in salads, sandwiches and stir-fries. As a bonus, they appear early in the year. The garlic flavour of ramsons (*Allium ursinum*) is more pronounced and both leaves and flowers can be used as a garlic substitute. Ramsons thrives in damp to wet soil, even in heavy shade, and is a fine sight – and smell – when the starry white flowers open in late spring. The equivalent in eastern North America is ramps (*Allium tricoccum*), which is also spring flowering.

Burdock (*Arctium lappa*) is a dual-purpose plant. The carrot-like roots are eaten in Japan as a vegetable, known as *gobo*, and both roots and seeds are used in herbal medicine to remove toxins associated with chronic skin conditions, arthritis, infectious diseases and heavy-metal poisoning. In addition to being a potent detoxifier, burdock is known to have antibiotic and anti-tumour effects, and to lower blood sugar.

There are few weeds more unpopular among gardeners than couch grass or twitch (*Elymus repens*), as it always manages to infiltrate choice

Weeds

STELLARIA MEDIA

perennials and shrubs where it is most difficult to eradicate. The rhizomes by which it achieves such invasiveness are, however, its saving grace, for they contain an antibiotic volatile oil and substances that have soothing, diuretic effects on the urinary system. They are taken in the form of a decoction, liquid extract, tincture or capsules, for urinary tract infections such as cystitis and urethritis, and to treat kidney stones and prostate enlargement.

Chickweed (*Stellaria media*) grows almost year round in rich soil, forming great mounds of tiny tender leaves that are an especially welcome addition to salads in winter. The name chickweed refers to its popularity as a food for birds and domestic fowl. In addition to providing nutritious greenery for human and avian diets, it is one of the most effective remedies for itching and irritated skin. It can be made into a lotion (using cold herb tea), a poultice of mashed fresh leaves, or an oil or ointment by heating leaves in oil or fat then straining them. Chickweed preparations can also be used to relieve varicose ulcers, rheumatism, gout and vaginitis.

Culpeper's comments on nettles (*Urtica dioica*) were that 'they need no description; they may be found by feeling, in the darkest night' and we all learn to recognize nettles at an early age. Nettles are important in healing, clearing toxins, reducing allergic reactions (including nettle rash) and controlling bleeding. They also make an excellent iron-rich, spinach-like vegetable, traditionally eaten as a spring tonic herb. Try them in soups, soufflés, or pasta sauces, or as a bland-tasting tea that can be mixed with ordinary tea. Pick nettles when only a few inches high; older leaves develop gritty particles of calcium oxalate that no amount of washing will remove.

URTICA DIOICA

Ground ivy or alehoof (*Glechoma hederacea*) was once used in brewing. Now it is more important in herbal medicine, as a remedy for catarrh, sinusitis and cystitis. It is a pleasantly aromatic, creeping plant with prettily scalloped leaves and lilac-blue flowers. Though unrelated, and very different in appearance, cocklebur (*Xanthium strumarium*) shares the same herbal uses as ground ivy. In addition, it relieves arthritic and rheumatic conditions. Cocklebur is a common weed in many warm to temperate regions. It is a large annual, resembling burdock, with similar spiny burs that cling to clothing and passing animals. First mentioned as a medicinal herb during the Tang Dynasty (AD618–907), cocklebur fruits are still a common ingredient in Chinese herbal remedies.

See also: *Achillea millefolium*, *Galium aparine*, *Plantago* species, *Taraxacum officinale*, *Tussilago farfara*.

GLECHOMA HEDERACEA

Vitis vinifera

GRAPE VINE

PORTRAIT
A perennial deciduous climber that uses tendrils for support. It has a twisted trunk, fibrous, peeling bark, and lobed, hand-shaped leaves up to 15cm (6in) across. Panicles of tiny pale green flowers are produced in summer, followed by pendulous bunches of green to purple, ovoid fruits about 2.5cm (1in) long. *Vitis vinifera* is native to southern and central Europe and western Asia. Wild plants reach 35m (120ft) but in cultivation are normally pruned to 1–3m (3–9ft).

HISTORY
The grape vine is central to Jewish and Christian rituals, a constant motif in art, and a symbol of abundance. It has contributed significantly to the development of agriculture and trade in the Mediterranean since the Early Bronze Age. Grape vines were taken to areas such as Burgundy and the Rhineland by the Romans, where they thrived until the nineteenth century, when European vineyards were devastated by an attack of *Phylloxera*, an aphid introduced from North America. The crisis was resolved by importing an American species of *Vitis* that is resistant to the pest, and to this day European vines are grafted on to American rootstocks. Though best known for its contribution to human diet, the grape vine has an equally long history as a medicinal plant. Culpeper wrote in the seventeenth century that 'wine is the greatest cordial amongst all vegetables'. He also recommended the ash of burnt vine branches as a dentifrice.

COOKING
In addition to the obvious uses of grapes as food, juice, wines, spirits and vinegar, the fruits yield molasses, the seeds are pressed for oil and an extract from the skins is used as a colouring in the drinks industry. The leaves are used for wrapping foods such as *dolmas*, and the residue from wine barrels is processed into cream of tartar. Flavours of most grapes and their products can vary greatly depending on the variety of grape, growing conditions and time of harvesting. There are hundreds of different varieties.

BEAUTY
Extracts of grape seeds (pips) are added to anti-ageing skin products because they contain anti-oxidant properties.

HEALING
Grape fasts are detoxifying; they improve liver function, and may have anti-cancer effects. An infusion of grape leaves is anti-inflammatory and astringent, controlling diarrhoea, bleeding, discharges and inflammations of the mouth, gums, throat or eyes. Red-coloured grapes and leaves are rich in anthocyanins that strengthen blood vessels, improving conditions such as varicose veins and haemorrhoids. Grape pips contain polyphenols that are potent anti-oxidants and standardized extracts of grape seed can be taken to counteract damage by free radicals, to improve cardiovascular health and to slow the ageing process. Regular, moderate amounts of red wine also benefit the cardiovascular system.

NOTES FOR GARDENERS

Grape vines need rich, well-drained soil in sun. Though hardy, some varieties yield much better than others outdoors in cool areas; choosing varieties therefore depends very largely on local conditions. Gardeners with limited space can even grow a vine in a pot. Varieties such as 'Black Hamburgh', 'Foster's Seedling', and 'Muscat of Alexandria' can crop well when containerized, especially if stood on a base that has castors and can be wheeled into the warmest, sunniest spot as the fruits open. Aside from vines that produce grapes for dessert or wine, there are several ornamental varieties that are worth considering for the garden. The Teinturier grape, 'Purpurea', has leaves the colour of red wine that turn even more spectacular colours in autumn. The small fruits ripen late and are good for making jelly. In contrast, the parsley-leafed grape, 'Ciotat', has finely cut foliage and small, round, pale green fruits that are sweet and early ripening. Both are vigorous but, like all grape vines, can be kept in check by pruning. Named varieties cannot be grown from seed. Instead, take hardwood cuttings in late winter, or cuttings with a single bud, known as 'vine eye' cuttings, in early spring.

WITHANIA SOMNIFERA

Withania somnifera

ASHWAGANDHA

PORTRAIT

An upright evergreen shrub with velvety stems and oval-oblong leaves, 5–8cm (2–3in) long. Clusters of inconspicuous pale green, bell-shaped flowers are produced in the axils almost all year round, followed by scarlet glossy fruits, 7mm (¼in) across, encased in a loose brown papery calyx. Ashwagandha occurs as a weed of disturbed ground or stony places from the Canary Islands through Mediterranean regions and the Middle East to Africa and India.

HISTORY

Ashwaganda is a plant with a very wide distribution and a correspondingly long and complex history of medicinal use in many different cultures. Its uses were described in Sumerian texts, thousands of years before the birth of Christ, and remains have been found among other medicinal herbs in ancient Egyptian sites. Not surprisingly, it has many different names, including winter cherry in English, *genegeneh* in Dhofari Arabic, *geneesblaarbossie* in Afrikaans, *amukkara* in Sinhalese, and *asgand* or *punir* in Hindi. Its original Sanskrit name, ashwagandha, is the most prevalent because of its use in Ayurvedic medicine.

HEALING

Ashwagandha is the Ayurvedic equivalent of ginseng — and much cheaper. It is a restorative, strengthening herb, widely used as a tonic for the elderly, for men suffering from impotence or infertility, and to revitalize those recovering from illness or surgery, or exhausted through stress or trauma. A great deal of research has been done into its chemistry, which is extremely complex. More than 80 compounds are known, including alkaloids that have sedative effects and lower blood pressure, and substances similar to our own steroid hormones, which are anti-inflammatory and protect against invasion by cancer cells. Different parts of the plant are used according to the condition being treated, and in Ayurvedic medicine it is usually combined with other herbs, milk or *ghee* (clarified butter). Western herbalists often prescribe capsules of powdered root for nervous exhaustion. The berries are not poisonous and in India are chewed as a tonic. Other parts are narcotic and should be treated with respect.

NOTES FOR GARDENERS

Withania somnifera is frost hardy only and in areas with cold winters needs protection. It can be grown in a container but under glass is prone to red spider mite, so plants are best kept outdoors in the summer. Propagation is easiest from seed sown in spring at about 18°C (65°F). It is not particularly fussy about soil or situation, other than needing well-drained conditions and a reasonable amount of sun.

Zanthoxylum americanum
Z. piperitum

TOOTHACHE TREE
JAPANESE PEPPER

PORTRAIT

The toothache tree is a deciduous shrub or small tree, reaching 8m (25ft) high, with spreading, spiny branches and dark green, lemon-scented leaves up to 30cm (12in) long, divided into between five and eleven oval leaflet with pale green, downy undersides. Small yellow-green flowers appear in spring before the new leaves, followed by clusters of globose red-brown capsules, 5mm (¼in) in diameter, containing black seeds. Japanese pepper is similar in habit, with aromatic leaves up to 15cm (6in) long, divided into anything from 11 to 23 toothed leaflets that turn yellow in autumn. It too bears yellow-green flowers but in this species the fruits are red. There are about 250 species of *Zanthoxylum* or prickly ash in various parts of the world; *Z. americanum* occurs in moist woods in eastern North America; and *Z. piperitum* is from China, Japan, Korea and Taiwan.

HISTORY

Prickly ashes are related to citruses and rue. Many species are used locally in medicine and for flavouring; they are strongly aromatic, often producing a burning sensation when swallowed or

307

Zea Mays L.

applied. The toothache tree or northern prickly ash was an important herb to native American tribes, who chewed the root bark for toothache, mixed it with bear grease for ulcers and sores, and made a decoction for sore throats, venereal disease and rheumatism. The remedy was adopted by settlers and was apparently used with great success in the cholera epidemics that struck Cincinnati in 1849 and 1850. Prickly ash was an ingredient of a formula devised by Harry M. Hoxsey M.D. and used in the Hoxsey Cancer Clinic in Dallas, Texas during the 1950s. Japanese pepper has long been an essential flavouring and condiment in Japanese cuisine.

COOKING

The dried fruit hulls of Japanese pepper or *sansho* are used to flavour soups, noodles and rice, and the seeds (*sansho-no-mi*) are blended with shoyu (soy sauce) and mirin (rice wine) to make the sauce *tsukudani*. The fruits are often ground using a pestle made of sansho wood, either with salt as a seasoning, or with chilli, orange peel, poppy seeds, seaweed, and black and white sesame seeds to make the spice mixture known as *shichimi*, which is sprinkled over soups and noodles. Young shoots and tender new leaves are also used for flavouring. The Chinese equivalent is Szechwan pepper, from *Z. simulans*.

HEALING

Zanthoxylum americanum is primarily a circulatory stimulant, now used mainly for rheumatic and arthritic conditions, Raynaud's disease, and intermittent claudication (cramp in the legs caused by narrowing of the arteries). It improves blood flow, which in the process removes toxins and ensures a better supply of oxygen and nutrients to the tissues. Both berries and bark are used; the latter is stronger. Southern prickly ash, *Z. clavaherculis*, is used in the same ways.

NOTES FOR GARDENERS

Both of these prickly ash trees are attractive, hardy and easy to grow. All they need is well-drained soil in sun or partial shade. They are not very common in cultivation but can be found in a few nurseries. The spineless form of Japanese pepper is worth acquiring but difficult to come by. Young Japanese pepper trees can be grown in containers, and before they reach fruiting size will at least produce aromatic foliage for the kitchen. Prickly ashes are propagated from seed sown when ripe, and from semi-ripe cuttings in summer, or root cuttings in winter. Some species self sow freely.

Zea mays   CORN

PORTRAIT

A giant annual, reaching 3m (10ft) tall, with pointed, arching, strap-shaped leaves up to 90cm (3ft) long. Male and female flowers are produced separately in summer; males in a tassel-like spike up to 40cm (16in) long at the top of the stem; and females in a cluster in the leaf axils, sheathed by overlapping leaves to form a husk about 20cm (8in) long, from which protrude pale green silky stigmas (cornsilk) that dry to threads when flowering is over. After flowering, the familiar cob develops, consisting of rows of angular seeds, pressed closely together, which may be anything from white and yellow to red, purple or blue-black in colour, depending on the variety. Corn or maize or is native to Central America.

HISTORY

Corn has been cultivated in the New World for more than 5,000 – possibly 7,000 – years and spread worldwide after the Spanish conquest. The Portuguese took it to Africa, where ironically its high yields and superior food value led to a population explosion that supplied the slave trade. It proved an adaptable crop and centuries of human intervention have resulted in numerous varieties that tolerate a wide range of climatic conditions. Indeed, it is so highly developed that plants are no longer capable of natural dispersal. On the medicinal side, corn was described in Aztec herbals, and used in Mayan and Incan folk medicine; cornsilk was used in spells and divination.

COOKING

In addition to being a staple food in large areas of the world, corn is the basis of fermented drinks such as *chicha*, popular throughout Central and South America. It also yields corn oil, used in salad dressings and cooking. Unripe cobs can be squeezed for juice; the juice from red corn cobs is made into corncob jelly, and that from green cobs is added to American sage cheese. Corncobs are burnt for smoking fish and meat in New England, and in Mexico the husks are used for wrapping food such as tamales, made from finely ground cornmeal .

BEAUTY

Cornmeal, which can be bought in any grocery store, can be mixed with a liquid, such as buttermilk, egg white, cucumber juice or a herb infusion, to deep cleanse the skin. In India, dry cornmeal is brushed through the hair as a conditioner.

HEALING

Cornsilk is a soothing diuretic herb, used for cystitis, prostate disorders, kidney and bladder stones, fluid retention, and other problems of the urinary system. It also lowers blood pressure and improves bile flow. Among its constituents are large quantities of potassium that compensate for the amount lost through increased urine output, and allantoin, the healing substance also found in comfrey (see p.264). The part used is the soft yellow cornsilk that is usually thrown away when the cob is removed from the husk. This is made into an infusion by putting it into a jug or teapot and covering with boiling water. Cornmeal is equally useful as a home remedy, mixed with water to form a paste and applied to boils, bruises, sores and skin problems. Gel extracted from maize is the main ingredient of a pharmaceutical dressing known as Sterigel, used for slow-healing wounds and lesions such as ulcers and bedsores.

NOTES FOR GARDENERS

Corn needs rich, well-drained soil in sun. Sow seed in late winter or early spring at 18°C (65°F), either in small pots ready for planting out when danger of frost is past, or in the open ground in warm areas. There are numerous varieties, including ornamental ones such as 'Strawberry Corn', which produces reddish-yellow rounded cobs, and 'Harlequin', with red cobs and leaves striped red, white, and green.

Zingiber officinale

GINGER

PORTRAIT

A deciduous, tender perennial, reaching 3–5ft (1–1.5m) high, with thick, branching rhizomes and reed-like stems that bear narrow, pointed leaves up to 15cm (6in) long, arranged in two rows. Occasionally an erect flower stem 15–20cm long is produced, terminating in a cone-shaped spike, 5cm (2in) long, of closely overlapping ochre bracts, from which emerge yellow-green, orchid-like flowers with a purple, yellow-patterned lip. Ginger is native to forests in Asia.

HISTORY

Ginger has an ancient history of use as a culinary and medicinal herb. Linguistic evidence – long before written records – indicates that ginger was important 6,000 years ago, as the word for ginger in many different languages is very similar, having its roots in an ancestral language spoken by

ZINGIBER OFFICINALIS

ZINGIBER OFFICINALIS

'Austronesians'. These early people migrated south from southern China and Taiwan, through the Malay Archipelago, across the Pacific to New Zealand and Easter Island, and as far as Madagascar to the west, taking ginger and their word for it, across oceans and continents. Historically, it was so valuable that Arab traders misled rivals as to its origin by inventing a place called 'Troglodyticall Arabia'. Being a precious commodity, the Romans taxed it *c.*AD200 – about the same time that it made its first appearance in Chinese herbals. The Romans brought ginger to northern Europe. It is mentioned in Anglo-Saxon herbals in the ninth century, and its cultivation was described by Marco Polo on his travels in the thirteenth century and later by Vasco da Gama (*c.*1469–1524). Taken by Europeans to the New World, it became an important crop, especially in Jamaica, which produces some of the world's finest.

COOKING

Fresh ginger is characteristic of south-east Asian and Chinese cooking, often stir-fried with seafood or meat. The more pungent flavour of dried ginger is better suited to spice mixes for pickles, chutneys, curry powders or pastes, and baking. Young fresh rhizomes are candied as stem ginger or crystallized. Ginger is also important as the principal flavouring for ginger ale, ginger beer and various cordials and herb teas. Pickled ginger is eaten with *sushi*, partly for flavour, partly as a gastric disinfectant when eating raw fish.

AROMATIC USES
Spicy, warming essential oil of ginger is used in perfumery.

HEALING
Ginger is of such importance in Ayurvedic medicine that it is known as *vishwaghesaj*, 'universal medicine', and occurs in about half of all prescriptions. Likewise in Chinese medicine, in which fresh and dried ginger are used for different purposes – the former for coughs and colds, diarrhoea and vomiting, and the latter for chronic bronchitis and coldness associated with shock. In western herbal medicine ginger is used for circulatory, respiratory and digestive complaints. Research has shown that it is especially effective for relieving nausea and it is now widely used to prevent travel sickness. Aromatherapists also use ginger for respiratory tract infections, digestive upsets, poor circulation and painful joints and muscles.

NOTES FOR GARDENERS
Ginger is easily grown from fresh rhizomes bought in a supermarket and planted just below the surface in humus-rich compost in sun or partial shade. It needs plenty of warmth and high humidity to do well, and a long growing season for significant increase in rhizome size. In cool, temperate regions, plant in a container in early spring and keep at a minimum temperature of 24°C (75°F) – perhaps in an airing cupboard or boiler room – until new shoots have appeared.

11

Amomum Zingiber.

Published by Dr Woodville, March 1.1790.

GLOSSARY

adaptogen a herb that supports the immune system and improves resistance to stress.

alterative increases vitality through detoxifying the tissues and stimulating their renewal.

apomictic reproducing asexually.

aril a fleshy or hairy, often brightly coloured covering around a seed.

axil the upper angle between a leaf stalk and the stem (or between a branch and the trunk).

ayurveda (adj. **ayurvedic**) a traditional Hindu system of medicine, using herbal remedies, diet, and yogic breathing to balance bodily systems.

bract a modified leaf at the base of a flower or flower cluster. Bracts vary greatly in size and form; they may be reduced and scale-like, leaf-like, or large and brightly coloured.

bulbil a small bulb-like structure, produced most commonly in a leaf axil or flower head, which detaches and grows into a new plant.

calyx the outer part of a flower, formed from the sepals, enclosing the petals in bud.

cladode a flattened, leaf-like stem.

compound leaf a leaf divided into two or more leaflets.

glaucous covered with a waxy or powdery bloom.

globose spherical.

nervine a herb that supports the functioning of the nervous system.

nod the point on a stem from which one or more leaves emerge, often indicated by a slight swelling.

ovate describing a leaf that is egg-shaped in outline, with the broader end at the base.

panicle a loosely branched cluster of flowers.

pinnate describing a compound leaf in which the leaflets are arranged in two rows on each side of the midrib.

propagule a vegetative structure that develops into a new plant when detached from the parent plant.

stamen the male part of a flower, typically consisting of a filament, bearing an anther that releases pollen.

standard (1) a tree or shrub with a distinct length of erect bare stem below the first branches, usually grafted or trained to give that effect. (2) one of the three inner segments of an iris flower. (3) the larger, usually upright back petal of a flower belonging to a plant of the pea family, Papilionaceae.

stigma the female part of a flower, borne at the tip of the style, that receives pollen.

stolon a creeping or arching stem that roots along its length or at the tip to form new plants.

stratification exposure of seeds from temperate plants to a period of cold in order to break dormancy, mimicking the natural process of winter.

style part of the female organ in a flower, forming a narrow, often elongated extension of the ovary, and terminating in the stigma.

subspecies a regional, often geographically isolated population in which 90 per cent or more individuals consistently differ in certain respects from the species, while sharing a majority of other attributes. Often abbreviated to **subsp.** or **ssp.**

umbel (adj. **umbelliferous**) an umbrella-shaped, flat-topped or rounded flower cluster in which individual flower stalks arise from a common centre. Characteristic of the parsley family, once known as Umbelliferae (now Apiaceae).

variety a rank subordinate to species that describes individuals within a population that differ consistently from the majority, usually in colour or habit. Often abbreviated to var.

vulnerary a herb used for healing wounds.

whorl an arrangement of three or more branches, leaves, or flowers, arising from the stem at the same point and encircling it.

INDEX

Page numbers in italics refer to illustrations.
Latin (botanical) names indexed below are in addition to those listed alphabetically in the contents.